UNCONTROLLED
RISK

THE LESSONS OF LEHMAN BROTHERS AND HOW SYSTEMIC RISK CAN STILL BRING DOWN THE WORLD FINANCIAL SYSTEM

MARK T. WILLIAMS

New York Chicago San Francisco Lisbon London Madrid Mexico City
Milan New Delhi San Juan Seoul Singapore Sydney Toronto

ISBN   978-0-07-163829-6
MHID   0-07-163829-6

To Kym, Amelia, and Sarah

"I have never adhered to the view that Wall Street is uniquely evil, just as I have never found it possible to accept with complete confidence the alternative view, rather more palatable in sound financial circles, that it is uniquely wise."

JOHN KENNETH GALBRAITH,
THE GREAT CRASH 1929

Contents

Acknowledgments

This book took form after a conversation with my twelve-year-old daughter, Amelia. In the middle of the Great Credit Crisis of 2008, she asked me a simple question: "Why did Lehman Brothers fail?" After one year of research and hundreds of hours of interviews, I was able to attempt an answer to this question. For planting this seed, I thank you, Amelia. I am also very grateful to McGraw-Hill, especially Leah Spiro for her guidance, and Knox Huston and Julia Anderson Bauer for shepherding the manuscript through the editing process. A special thanks to Troy Froebe for editing and for teaching me that writer's block can be overcome with a competitive game of pool.

I received invaluable comments on drafts from Ed DeNoble, Peter Lindner, Charles Webster, Roger Goodspeed, Chuck Langenhagen, Richard Hurd, Pat King, Geoffrey Stein, Paul Paradis, Greg Wilson, Scott Oran, Daniel Wagner, Scott Bobek, and others who prefer to remain anonymous. Thanks to all of you for important insights that greatly improved this book. I owe a special thanks to Dean Louis Lataif, Senior Associate Dean Michael Lawson, Jack Aber, and Don Smith of Boston University School of Management for their unwavering support as I wrote this book. Also, Douglas Chamberlain of Appleton Partners provided much encouragement. Of particular inspiration were Harry Markopolos and Finnur Oddsson, who both energized me with added purpose.

In researching this book, I interviewed numerous traders, investment bankers, risk managers, corporate executives, regulators, and others—most of whom understandably wished to remain anonymous. I have honored their wishes. I am grateful to each and every one of them.

This book could not have been completed without the help of a dedicated group of researchers, including Shaun Mahal, Giuseppe Morgana, Michelle Ai, and several others. For any mistakes that remain in the book, I take sole responsibility.

Finally, to the many former Lehman employees who were willing to talk to me about a painful and personal tragedy—and who, for obvious reasons, remain anonymous—a sincere thank-you.

Chapter 1

The Inquisition

After a month of financial turmoil that rocked the world, it was time for answers. October 6, 2008, signified a dramatic change in circumstances for legendary Wall Street firm Lehman Brothers and its once lionized leader, Dick Fuld. Now it was time for the disgraced former CEO to face the music as he sat before the U.S. Congress. The American people were outraged that Wall Street had hijacked Main Street, causing a global economic collapse and financial harm to countless individuals. President Barack Obama characterized it as "wild risk taking" on Wall Street. Now California Congressman Henry Waxman, chairman of the U.S. House Committee on Oversight and Government Reform, was charged with exacting some form of revenge. CEO thievery from the economy would no longer be permitted.

On this autumn day, Fuld found himself suddenly thrust into unfamiliar and unfriendly surroundings. No longer was he in the comfort of Lehman Brothers' clubby midtown headquarters in New York where his word was law. The official purpose of this hearing, which aired live on CSPAN, was to determine how Lehman failed. However, the real reason became readily apparent as soon as Waxman commenced with his opening remarks. He wasted no time in putting Fuld on the hot seat, holding him singularly responsible for the fall of Lehman, the loss of jobs, and the significant financial losses sustained by shareholders and bondholders. Justly or not, Fuld would be the fall guy, put on stage to symbolize what was wrong with Wall Street.

In this unfriendly spotlight, Wall Street's longest sitting investment-banking CEO now appeared confused and guilty of massive wrongdoing. His hunched posture, grim-faced expressions, and defensiveness seemed like further evidence of his guilt. Most of the public believed he deserved his comeuppance. And why not? Conventional wisdom accused Lehman of creating toxic mortgage-backed securities and selling enough of them to make the entire financial system sick. Someone needed to be held accountable. But weren't there other firms on Wall Street that had employed similar practices?

Proposed by a Republican senator and signed into law under a Democratic administration, the 1999 repeal of the Glass-Steagall Act surely influenced the level of wild risk taking. Shouldn't the politicians and the former Federal Reserve (Fed) chairman who advocated the repeal of this Depression-era legislation be held at least partially accountable for what happened? Where were the financial regulators charged with protecting the safety and soundness of our banking system? During the last two decades "regulation-light" was the mantra. Banks overdosed on risk not overnight but over time as regulators and policymakers watched. There were other watchdogs that did not bark. Why wasn't Lehman's accountant able to detect the firm's deteriorating financial health? The bulk of financial journalists missed this growing storm cloud as well. Lobbyists played their role by doing what they do best—turning money into influence. The credit rating agencies that investors depended on to provide an independent seal of approval failed as bond ratings that appeared to be AAA quickly sank to junk.

Then there was the House Financial Services Committee, a committee whose main responsibility was oversight of the banking industry. Its chairman, Congressman Barney Frank, claimed no accountability for the Great Credit Crisis of 2008. He argued that compensation practices contributed to excessive risk and that company boards and CEOs failed at their fiduciary duties because they were combined at the hip.

Granted, there were deficiencies in corporate governance and compensation. But was it really so simple, or was there also political deflection? Years of various congressional policies led to the conditions that made the crisis possible. Government support of the U.S. mortgage industry pumped trillions into a market that grew out of control from a policy of greater home ownership, artificially low interest rates, lax lending standards, and securitization. Since 1984 and the multibillion-dollar bailout of Continental Illinois Bank, the U.S. government had sporadically supported a "too big to fail" doctrine that did nothing to discourage large and interconnected firms from increasing risk. Such a policy created "moral hazard" by encouraging financial institutions to take more risk than they would if they were not backstopped by the government. Most people undoubtedly assumed that Lehman fell into this category, yet the U.S. government made the phone call to the board telling them to file for bankruptcy. And how could Lehman be held responsible for the systemic risk unleashed after its demise? Lehman didn't opt for bankruptcy.

Referring to the ripple effect that occurs when one institution's failure rapidly affects counterparties, *systemic risk* is the very concept that underscores the too big to fail doctrine. The overarching theory holds that the failure of one big bank can bring down the entire financial system. At the end, by not backstopping a Lehman partnership, the U.S. Treasury and the Fed tested this theory, with fairly disastrous results. It turned out Lehman was a central cog in an interconnected global financial wheel. In Fuld's mind, Lehman was more of a victim than a culprit.

"THE PERFECT STORM"

The hearing lasted for almost five hours, with Fuld responding to sharp criticism from a hostile panel. As part of the public spectacle, Fuld was allowed to read a prepared statement into the congressional records. His statement was thirteen pages in length and could have been aptly titled "The Perfect Storm." Using a deliberately monotone voice, Fuld indicated there was a "storm of fear" on Wall Street. He implied that Lehman had been a boat in a turbulent sea with many destabilizing factors and some navigation errors had occurred. But in reality this storm of storms was much larger than anyone had predicted. Lehman was just the unfortunate investment bank that hit the rocks. As the captain, he took "full responsibility" for the wreck but spent most of his time listing all the maneuvers attempted to avoid the rocks.[1]

Fuld insisted he did all he could to protect the firm, including closing down the mortgage origination business, reducing leveraged loan exposure, decreasing commercial and residential loan exposure, reducing firm leverage, raising additional capital, making management changes at senior levels, cutting back expenses, seeking a merger partner, and encouraging regulators to clamp down on abusive short-selling practices. All this tacking and jibing was to no avail. Fuld also chastised the Fed for not responding to Lehman's distress signal quickly enough and not launching a timely emergency rescue to shore up market confidence in the overall financial system.

Then Fuld placed blame on the opportunistic pirates, the naked short-sellers who spread false rumors, shorted Lehman stock, and walked away with vast profits. Additional blame was placed on the Securities and Exchange Commission (SEC) for lifting short-selling restrictions that would have provided Lehman safe harbor during the financial storm. Fuld concluded his statement by focusing on the need to revamp the existing Depression-era system of banking regulation to meet the more complex needs of today. And while many of his points were valid and worthy of further analysis, the committee was more interested in drawing attention to his oversized compensation.

Wasting no time, Waxman quickly highlighted the approximately $500 million in compensation Fuld had pulled out of Lehman during an eight-year period. The congressman proceeded to zero in and pepper Fuld with such pointed questions as "Is it fair, for a CEO of a company that's now bankrupt, to make that kind of money? It's just unimaginable to so many people."[2] In case the picture was not vivid enough, Waxman added, "While Mr. Fuld and other Lehman executives were getting rich, they were steering Lehman Brothers and our economy toward a precipice." Although Fuld attempted to answer Waxman's questions and those of other committee members, on numerous occasions he was interrupted or entirely cut off. Fuld was not on stage to answer or debate important risk management questions—he was there only as political fodder. And why should they show deference? Fuld was the CEO of the largest bankrupt company in U.S. history.

The fall of Lehman was complex and could not be boiled down into 30-second CSPAN sound bites. In Fuld's opinion, it was a confluence of events, a litany of bad judgment combined with bad luck—but not unbridled greed. As the hearing progressed, Fuld responded to several questions by providing financially technical and lengthy explanations. Most committee members were not in the mood to receive a lecture on the complexities of financial markets and were frustrated by Fuld's demeanor. John Mica, Republican congressman from Florida, injected levity to the proceedings by saying, "If you haven't discovered your role, you're the villain today, so you've got to act like the villain here."[3]

On the same day, other experts in the financial markets were wheeled in before the committee to opine on why Lehman failed. One expert, Luigi Zingales, a professor from the University of Chicago, felt the firm's use of aggressive leverage, emphasis on short-term debt financing, bad industry regulation, lack of transparency, and market complacency due to several years of juicy earnings were the root causes. Zingales indicated that mortgage derivatives were evaluated on historical records, and firms had subsequently failed to factor in an *ahistorical* decline in lending standards and fall in real estate prices. He also pointed out that the mortgage-backed securities market in which Lehman participated was bankrolled by quasi-governmental agencies, including Freddie Mac and Fannie Mae. In his concluding remarks, Zingales suggested that "Lehman's bankruptcy forced the market to reassess risk."[4] Although only an abbreviated three-page testimony, it was a thoughtful assessment and deserved more committee attention. But the sport of the day was roasting Fuld. A crash course in how risk management worked (or did not work) would have to be left for later.

For Fuld, sitting in front of his accusers must have been a surreal experience. The circumstances leading up to and following the demise of his firm were nothing short of remarkable. Only six months prior, Lehman was one of the main players that made Wall Street tick. The Lehman bond indexes were the gold standard of the investment management industry—relied on by managers around the world. It had been one of the country's elite five stand-alone investment banks. Yet, as Fuld spoke into the microphone that October day, none of the elite five—Goldman Sachs, Morgan Stanley, Merrill Lynch, Lehman Brothers, or Bear Stearns—were left standing. The industry he had worked so hard to shape and nurture was gone. Goldman Sachs and Morgan Stanley, under severe duress, had recently gained bank-holding company powers; Merrill Lynch had been purchased by Bank of America; Lehman Brothers had failed; and Bear Stearns had been taken over by J.P. Morgan Chase.

To Fuld, Lehman was more than a job. Fuld had started at Lehman almost right out of college. He called himself a Lehman lifer. Fuld was proud—"damn proud"—he was not at Goldman Sachs. Lehman had its own unique culture. Why didn't these congressmen understand this? Yes, Fuld was once a billionaire, but he was part of the American dream, a success story. It was true that through the years, as Lehman's wealth grew, so did Fuld's. He had houses in posh places such as Greenwich, Connecticut, West Palm Beach, Florida, and Sun Valley, Idaho, but it was customary for Wall Street titans to have trophy homes. Why didn't Waxman's committee look at the firm value created over Fuld's long career? Unlike other recent well-documented failures such as Enron or Worldcom, Lehman had real earnings. Prior to the "Perfect Storm," Fuld had created, rather than destroyed, vast amounts of shareholder wealth. These billions in earnings had resulted in multimillion-dollar payouts to bankers who in turn paid taxes and helped fill the U.S. Treasury's coffers.

With Fuld at the helm (prior to recent events), shareholders had been rewarded with an impressive annual return on equity of more than 24 percent. Did the congressmen not understand the importance of the investment banking industry? Investment banks were the gatekeepers of capital flow in our economy. Investment banking helped to build this country, and Lehman had played a vital role. During the past 158 years, when the U.S. government needed to raise capital in times of war and peace, Lehman was there. And this ability to raise capital fostered the growth of many major corporations. Lehman helped take companies like Sears Roebuck and Campbell Soup public. What, for God's sake, could be more apple pie than that?

FULD'S TRACK RECORD

Under Fuld's term as CEO, Lehman's empire stretched the globe with more than sixty offices spanning twenty-eight countries. After the spin-off from American Express in 1994, annual earnings increased from $75 million to more than $4 billion. The Lehman army grew from less than nine thousand employees to more than twenty-eight thousand strong. By 2007, Lehman's assets exceeded $690 billion with equity of more than $28 billion. Management and staff believed in Lehman. Employees were the single largest shareholders, owning 30 percent of the firm's stock. At the apex of Fuld's career, he was praised as an intense and capable CEO. Regardless of market turbulence or executive infighting, he always landed on top. He had proven he was a survivor.

Yet Waxman's committee seemed to disregard these accomplishments. War was declared on Wall Street on October 6, 2008. As the day progressed, Fuld became irritated as the focus remained on his compensation, ignoring the fact that he was the single largest shareholder. He repeatedly reminded committee members that he was paid heavily in stock (now worthless) and not all cash. It is estimated that when Lehman failed, Fuld lost more than $650 million. Was this not punishment enough? Waxman attempted to hold Fuld accountable, saying, ". . . you made all this money taking risks with other people's money."[5]

This statement demonstrated a fundamental naiveté about investment banking. Risking other people's money—from shareholders and bondholders—is how investment banks have always made money. This is part of the money machine that drives earnings. But Waxman was trying to use "other people's money" against Fuld, as if Fuld had done something dirty with it. In essence, Waxman was criticizing Fuld for thinking, acting, and talking like an investment banker. What Fuld should have been criticized for was the leverage, type, and size of risky bets that he allowed to be placed with insufficient capital. Lehman's bankers took excessive risk, and they either grossly misjudged it or they just plain ignored it in the pursuit of excessive returns. At the hearing, Fuld was not held accountable for Lehman's state of *uncontrolled risk.*

After the congressional hearing, as Fuld was escorted outside to his waiting driver, he walked by a smattering of protestors holding placards with "Greed" and "Shame" written on them. Some pelted the fallen CEO with insults, calling for his jailing. Undoubtedly this day, combined with other not-so-distant events, would be permanently etched in Fuld's mind. While it was widely rumored that an employee punched him in the nose shortly after the September 15, 2008, bankruptcy, the pain and embarrassment he must have felt after facing Congress would most certainly last much longer.

After all the grandstanding, the U.S. House Committee on Oversight and Government Reform hearings failed to provide any valuable insight into what actually caused the Lehman bankruptcy. While it is evident that greed was a contributing factor, there were many more complicated and equally important causative reasons. Billions of dollars in shareholder wealth were destroyed. Although politically expedient, it is intellectually irresponsible to hold Fuld singularly responsible. When Lehman collapsed, it had more than twenty-eight thousand employees. To suggest that a single CEO caused the entire firm to "Fuld" is a gross misrepresentation. But it does seem puzzling that a company made up of so many intelligent and market-savvy people, a firm that was able to weather numerous calamities during its 158-year history, was unable to survive the Great Credit Crisis of 2008.

At one point during the hearing, Waxman suggested, "[W]e need to understand why Lehman failed and who should be held accountable. . . . The taxpayers are being asked to pay $700 billion to bail out Wall Street. They are entitled to know who caused the meltdown and what reforms are needed."[6] Waxman was right on target. To truly understand the events leading up to and after Lehman's bankruptcy requires a clear understanding of Lehman's history, the investment banking industry, its changing regulation, the evolving landscape of financial markets, and what decisions Lehman made as it defined its risk-taking culture under Dick Fuld. Only an understanding of all of these events will provide a clear view of what happened to bring down the House of Lehman. The pages that follow are devoted to exploring the facts that led up to and caused the largest bankruptcy in Wall Street history.

Chapter 2

From Humble Roots
to Wall Street Contender

The House of Lehman began not in the powerful financial centers of the North but in the rural agrarian South. Starting in 1844, the Lehman brothers one by one—first Henry, then Emanuel (1847), and finally Mayer (1850)—emigrated from Bavaria, Germany, to Montgomery, Alabama. They were Jewish immigrants with one simple goal: open a profitable dry goods store.[1] Having grown up in a family where their father, Abraham, was a cattle merchant, sales and brokering was a familiar business concept.

In 1845, shortly after his arrival, Henry opened H. Lehman on Commerce Street in downtown Montgomery, a stone's throw from the town's slave auction block. In 1848, one year after Emanuel's arrival, the business was renamed H. Lehman & Bro. Initially the small store specialized as a place to sell cotton goods such as shirts, sheets, cotton twine, and rope as well as a place for Henry to sleep. Beyond providing daily necessities, the Lehman brothers advertised themselves as "wholesale and retail dealers in dry goods, clothing, groceries, hardware, boots, shoes, hats, caps, bonnets, cutlery, flowers, combs, etc., etc., etc., making them probably as 'general' as merchants could be."[2] Many of their regular customers made their living by planting, harvesting, and selling cotton. As the prosperity of these customers grew, so did the prosperity of H. Lehman.

The arrival of Mayer reunited all the brothers. In acknowledgment of Mayer's arrival in 1850, the name of the family business was changed to Lehman Brothers, a name that would endure through 158 years of both tumultuous and stable business cycles—ultimately ending in bankruptcy on September 15, 2008.

MANAGING RISK

The essential business decisions confronting the Lehman shopkeepers were similar to those of any small dry goods store: what products to stock, what level to maintain, where to source merchandise, how to collect bills, and how to survive economic downturns. The brothers followed the golden rule of retail—products sold today are worth more than products sitting on the shelf. The success of H. Lehman also hinged on the primary risk of whom to extend credit to, how much of that credit to extend, and when to cut it off. Also important was diversifying exposure to any one segment of its customer base. In 1845, using the modern-day parlance of risk management, H. Lehman had to take market risk, credit risk, and borrowing risk to gain profit. As shopkeepers, market risk involved owning merchandise that might lose value, not sell, or even rot on the shelves. They took credit risk by extending store credit to customers who may not have had the ability or willingness to repay their debts. Lehman also assumed borrowing risk when obtaining capital to fund store operations and negotiating the terms on which they borrowed.

It is a well-known business principle that firms need to take risk to earn return. Companies that take no risk go out of business just as easily as those that take too much risk. Appropriate risk levels can be interpreted differently and depend on who is taking it. A key driver of risk is determined by each company's risk tolerance. Since companies are made up of individuals with distinct personalities, risk tolerance is directly linked to those who run the company. At H. Lehman the most conservative of the three brothers in terms of risk taking was Emanuel, while Mayer was a polar opposite—a risk taker. It was a symbiotic relationship that worked well. Mayer made money, and Emanuel made sure it wasn't lost. The modern equivalent is the relationship between the risk-taking CEO and the risk-adverse chief risk officer. Whether you are a dry goods store with three employees or an international investment bank with more than twenty-eight thousand, the core challenge of success is fundamentally the same: *how much risk* to take when pursuing profit. Risk management is the business discipline that balances this natural conflict between risk and return. A central part of risk management is to ensure that profits accurately compensate the level of risk taking. Firm capital also needs to be adequate to support the level of risk activities. Although few financial records are available from H. Lehman's early years, what is clear is that an appropriate amount of risk was taken, and store profits grew at a rate high enough to expand the size of the original store while supporting the salaries of all three brothers.

WHY MONTGOMERY?

The Lehmans' timing was fortuitous. They started their dry goods business during a period of great economic expansion and optimism in the United States. From 1840 to 1850, the U.S. population increased by approximately 36 percent, with 85 percent living in rural areas. The South had about 42 percent of the nation's population but only 18 percent of the manufacturing capability of its northern neighbors. What the South lacked in population, it made up for in ideal growing conditions, fertile soil, and plenty of slave labor to harvest cash crops. What initially attracted these brothers to a seemingly obscure city in the South could be summed up in six letters: c-o-t-t-o-n.

Montgomery was conveniently situated on the Alabama River. This inland waterway flowed into the Gulf of Mexico and was a major highway for shipping cotton to Mobile and New Orleans as well as on to major foreign markets such as Liverpool, Rotterdam, Antwerp, and Hamburg. In Montgomery, one of the most important cotton markets at the time, owning cotton was the equivalent of having cash. The Lehman brothers initially viewed cotton as a commodity its customers converted to cash prior to purchasing store merchandise. But this view changed as H. Lehman routinely began accepting cotton bales as payment for merchandise. Cash did not have the ability to appreciate in value while cotton did. As a natural outgrowth of accepting cotton in lieu of cash, Lehman began a second successful business. Owning and trading cotton would become the most significant part of their operation.

KING COTTON

By the early nineteenth century, the Industrial Revolution that had first taken hold in Great Britain made its way to America. Numerous labor-saving inventions drove this change from an agrarian to an industrial economy. Machines took the place of humans, decreasing the cost of production and increasing the overall amount of goods available for sale. One of the most important inventions was Eli Whitney's cotton gin in 1794. Almost overnight, more cotton could be harvested with fewer hands at a lower cost. Cheaper cotton meant that cotton fabric and related products were also more affordable to a broader market. The cotton gin went from being powered by hand, then by horse, and eventually by water, each time increasing output, reducing cost, and strengthening the South's global competitive position.

By the early to mid-1800s, many inland and coastal cities across the South were experiencing a "cotton boom." Cotton became so important to the economic livelihood of the South and to the U.S. economy that it earned the name King Cotton. By 1850, approximately two-thirds of the world's demand for cotton was supplied by the United States, the majority of which was generated in the South. Cotton not only remained the single largest U.S. export until the 1930s, but it also was the largest source of the country's growing wealth.[3]

Even before the cotton boom, cotton was a commodity with a price set by global forces. Cotton prices routinely experienced rapid volatility, with both buyers and sellers subject to price risk as a result of many factors, including the costs of production, shipping, storage, taxes, and selling fees as well as the give and take of supply and demand. With globalization came increasing complexities including spoilage, tariffs, and other fees. In 1818, European demand for American cotton sent prices as high as 32.5 cents a pound only to collapse to 14 cents the following year when alternative sources were found. For the next seventeen years, the average price per pound remained less than 10 cents until prices soared again in 1857, reaching 15 cents. From 1850 to 1860 the average price increased by 23 percent, and from the mid-1870s through 1900 the annual price volatility of cotton was more than 20 percent. In other words, trading in cotton was risky. High volatility also meant high potential profit.

COTTON MERCHANTS VS. GENERAL STORES

In 1851, there were only three banks in Mississippi and Alabama combined, making obtaining capital in these important cotton states difficult.[4] Dry goods stores such as H. Lehman filled this gap by extending store credit, serving an important banking function. For smaller cotton farmers, Lehman might serve as the only market for their cotton. Yet, opting to pay general stores with cotton was cumbersome because it required transporting the cotton to make a purchase or settle a bill.[5] With one bale of cotton equal to 500 pounds at the time, this could be a labor-intensive process. Such a local barter system also forced the seller to take the prevailing market price instead of waiting for the best price during the selling season.

Initially, Lehman did not take consignment of large quantities of cotton or receive a fee for its services. But, in allowing its customers to settle account balances in cotton, Lehman was exposing the store to cotton price declines. To convert its cotton holdings into cash, Lehman employed the services of a cotton merchant—a specialist—who acted as an agent for a fee in completing the final sale. These merchants, used by most large-scale planters, provided loans in cash based on a percentage of the perceived further sale value.[6] If the proceeds for one year's harvest did not cover all advances, then the debt would roll over into the next crop season. While Southern growers provided collateral, the glue that kept this financial structure together was the willingness of cotton merchants to fund such activities. Cotton merchants eventually controlled the bulk of the market, and the role for Lehman's dry goods store as a cotton intermediary diminished.

As the size of the global cotton industry grew, the dollar size and sophistication required for financing also grew. Payment in larger transactions began to take the form of bank drafts drawn off of New York City banks. Many cotton merchants even argued that the financial center in the South was now the North.[7] In 1858, to transform itself from a general merchant into a cotton trader, Lehman established a New York branch office in the heart of the growing Wall Street financial district, at 119 Liberty Street.[8] To manage this northern outpost, Emanuel, the older and more conservative of the brothers, moved to New York.

In just thirteen years, Lehman had transformed itself from a general merchant to a cotton trader, expanding its business footprint northward to New York. Although not yet an investment bank, the brothers were building the critical in-house expertise, name recognition, business contacts, and infrastructure needed to become an expert in the rapidly developing U.S. commodity and financial markets.

THE CIVIL WAR

The first major business challenge facing Lehman was the Civil War. Once South Carolina broke from the Union on December 20, 1860, other Southern states including Alabama soon followed. The Lehman brothers had prospered in the South and were partisans of the Confederacy, even acquiring their own slave in 1854.[9] At the start of the war in April 1861, President Abraham Lincoln imposed the first of many economic blockades that would impact the Southern cotton trade beholden to Northern mills and ships. Pre-war, as much as 95 percent of Southern cotton was exported or shipped north. Cut off from its Northern merchandise suppliers, Lehman began to concentrate its business efforts "more intensively to cotton" and away from its general dry goods business.[10]

Once war was declared in 1861, Montgomery served as the first capital of the Confederate government. Lehman now was headquartered in the cradle of the Confederacy. Mayer continued to handle the day-to-day operations in Montgomery as Emanuel shuttered the New York office. As the war progressed, Southern growers continued to cultivate cotton and store their harvests in hidden warehouses and cotton sheds.[11] However, between 1861 and 1864, annual crop yields plummeted from a high of 4.5 million bales to a low of 300,000 bales. With the decline in supply, global cotton prices spiked. Higher prices meant there was money to be made for those willing to take the trading-related risk. Having repositioned itself to concentrate on cotton trading, Lehman was one of those firms willing to take the risk.

In 1862, Lehman established a joint venture with John Wesley Durr, a well-known Southern cotton merchant. The new business, Lehman, Durr & Co., included the purchase of a sizable Alabama warehouse to store cotton. With this increased storage capacity, Lehman could purchase cotton when prices were low, hold bales until prices went higher, and then sell. By 1863, Lehman, Durr & Co. was among the five leading Montgomery cotton firms.[12]

In the final days of the war, Lehman actually burned much of its cotton inventory to prevent this valuable commodity from reaching Union hands.[13] Despite the economic hardship in the South, with the surrender at Appomattox Court House on April 9, 1865, King Cotton returned as the South's main cash crop. Post-war, more than half the cotton produced in the South came from western Alabama, Mississippi, and Louisiana. Through its partnership with John Wesley Durr, Lehman was instrumental in refinancing some of Alabama's debt during Reconstruction. This financial success allowed Lehman to reestablish the New York office. The profound economic shift that had begun prior to the war was turning out to be permanent. The trading center of cotton had moved from the South to the commission houses of New York City.

By 1868, the New York Lehman office was busy enough that Mayer joined Emanuel, and they decided to make New York their permanent base of operation. Lehman also expanded to other commodities, including coffee, sugar, grains, and petroleum.[14] In 1870, Lehman became one of the founding members of the New York Cotton Exchange, and Mayer served on the board until 1884. Lehman was also an active member of the Coffee Exchange and the New York Petroleum Exchange. Once in place, these exchanges increased the volume of trading in these products, which was financially advantageous to such firms as Lehman.

GATEKEEPERS OF CAPITAL

During the early twentieth century, using debt and stock ownership as a means of raising capital was still a relatively new concept. Unlike the capital markets of today, widespread inefficiency often plagued the market. Key to the success of capital flow was the number of banks and their willingness to lend. As the economy grew, the number of banks also grew. In 1860, there were approximately 1,400 banks in the United States; by 1921 this number had grown to about 30,000.

One of the main capital gatekeepers of this time was the banking behemoth later known as J.P. Morgan, founded in 1871 as Drexel, Morgan & Co. by J. Pierpont Morgan and Philadelphia banker Anthony Drexel. This venture started as a vehicle for Europeans to invest in and profit from the American industrial expansion. A major part of the securities business was underwriting new issues of stocks and bonds for cash-hungry borrowers such as railroads. In 1879 J.P. Morgan successfully issued New York Central Railroad stock for owner William Vanderbilt. At the time, this was the largest stock offering of its kind, and it made J.P. Morgan's reputation. It became the primary bank that railroads went to for capital. J.P. Morgan next provided funding to numerous large-scale industrial mergers such as U.S. Steel, General Electric, and International Harvester.

ANTI-SEMITISM ON WALL STREET

J.P. Morgan's early successes positioned it to pick and choose its customers, and it wasn't shy about avoiding Jewish clients or partnerships. In fact, J.P. Morgan and other prominent lenders were widely known as having a policy of *not lending* to "Jewish companies." Such discrimination forced Jewish-run firms to tap European financial houses as their primary source for capital and allowed them to develop a close web of family connections.[15] In some ways, the international money that firms like Lehman accessed provided them room to grow with minimum competitive threats from traditional Wall Street firms. This model of family-controlled leadership continued at Lehman until the late 1960s.

To smaller firms like Lehman and Goldman Sachs & Co., the lucrative market segment that included heavy industries like railroad and steel was tightly controlled by an underwriting oligopoly.[16] However, according to former Harvard historian Vincent Carosso, "the growing financial needs of companies in light industry, retail stores, and other small enterprises seeking to go public were not being met by the major investment banking firms."[17] Quite simply, U.S. consumers had more disposable money to spend, and the dramatic growth of department and chain stores were an attempt to meet this demand. For bankers kept out of well-established underwriting, this trend provided an opportunity to finance smaller niche enterprises.

Perhaps most important, these discriminatory practices also provided the impetus for investment banking firms to develop joint businesses and use more creative financing. Author Charles Ellis has suggested that "[i]n a rapidly expanding firm-to-firm partnership, the Goldmans provided the clients and the Lehmans provided the capital."[18] Working in collaboration with Lehman, Goldman Sachs pioneered the use of commercial paper as a lending tool. Such techniques were viewed as speculative because a loan was provided based on payment of a larger amount in the future. These IOUs would then be traded like securities among the nondiscriminatory investment banks. It is striking that today this $2 trillion commercial paper market, which plays such a critical role in providing corporations with shorter-term financing, was the brainchild of these two, at the time, marginalized firms. Ironically, this same market Lehman helped to create would later grind to a complete halt upon the firm's dramatic bankruptcy.

Lehman continued to be opportunistic. Another shrewd move was the acquisition of a seat on the New York Stock Exchange (NYSE) in 1887. Although Lehman had some previous bond experience serving as fiscal agent for Alabama, buying a seat on the NYSE placed Lehman at the epicenter of a burgeoning capital market.[19] Since May 17, 1792, when the NYSE was founded, Wall Street had played a role in raising capital. But the amount of capital needed to support the growth of the post-war industrial economy meant that Wall Street and its banking firms were playing an ever-increasing role. Lehman now had a seat on perhaps the busiest capital intersection in the world and was well positioned to become a contender in the investment banking community.

SECOND GENERATION OF LEHMANS

With the death of Mayer (the risk taker) in 1897 and Emanuel (the risk manager) in 1907, the day-to-day responsibilities of running Lehman officially passed to the next generation, Emanuel's son, Philip. With the passing of the torch, the partnership was expanded to five family members: Philip, Sigmund, Arthur, Meyer H., and later Herbert H.[20] The firm was constrained by its capital size, which was directly related to the number of partners.[21] As the fee-driven business model of securities underwriting began emerging during this time, Lehman still did not have adequate capital size to put firm capital at risk.

Changes in corporate law were also under way. Previously, a business owner's personal net worth was on the hook. Risk management was essential, not only to keep from losing money at work but also to keep from losing the family home. Now the growth of modern capitalism was being bolstered by a legal separation that created limited liability for corporate owners. These favorable new conditions eventually helped catapult the Lehman family partnership into the rankings of an investment bank.

LEHMAN'S BIG BREAK

The economy was booming, and Lehman was positioned perfectly. By 1899 the firm helped in the sale of the Rubber Tire Wheel Company (predecessor to Goodyear Tire and Rubber Company), a large producer of tires used for automobiles. Shares of this company were subsequently distributed in a public offering.[22] Lehman then underwrote its first public offering in March 1899, involving International Steam Pump Company. This offering included $15 million in common stock and $12.5 million in preferred stock.[23]

This early success whetted Lehman's appetite, but transformation to a full-fledged investment bank was not quite complete. The next major joint-underwriting opportunity came several years later, in 1906, with United Cigar, later known as General Cigar. As a Goldman Sachs client, United Cigar had done short-term commercial borrowing to finance inventory, but this time it needed to raise long-term capital. Unlike the standard railroad financing, United Cigar's value was not based on balance sheet assets but on earnings power. The uncertainty of this emerging retailer made it risky to underwrite. The company decided to use stock instead of debt as a funding strategy—a speculative move. As part of this transaction, Lehman and Goldman Sachs agreed to underwrite $4.5 million in stock and eventually were able to sell this stock to investors at a 24 percent markup—a tidy profit for both firms.[24] The bet not only paid off but created the opportunity for underwriting other consumer retail companies that fell outside the traditional balance sheet model for lending.

One of these fast-growing retail start-up companies was Midwest-based Sears, Roebuck & Co. Retailing directly to the consumer via mail order was a relatively new business concept, and underwriting such a company posed inherent risk. While it first went slowly, by April 1906, in yet another example of a successful firm-to-firm partnership, Lehman and Goldman Sachs underwrote $10 million of Sears securities. By 1910 Sears stock had doubled in value, validating the company's retail business model and the methods used by Lehman and Goldman Sachs to underwrite the stock. In 1912 Lehman also underwrote F.W. Woolworth Co., the first variety chain to be sold to the public. With the notoriety achieved from these early successes, Lehman and Goldman Sachs began to build a sizable book of business.

By 1912 Lehman had sold all of its interest in its cotton operations, concentrating its efforts on the more lucrative underwriting fee activities from its New York headquarters. This break with its roots in the South was not only symbolic but also freed Lehman to focus on investment banking. In this new era of mass merchandizing, many companies were being formed. Between 1906 and 1925, Lehman was involved in underwriting approximately one hundred securities issues.[25] Lehman, in partnership or on its own, became the banker for many future prominent retailers, including R.H. Macy; Gimbel Brothers; Brown Shoe Company; and May Department Stores Company. Lehman also helped to underwrite Studebaker Corporation (1911); Continental Can Company (1913); B.F. Goodrich Company (1920); Campbell Soup Company (1922); American Metal Co. Ltd. (1922); and the Anglo-Chilean Nitrate Corporation (1925).[26] The flood of underwriting fees, without putting significant firm capital at risk, helped build the House of Lehman. At last, Lehman was truly an investment banking firm. Southern cotton paid for the initial ticket, but now Lehman had earned a front row seat.

THIRD GENERATION OF LEHMANS

Under the leadership of Philip Lehman,[27] the second generation transformed the firm from a commodities house to an investment banking house. One of the last important decisions made under Philip was to expand beyond the firm's family-only partnership philosophy. In 1924, decades after Lehman's founding, it finally permitted an outsider to become a partner with the addition of John M. Hancock. Partnership size was no longer constrained by family lineage. Partners with varying experience and expertise could be hired. By 1950, Lehman had expanded to seventeen partners, only two of which were family members.

Philip officially relinquished day-to-day duties in 1925 when he handed leadership to his son, Robert "Bobbie." Under Bobbie's guidance, the firm expanded equity and bond underwriting, investment advising, and brokering. A great bull market helped make this growth possible. From 1920 to 1929, stocks more than quadrupled in value. Convinced stocks could only go up, many investors borrowed heavily on this bet.[28]

CRASH OF 1929

The Civil War presented Lehman with its first significant challenge. This initial test unexpectedly turned fortuitous, providing the impetus to morph into a New York–based investment bank. The stock market crash of 1929 proved to be an even more daunting challenge. In a matter of months, stock market declines wiped out billions in depositor money and investment capital, destroyed investor confidence, and triggered a rise in unemployment, which eventually topped 20 percent. Banks that had enabled investors to speculate on the market were now trying to call in their loans. As word spread that many banks were sitting on bad loans and worthless stocks, bank runs forced many banks into bankruptcy. The stock market would not hit bottom until it dropped by 80 percent from the 1929 high. On July 8, 1932, the Dow Jones Industrial Average (Dow) dipped to its lowest level overall in the 1900s. In the most dramatic and protracted financial meltdown in U.S. history, the capital spigot vital to emerging companies was turned off. The equity underwriting that had been Lehman's main engine of growth over the previous two decades, and which only months earlier had been so profitable, was no longer working. Lehman had to once again readjust.

In response to the 1929 crash, Congress issued an investigation to determine why such a dramatic financial collapse took place and how to prevent one from happening again. Beginning under the Hoover administration, continuing under Franklin Delano Roosevelt (FDR), and lasting until 1934, Judge Ferdinand Pecora led the Senate committee hearings that probed the causes of the crash. The findings of the Pecora Commission destroyed the favorable public image that investment bankers had previously enjoyed and paved the way for widespread regulation.[29] As the stock market had heated up in the early 1920s, it was true that numerous commercial banks had entered the equity underwriting business and used customer deposits to support very risky activities. Other speculative excesses included aggressive trading practices by investment banking houses. In April 1932 the Senate Banking and Currency Committee questioned Walter Sachs, a general partner in Goldman Sachs, about such business practices. This hearing revealed that the firm had placed client funds in stocks near the height of the market, but by 1932 these stocks were worth a mere 1/100th of the initial investment. Thirty percent of American banks failed, and approximately $140 billion was lost. Public outcry for sweeping reform was hardly surprising.

THE NEW DEAL

In response to the crisis, FDR's first act as president was to declare a national bank holiday, which closed the banks for a three-day rest period to prevent bank runs. The most memorable line from his speech targeting this crisis—"The only thing we have to fear is fear itself"—has been echoed numerous times and even dusted off in response to the Great Credit Crisis of 2008.[30] This was more than just a political sound bite. Strong words were needed from the president to calm an anxious public, and, more important, to prepare it for the looming changes. It was in this heated political climate that Congress passed the far-reaching and reform-minded Banking Act of 1933. The centerpiece of this reform was the Glass-Steagall Act, which prohibited commercial banks from underwriting the securities of corporations. In a single stroke of a pen, the relationship between investment banks and commercial banks was severed. This act radically changed the face of Wall Street, forcing commercial banks and investment banks to pick their industry. According to Professor Robert Sobel, "[b]anks and bankers molded their destinies throughout the rest of the decade."[31]

To better protect depositors and reduce the chance of future bank runs, the Banking Act of 1933 also established the Federal Deposit Insurance Corporation (FDIC). This new agency required deposit institutions such as commercial banks to pay an insurance premium into a general fund based on deposits held. The FDIC was then charged with ensuring the safety of depositor money and given the power to close banks if necessary. In a move to reduce the chance of financial panics, banks were also prohibited from investing depositor money in stocks.

A third important reform was the creation of the Securities and Exchange Commission (SEC) to regulate the sale of securities to the public. Overnight, the SEC became the top securities cop. To head this watchdog organization, FDR appointed Joseph P. Kennedy. When asked why Kennedy, FDR responded tongue-in-cheek by saying, "It takes a thief to catch a thief." In a sweeping reform, firms that issue and underwrite securities were required to comply with full-disclosure requirements. Companies had to register with the SEC before selling stocks to the public and provide an official financial report, or "prospectus." This report had to incorporate the advice from experts such as investment bankers, lawyers, and accountants to explain the offering and its risks in detail. Only when the SEC was satisfied with the prospectus could a company go ahead with the offering.

These three radical Depression-era reforms forced Lehman and other financial firms to reassess their banking activities. Rarely had an industry been obligated to accept so much change in such a short period of time. Corporate makeovers and business disruptions were the norms for firms pulled apart by the Glass-Steagall Act. For example, once J.P. Morgan chose to stay in commercial banking, several employees left and formed the investment bank Morgan Stanley. J. W. Seligman Company, a well-known investment bank similar to Lehman, divested of banking activities, including taking in deposits.[32] Other corporate makeovers included the combination of Chase National and First National of Boston (First Boston Corporation), and investment affiliate Guaranty Trust of New York merging with Edward B. Smith & Company (Smith Barney & Company).

For Lehman, which by the 1930s was primarily an investment bank, the choice was clear. It quickly relinquished all ties to commercial banks and deposit-taking activities with affiliates. In two years, Lehman went from operating in a virtually regulation-free environment to operating under what would have been considered at the time heavy federal regulation. As the nation slowly pulled itself out of the Great Depression, Lehman began to see an expansion in underwriting activities, including the initial public offering of the country's first television manufacturer, Dumont. Yet, as a percentage of the nation's total underwriting activities for both stocks and bonds, Lehman was still not one of the top-tier investment banks.

END OF FAMILY-RUN LEHMAN

During World War II, Lehman sold government bonds. Daily operations were compromised because many people from the firm served in the armed forces, including nine of the existing fourteen partners who served active duty. Post–World War II, the United States experienced an economic boom as troops returned home, and capital was once again available for business enterprise. Lehman's underwriting successes before the war gave it an expertise that was now in high demand. By the 1950s, a growing number of retail, real estate, electronic, and aviation companies were selling new shares to the public.

In 1954 a major psychological hurdle was surpassed when the market finally overcame its 1929 pre-crash levels. By 1955 the Dow reached 488, and by the end of 1959 it hit 679, almost a 300 percent increase from the beginning of the decade.[33] During this period, the trade volume on the NYSE also took off. Between 1945 and 1959, the volume of shares traded almost tripled. The U.S. economy had rebounded, and Lehman, along with the rest of the nation, benefited. According to Ken Auletta, "[b]y 1967, the House of Lehman was responsible for $3.5 billion in underwriting."[34] Measured in underwriting volume, Lehman now ranked among the top four investment banks, and for the most part, it would remain in this top-tier position until its spectacular collapse.

Chapter 3

From Private to Public

After a protracted illness, Bobbie Lehman, family patriarch and leader of the fourth largest investment bank on Wall Street, died in 1969. When the bull market of the 1920s came to an abrupt end with the crash of 1929, the ensuing Great Depression tested whether the third generation of Lehmans had the leadership skills to navigate a crippled banking system and a stock market that would not rebound until the 1950s. Under the steady hand of Bobbie, the firm grew from six to forty-four partners and attained the lofty status of a top-tier investment bank. Referring to the firm under Bobbie, author Ken Auletta wrote in *Greed and Glory on Wall Street*, "You felt that if there was any such thing as a business aristocracy, and at the same time a highly profitable venture, that was it."[1] But by 1969, the following could have been just as easily inscribed on Bobbie's tombstone: *Here lay a man who did not groom a successor.*

After Bobbie's death, the firm went through a period of chaos and uncertainty. The partner initially chosen to succeed Bobbie as chairman was Joseph A. Thomas. Although he had been with Lehman since 1930, Thomas lacked the physical stamina needed for the job. Suffering from emphysema and generally poor health, within months of becoming chairman, he took seriously ill. Lehman partners responded in panic mode and began withdrawing their capital. For a private partnership, such capital withdrawal is the equivalent of a bank run. Infighting ensued, and business began to drop off dramatically. Lehman was significantly wounded.

In 1971, sixty-five-year-old Frederick L. Ehrman, who had a reputation for being talented but gruff, became chairman. During Ehrman's tenure, Lehman's business continued to decline and was damaged further by the recession triggered by the oil embargo of 1973. More partners jumped ship. These added defections hurt corporate morale and highlighted the importance of replacing Ehrman. Someone needed to save the faltering House of Lehman. For the first time in its history, the firm needed to go outside its own management ranks to find a suitable leader.

PETER G. PETERSON

At first glance, Peter G. (Pete) Peterson did not appear a likely candidate to steer Lehman. Born in Kearney, Nebraska, to Greek immigrant parents, this Midwesterner attended Northwestern University and the University of Chicago. He was truly an "outsider" not just to Lehman but to Wall Street. Not an investment banker by training but a corporate executive who liked politics, Peterson was the former CEO of Chicago-based Bell & Howell, at the time a manufacturer of movie cameras. He had also served in the Nixon administration as secretary of commerce. Peterson seemed more like a corporate executive Lehman might find useful as a business contact rather than a candidate to run the bank. But it took an outsider to understand the problems that needed to be solved.

Peterson thought Lehman was resting on its laurels and needed to aggressively solicit and attract new corporate customers. The banking industry was experiencing a pronounced change in customer behavior in which corporations had begun to shift toward multiple investment banking relationships. For example, General Motors (GM) had historically used only Morgan Stanley but was now adding additional bankers to its roster. As competing firms began soliciting key Lehman customers, the collegial bond between sole banker and client was disappearing.[2]

Arriving at Lehman in 1973, Peterson immediately focused on expanding product development and broadening the financial services offered. He also cut expenses and reduced the number of employees from 955 to 663 by the following year.[3] In short order, this assertive new business solicitation and cost cutting swung Lehman back to profitability. In November 1975, Peterson appeared on the cover of *Business Week*. The lead story, which he could not have written any better, was titled "Back from the Brink Comes Lehman Bros."[4] Peterson was able to lead Lehman from significant operating losses to five consecutive years of record profits.

STRUCTURAL CHANGES

By the 1970s, the financial landscape on Wall Street was changing with the rise of institutional clients, including mutual funds, pension funds, insurance companies, and even investment banks. Fast-rising firms such as GM had ever-growing employee ranks and sizable pension funds that needed to be managed. This new group of financial players increasingly had the capability to trade large blocks of stock. Investment banking, which had historically built its reputation and size on long-standing business relationships, was becoming more of a transaction-by-transaction industry. In many ways, investment banking was making the transition from a less genteel business to a more competitive industry. The new business model followed a simple formula: underwrite the largest number of shares and receive the largest commission. The industry rankings, also known as "league tables," supported the view that bigger trade volume and bigger underwriting deals meant higher rankings. The increased size of deals and competition added pressure on firms to place greater amounts of capital at risk. On Wall Street, a clear distinction developed between the deep-pocketed firms and smaller firms that were less capitalized. Under Peterson's stewardship, Lehman's capital increased fivefold, yet compared to other top-tier firms, it still was not keeping pace.

Acknowledging that more capital strengthened competitive position, firms continued bolstering their capital. Even as far back as the late 1950s, Salomon Brothers began building up its capital war chest. From 1960 to 1970, its capital base increased from $10 to $60 million, and by 1980 it had reached $236 million. Having faith that more firm value would be created in the future under this strategy, Salomon Brothers grew its capital by paying out less to partners on an annual basis.[5] This put Salomon Brothers on solid footing as it moved into more underwriting activities and competed head-to-head with firms like Lehman.

The competitiveness extended beyond capital war chests. In an effort to attract the deep-pocketed institutional investors, margins started falling in traditional underwriting and merger and acquisition fees. These fees had been Lehman's bread and butter. In some services, investment banking was taking on the characteristics of a commodity business where bankers made money on volume, not on pricing. Compounding this was a simultaneous compression in brokerage-related fees. On May 1, 1975, the Securities and Exchange Commission (SEC) lifted the fixed-rate commissions and ushered in a new era of greater commission rate competition. This meant institutional clients that traded large blocks of stock could now negotiate the rate they paid. Many investment banks responded by increasing the types of services offered to find new higher-margin sources of revenue, in addition to maintaining relationships with important clients. Business writer Rachel S. Epstein has suggested that "[b]efore the SEC ruling, clients had stayed with their brokers or investment bankers 'for life'; now companies shop[ped] around to negotiate the best deal."[6] Central to all of these new strategies was the increasingly prominent role played by trading.

THE RISE OF TRADING AND CHANGING RISK PROFILE

Lehman in the 1970s was one of many investment banks that decided to expand their trading activities in an effort to diversify their revenue stream. Given that investment banking revenue was so susceptible to the economic cycles, Lehman pushed to find ways to generate more predictable year-on-year revenue. Trading and putting more firm capital at risk was part of the answer. Heading up this effort was partner and trading boss Lewis L. Glucksman. Born into a second-generation Hungarian-Jewish family in New York City, Glucksman served as a teenage volunteer with the navy in World War II. Afterward, he attended William and Mary College before earning a master's in business administration from New York University (NYU). In 1962 Glucksman joined Lehman and quickly distinguished himself as an adept trader, eventually being promoted to head of sales and trading. He also oversaw a little-known junior trader, Richard "Dick" Fuld Jr., who would rise to run the company a decade after his mentor, Glucksman, vacated the position.

DICK FULD

Born in New York City, Fuld was raised in an upper-middle-class family. He attended the University of Colorado (Boulder), and his first career in the air force was short-lived because of a fistfight with the commanding officer. Hired in 1969, the same year that Bobbie Lehman died, Fuld started his career at Lehman by trading commercial paper—a low-risk business in comparison to today's derivatives market. In 1973, similar to his boss, Fuld completed a master's in business administration at NYU. Over time he developed a reputation as being an accomplished fixed-income trader.

Under Glucksman's leadership, Lehman's trading area put a growing amount of firm capital at risk. This bet paid off, and Glucksman's traders began to generate an increasing amount of the firm's overall profit. As trading profits grew and outpaced investment banking profits (i.e., fees from mergers and acquisitions), tension between these two factions become apparent. Unlike at rival investment banking firms such as Goldman Sachs or Salomon Brothers, at Lehman there was no previous history of significant trading prior to Glucksman's arrival in the early 1960s.[7] At Lehman, Glucksman and the younger Fuld were in the first generation of true traders, and, significantly, within the Wall Street community they began to represent the new face of the company. On the trading floor, Glucksman developed a reputation as being volatile, and it was rumored he even ripped off his shirt in an agitated state. Fuld earned the nickname "Gorilla" from his grunting on the trading floor and his obsession with staying physically fit. Pleased with this caricature, Fuld kept a stuffed namesake in his office. These two men, a decisive departure in character from the early years of Lehman Brothers, would come to epitomize the rough-and-tumble sport of trading.

As trading in fixed income and to a lesser extent equity instruments took a more prominent seat in the firm, the level of risk taking changed dramatically. Trading, unlike investment banking, required greater amounts of firm capital and the willingness to risk big to win big. Salomon Brothers, in particular, would come to represent this new breed of investment bank with a firm focus on placing large trading bets. Unlike Lehman, Salomon Brothers had amassed sizable capital that allowed it to take such bets. It was an early advocate of bringing in mathematicians and physicists from schools such as Massachusetts Institute of Technology and training them to become bond traders. By the 1980s the domestic fixed-income arbitrage group of Salomon Brothers, headed by famed trader John Meriwether, was bringing in the majority of the firm's overall revenue. At Salomon Brothers, the success of this single trading area created envy and resentment across the firm. At Lehman, the same trend was becoming increasingly true. These two business lines not only represented a philosophical difference—they were also literally separated by two different physical locations. It would not be until 1980, when Lehman moved its investment banking operation to 55 Water Street, that both business lines would be consolidated under one roof.

It was not surprising that Peterson, who sat in the same headquarters as Bobbie Lehman once had at One William Street, was not initially inclined to move the business.[8] Peterson, the consummate statesman (and to some the arrogant leader), still saw the firm through the eyes of his respected predecessor and not through those of brash traders like Glucksman or Fuld. Inevitably, these two distinct cultures would collide. Author Jonathan A. Knee wrote that "[a]t Lehman, it was the supremacy of fixed income over investment banking or vice versa."[9] Lehman's future direction was hanging in the balance of which one of these factions would win out.

PETERSON'S DEMISE

In May 1983, in an attempt to bridge the growing chasm, Peterson extended an olive branch, promoting Glucksman to the newly created position of co-CEO. Though well intended, this approach backfired, fueling more hostilities and speculation between the firm's two warring factions. Peterson was not able to serve as a counterbalance. Once given additional power, Glucksman quickly made personnel changes, including how bonuses and partnership interests would be determined. These moves, combined with his already abrasive management style, appeared to many to be a power grab, with the ulterior motive of a redistribution of power favoring Lehman traders at the expense of its investment bankers.

A financial storm also brewed outside the walls of Lehman's headquarters. The economy was going through its first significant recession in more than a decade, putting downward pressure on Lehman's profitability. In short, Lehman was a powder keg ready to explode, and the weakening economy was the remaining event needed to light the fuse. The tension continued to escalate, culminating in a bitter power struggle in which Peterson was finally ousted and Glucksman became the firm's sole CEO.[10] Trading and putting greater firm capital at risk had won; investment banking had lost.

THE SUPERNOVA

Glucksman's tenure at the top lasted less than one year. Though a success-ful trader, Glucksman did not have the demeanor or required skill to turn Lehman around as its CEO. During his brief stint, he presided over a firm with sinking earnings and increasing defections in a weakening economy. In Glucksman's defense, an additional powerful force outside of his control also came into play. Wall Street was undergoing fundamental changes that had started in the previous decade. Underwriting transactions and trading lot sizes continued to put additional pressure on firms to increase capital as they competed for a share of this lucrative business. A combination of all of these factors—declining firm profits, questionable management skills, a weak economy, and competitive pressures requiring larger capital—contributed to a loss of confidence in Glucksman. By 1984 Lehman was forced to sell not to the highest bidder, but to the only bidder.

For 134 years, Lehman's formula for success centered on a small group of partners running a privately owned company. During this period, partners risked their own capital in the company and, for the most part, were attentive to the risks being assumed. Profits generated from a limited capital base supported company growth. By 1984 a weakened Lehman was hobbled by the fact that while a top-tier investment bank, its capital paled in comparison to its competition. This smaller capital base not only put Lehman at a disadvantage when competing for larger transactions, it meant there was less cushion to protect against losses. Lehman was backed into a corner. It had to reduce the risk-taking activities and shrink the firm, raise additional capital to remain independent, or sell itself outright.

In desperation, on May 11, 1984, Lehman was sold to Shearson/American Express for $360 million, considerably less than the $600 million price Glucksman was informally offered a year earlier.[11] The combined company was called Shearson Lehman American Express. This merger marked the death of Lehman's private partnership structure and the merger of a storied investment bank into the retail culture of Shearson. Lehman gained needed capital, but from the start the cultures did not mix.

Despite the clash, the new company continued to grow, and in 1988 it acquired E. F. Hutton & Company to form a retail brokerage and investment banking powerhouse. However, by 1993, under the guidance of newly appointed CEO Harvey Golub, American Express decided to exit the brokerage and investment banking business. Initially, it sold the retail parts to Smith Barney (later absorbed by Citigroup in 1994), and in June 1994, Lehman was spun off to the public as Lehman Brothers Holdings, Inc., a stand-alone investment bank. This new public company traded on the New York Stock Exchange under the symbol LEH, the ticker it kept until its final demise.

Under the new public spotlight, Lehman had to reassess itself and determine its core operations. One consequence of breaking up Shearson Lehman was that the Lehman portion was not as strong in investment banking or equity research. Post spin-off, many on Wall Street viewed Lehman as simply a fixed-income shop. The timing, however, of Lehman's initial public offering was good. The U.S. economy was finally coming out of a deep recession. After hitting bottom in 1991, the Dow was experiencing a forty-month stock market advance. On April 17, 1991, the Dow broke a new record, climbing above 3,000; in 1995 it rose above 5,000; and by mid-1997 it reached 8,000. Lehman again showed it could adapt to change and re-created itself with a growing tailwind from this stock market. Picked to lead Lehman was former fixed-income trader and Glucksman protégé, Dick Fuld. With Fuld at the helm, Lehman's future direction—an emphasis on trading and the inherent risk that came with it—was apparent.

Chapter 4

History of Investment Banking

B efore continuing with Lehman's trajectory, it is useful to explore the history of the industry in which Lehman competed—and also helped to define and build—as well as the history of the governmental and regulatory players within that industry. Banking is synonymous with money. Since the birth of America, investment banks and commercial banks have played an interconnected role in its economy. The boom-and-bust cycles of America's economy, and, indeed, the prosperity of banks have tracked the economic growth of the nation. During these cycles, legislation and the level of state versus federal regulation have had a major influence on banks' risk-taking activities. Since their inception, Wall Street banks and the bankers that run them have been envied, ignored, or vilified. This group continues to symbolize immense power and wealth.

INVESTMENT BANKING BASICS

Historically, commercial banks have been regulated heavily while investment banks have been regulated lightly or not at all. Some of the regulatory challenges that have confronted policymakers during the past two hundred years are still debated today. Regulation has played a defining role in the health of American banks and the economy, yet the U.S. government has failed to find the perfect balance between excessive regulation—viewed as stifling to bank profitability and economic growth—and lax regulation and oversight—viewed as a recipe for financial and economic instability.

In investment banking, similar to commercial banking, perception is everything. Investment banks are built on confidence in their ability to honor contractual obligations. Reputation and perceived financial strength determine the ability of a bank to tap capital markets, meet immediate- and longer-term funding needs, and attract and keep customers. For investment banks, job number one is keeping market confidence. A rumor that questions financial solvency, even if false, can prove devastating if not quickly silenced. Once market confidence is lost, an investment bank's ability to conduct day-to-day business can be instantly destroyed.

Investment banks serve as financial intermediaries in the transfer of capital from those who have money to those who need it. The cost of capital and access to it are important factors that prime the economic pump. Households (individuals; residential units of economic production and consumption) are the primary suppliers of capital, and corporations and government are the primary borrowers. Banks play a gatekeeper role to ensure that borrowers are able to obtain capital at competitive terms and lenders lend at competitive terms. This cost of capital is directly linked to the investment's perceived risk level. Lenders and borrowers have a natural conflict as they seek to balance risk and return. Lenders desire high return and low risk while borrowers seek low-cost funds. This is where investment banks come into play—they price and manage risk, which facilitates proper risk allocation among market participants.

If risk is not properly priced, capital is destroyed. Despite the evolution of market sophistication, with the help of banks, many bad investment decisions have been made throughout history. Yet, imagine a market without banks. Capital would not flow to its highest and best use, making it difficult for investors to find good investments and for borrowers to find adequate capital to support company growth. Financial products that provide risk mitigation or allow for speculation would be diminished. The significant growth of American industry during the past two centuries would not have occurred without investment banks taking risks.

Investment banks help corporations, governments, and municipalities sell their new securities (equity or debt) to finance capital needs, a process called underwriting. In addition, once securities are sold, investment bankers create secondary markets by acting as brokers and dealers between buyers and sellers unrelated to the issuer. Additional investment bank services include advising on mergers and acquisitions, consulting, merchant banking, and developing new financial products, including derivatives such as mortgage-backed securities. As investment banks evolved, many of them also became active in providing brokerage services to wealthy individuals and added asset management operations to their core areas of activities. It is common for investment banks to have trading floors to accommodate client needs as well as to trade for their own accounts. These trading activities can involve stocks, bonds, real estate, commodities, and derivative-related instruments. Trading activities put firm capital and, more recently, shareholder equity at risk to pursue profit.

While this modern description may capture the essence of investment banking today, the origins of the specialized services they provide are much older than Wall Street, the stock exchanges, or even the founding of the United States. In the history of global finance, investment banks are relative newcomers—the term "investment banking" was coined in America—and can trace their roots back to the Italian merchant bankers of the Middle Ages. Merchant bankers, simply a melding of *merchant* and *banker*, were once family-owned merchants that specialized in import-export, dry goods, or commodity trading. Eventually, merchants developed ancillary businesses from which they began using their excess capital to finance ventures in exchange for part of the profits. Merchants were willing to take risk by backing business ventures that other lenders and investors shied away from. Many of these bets entailed long and uncertain sea voyages, meaning that the initial investments could remain illiquid for indefinite amounts of time. Uncertainties included bad weather, inexperienced crews, goods damaged in transit, war, and piracy.

Organized stock exchanges such as those in Amsterdam and money markets in Antwerp and Lyon helped to facilitate the merchants' risk-taking activities by improving their ability to raise capital and finance investment activities. Merchant banking in Europe eventually began to consolidate, and, by the end of the eighteenth century, it was no longer a sideline business but a thriving banking specialty. Exchanges provided a ready source of capital that could be invested in a growing amount of ventures. Many of the American banks that sprouted in the 1800s were based on this European banking model.

It was not uncommon for merchants to act as *loan contractors*—a precursor to modern investment banks—by buying and reselling securities to make profit.[1] An example of this type of transaction occurred in 1813, when the U.S. Treasury, to finance America's war against England, enlisted the help of several financial intermediaries to raise money. One such syndicate included Barings, a London-based investment bank. Risking its own capital, Barings purchased war-related U.S. bonds, assumed the market risk, and successfully sold the bonds at a profit through its widespread business network. Today, this common transaction of an investment bank risking its own capital is referred to as *firm commitment*.

EARLY AMERICAN INVESTMENT BANKING

Immediately after the American Revolution, the pace of banking in the United States was slow because most investments were small and did not require the services of a financial intermediary.[2] In 1790 there were no investment banks, and only four of what are known today as commercial banks existed. That year the first brick to build what is now Wall Street was laid when the newly formed U.S. government refinanced $80 million of federal and state Revolutionary War debt. This single event resulted in the first public security offering, a debt transaction many financial historians mark as the birth of the U.S. capital market. Two years later, in 1792, the New York Stock Exchange (NYSE) opened, planting the seeds for investment banking in America.

Where there are stock exchanges, there are investment bankers. Similar to how merchant banks benefited from the great market exchanges of Europe, NYSE traders agreed to establish a formalized exchange for buying and selling securities and debt. The new exchange created a mechanism that investment banks could use for raising capital. In the exchange's first year, five securities were traded—three government bonds and two bank stocks. By 1800, the number of commercial banks listed on the exchange increased to twenty-nine, and the foundation of what would become the modern capital market was laid.

By 1830 the first railroad stock, Mohawk & Hudson, was traded. Railroad entrepreneurs needed capital to support their ambitious expansion plans. Bankers facilitated these ventures by raising capital through a growing domestic and foreign investor base by issuing stocks and bonds—an innovative move for the time. Over the long run, many investors profited as stock value increased. Exchange-traded securities continued to expand, and railroad stocks and bonds dominated trading through the rest of the nineteenth century. A formal exchange, an entrepreneurial spirit, and an increasing flow of foreign capital combined to establish ideal growing conditions that allowed investment banking to help build a new nation.

COMPANY OWNERSHIP, COURTS, AND CORPORATE GOVERNANCE

Expanded investment banking activities also created the need for defined corporate legal structures. The advent of equity and bond financing created a new concept of corporate ownership that was relatively foreign to most investors and required them to place faith in a board of directors, management, and strong legal system to support shareholder and bondholder rights. Of the thirteen original colonies, Delaware took the lead with a business court dating back to 1792. Based on English law, this legal system provided legal precedence that allowed for the development of corporations as stand-alone entities. Delaware's Court of Chancery still presides over cases of corporate fiduciary duty. Corporate management and boards of directors are held to a standard of conduct that demands they act in the best interest of shareholders. Though the complexity of business has grown during the past two hundred years, this principle still guides the court today. The majority of Fortune 500 companies and several Lehman Brothers subsidiaries were incorporated in Delaware.

Throughout the nineteenth and early twentieth centuries, it was not uncommon for shareholders to actively participate in the governance of U.S. corporations.[3] With the advent of stock exchanges and banks and the rapid growth of corporations that wanted to raise additional capital, issues surrounding corporate governance became increasingly important. Initially, shareholders derived power by electing a corporate board of directors, which in turn hired the CEO and other top management. Shareholders' active participation influenced company strategy and its level of risk taking. Near the end of the twentieth and into the twenty-first centuries, shareholders became less hands-on and showed displeasure not by voting out directors but rather by selling stock. As shareholders became more removed from deciding how companies were structured and run, CEOs enjoyed more latitude in their decisions. Typically, directors are elected by shareholders and get paid for providing such stewardship. To attract strong directors, companies offer competitive salaries, non-monetary perks such as fancy meeting venues, and legal protection by providing errors and omission insurance. Effective boards are a counterbalance to management and provide valuable oversight, helping to ensure that shareholder or partnership value is created and protected, not destroyed.

Unfortunately, some boards have developed into an extension of a CEO's friendship network instead of an independent governing body that ensures shareholder interests are put first. In 2002, in response to poor corporate governance at failed firms such as Enron, WorldCom, and Tyco, Congress passed the Sarbanes-Oxley Act. Part of the law requires greater transparency in financial reporting. Chief financial officers (CFOs) are also required to sign off on financials and are legally liable if reported numbers do not comport to generally accepted accounting principles (GAAP). As a publicly traded company, Lehman had to comply with this act. In spite of this legislation, Lehman was not immune from the trend of weak corporate governance.

EARLY AMERICAN COMMERCIAL BANKING

By the 1800s the economy expanded and banks did too. These banks followed a predictable path. If merchant bankers gave early American investment bankers a solid business model to follow, chartered banks were the less nimble lenders that gave investment bankers their competitive advantage. Chartered banks, the close equivalent of commercial banks today, tended to be more conservative in their lending practices. In most instances, even small risk taking was left to merchants and other speculators. In general, chartered banks followed a simple model: customers deposited money to earn interest, and the banks then loaned the money out to others for a higher rate of return.

Chartered banks also issued bank notes, and there were some chartered banks that engaged in investment-related activities including security underwriting. As noted by historian Vincent Carosso, "By the mid-1830s chartered banks in several states were successfully bidding for new issues and reselling them in smaller lots either to subcontractors or directly to investors."[4] What, then, distinguished chartered banks from investment banks other than a more risk-adverse approach to lending? The distinction has varied throughout history. To appreciate the relationship that has defined these two banking disciplines requires briefly examining the origins of the U.S. banking system.

Among the U.S. founding fathers, there was a deep-seated concern whether the banking system should be centralized or decentralized. This heated debate was not trivial. Hanging in the balance was whether banks would be under federal or state control. Proponents of federal control thought that a centralized bank would provide consistency and better oversight. Those opposed felt a central bank similar to the Bank of England would be too controlling and have an unfair advantage over smaller, state-chartered banks. The first two attempts to form a central bank (The Bank of the U.S.) were met with such resentment that they ended up being fairly short-lived.

It was not until 1863—when there were more than ten thousand different types of banknotes circulating in the United States and counterfeiting was commonplace—that Congress passed the National Currency Act. In addition, major amendments to the act in 1864 and 1865 gave national regulation and oversight powers to a newly formed federal regulator, the Office of the Comptroller of the Currency (OCC). The act allowed for the chartering of national banks and created a dual banking system of state and national banks.

A standardized national banknote replaced existing banknotes. The new system enhanced banking safety but did not address how to centralize monetary policy. Under the act, the money supply would increase or decrease by the value of underlying government bonds held by national banks and not in relationship to the needs of those that wanted to borrow. This stipulation caused the economy to gyrate, contributing to banking panics in 1873 and 1893. Still, no centralized bank was created to conduct monetary policy.

Not until the banking panic of 1907, which caused bank failures and inflicted national financial pain, did Congress again push for banking reform. It was believed that adopting a central bank approach would bring stability to the fragile system. This view was reinforced by the findings of the Pujo Hearings in 1913, which concluded America's banking system rested in the hands of a tiny group on Wall Street, the so-called "money trust," a criticism that continues to be raised today.[5] The election of Woodrow Wilson, a democratic president who appointed William Jennings Bryan as secretary of state, was the final straw. Bryan had a strong reputation as anti–Wall Street and pushed for national control over banks. In 1913 the Federal Reserve Act was signed into law, creating the third central bank—the Federal Reserve (the Fed), which remains in place today. This act established a system consisting of twelve regional banks stretching from Boston to San Francisco and a board of governors that served as the central policy, monetary, and regulatory oversight arm of the banking system. Led by a presidentially appointed chairman, each of the Fed's regional banks has a sitting president and a separate board and is responsible for monitoring and regulating state-chartered banks, bank-holding companies, and Edge Act corporations operating abroad.[6] Since February 2006 the sitting Fed chairman is Ben Bernanke, who replaced long-tenured Alan Greenspan.

While the Fed's monetary policy goals have varied through the years, the two primary ones include maintaining low inflation and high employment. Tools used to achieve these goals include influencing interest rates through open market operations, use of the discount window, and setting minimum bank reserve requirements. In addition, the Fed can influence the strength of the banking system as it interprets law, makes policy, enforces compliance, and examines banks under its jurisdiction. Fed field examiners physically inspect bank operations and assess bank capital adequacy relative to the level of risk-taking activities. Once examinations are completed, the Fed assigns a risk rating score, writing a formalized report that is then given to the examined bank.

Banks that have escalating risk profiles and shaky stability are put on notice through a "cease and desist" order. Through the years, the Fed's ability to issue and revoke bank charters has provided it with substantial powers. Although the Fed regulates two-thirds of U.S. banks, the OCC, established in 1863, regulates banks that have national charters. A third layer of regulation is state banking commissioner–sponsored examinations. The Federal Deposit Insurance Corporation (FDIC) is a fourth and final layer of regulation.

GOVERNMENTAL WATCHDOGS

In 1865 Congress established what is now known as the U.S. House Committee on Financial Services (House Banking Committee) to oversee a growing and increasingly complicated banking system. Today this important committee operates as six subcommittees and oversees the nation's financial services and housing sector, including banking, real estate, insurance, public and assisted housing, and securities. Since 2007 Barney Frank, a Democratic congressman from Newton, Massachusetts, has chaired this committee. From 2001 to 2007, it was chaired by Ohio Republican Mike Oxley. Since inception, the House Banking Committee has increasingly gained an important stewardship role over key institutions that impact the country's economic health and well-being.

In 1913, the U.S. Senate created the equivalent oversight committee, the Senate Committee on Banking, Housing and Urban Affairs (Senate Banking Committee). This twenty-three-member committee has jurisdiction over the nation's financial institutions, housing, urban development, and transportation. It also approves the nomination for chairman of the Federal Reserve Bank Board. Since 2007 Christopher Dodd, a Democratic senator from Connecticut, has chaired this committee. Prior to Dodd, Richard Shelby, a Republican from Alabama, was chairperson.

CHARTERED BANKS AND REGULATION

Chartered banks played a particularly vital role in issuing paper money when there was no national currency prior to 1863. Typical bank assets then included specie (gold and silver in coin and bullion), the banknotes and deposits of other banks, public securities, mortgages, and real estate. Unlike today, loans were discounted to face value and full-payment was required at maturity.[7] No liquid market for these loans existed, forcing banks to hold them to maturity, instead of selling them to other banks. Such loan arrangements did not include calculations of interest owed or monthly payments to maturity. This created a liquidity challenge for chartered banks because they could meet their obligations only by using specie, notes held, or loans that had matured. Not being able to get out of a loan obligation early or knowing whether it would even be paid in full created added uncertainty. In an attempt to manage credit risk, chartered banks made loans for only short periods, usually thirty to sixty days. These early restrictions influenced the eventual regulatory oversight and current practices of commercial banks.

In contrast, investment banks operated with almost complete autonomy and could engage in a multitude of activities with one exception: they could not issue paper money. They were not required to obtain charters from any of the various incarnations of American bank regulators, including the Fed. Often formed as partnerships, they also avoided the regulation that applied to corporations. Typically these investment banks, referred to as "private banks," accepted deposits, traded commodities, and engaged in underwriting and security trading. Prior to the Civil War, few firms were devoted solely to investment banking. The war changed this—never before had the U.S. government been forced to raise so much money in such a short period of time. As Barings had learned in the early 1800s, in times of conflict financial middleman are in great demand and can reap great fortunes. But the truly Golden Era of investment banking, which would propel firms like Lehman to financial prominence and lure commercial banks into riskier ventures, occurred after the Civil War when the nation experienced rapid industrialization.

When Lehman was formed, investment banks were still operating as separately functioning banks, providing lending and investment services that many chartered banks felt were too risky. But as investment banking activities—including raising capital and issuing securities—became visibly profitable, many other participants were eager to enter the market. Early commercial banks that had been issued bank charters were expanding their financial services. In response to competitive pressure, states began to allow their state-chartered banks to engage in selective investment banking activities.[8] Banks that held national charters were also applying similar pressure to their regulator, the OCC, and these banks slowly but surely gained expanded rights to underwrite and trade in corporate securities.

Through persistence and strong lobbying efforts, national banks were finally permitted to establish state-chartered affiliates that could engage in full-service investment banking. The result was a blurring of banking. As author David S. Kidwell wrote, "Thus, by 1930, commercial banks and investment banks were almost fully integrated, and they or their security affiliates were underwriting more than 50 percent of all new bond issues sold."[9] Capital was in demand, and the acceptable intermediaries to funnel capital were both commercial and investment banks. This period of banking harmony turned out to be short-lived because bankers took much of the blame for the Crash of 1929 and the ensuing Great Depression.[10]

THE CRASH OF 1929 AND THE RISE OF GOVERNMENT REGULATION

In the wake of the Crash of 1929, confidence in banks waned and bank runs ensued. By 1933 one in every five American banks had failed. Many blamed bankers for market speculation and lax lending standards that precipitated the crash.[11] In response, the government enacted far-reaching legislation by forming the FDIC and SEC and passing the Banking Act of 1933. By providing these financial guarantees, the government was suddenly in the bank risk-management business. It now had direct financial exposure to bank failures. Initially the FDIC insurance limit was $2,500. By the 1980s, this amount had increased to $100,000.[12] And while the government extended this insurance to commercial banks, investment banks were on their own. Investment banks such as Lehman fell under the regulatory and oversight framework of the SEC.

The last protective action, better known as the Glass-Steagall Act, walled off investment banking activities from those of commercial banking. The act inoculated banks by restricting permissible risk-taking activities. This legislation was unusual compared to that of other major countries, which did not, in general, make such distinctions. Excluding Japan, "universal" banks provide a wide range of services from commercial to investment banking in most nations. By the end of the twenty-first century, policymakers believed the universal model was better suited for a nation that purported to be capitalist.

BOND RATING AGENCIES

Credit rating agencies and the power they wield are relatively new phenomena. In 1909, John Moody charged for the first public corporate bond rating; by the 1920s there were three other firms performing similar business. It was not until after the Crash of 1929 that regulators began *requiring* banks, insurance companies, and pension funds to pay more attention to bond ratings. Bank regulators in particular used these ratings when assessing capital adequacy.

By 1975 the SEC wanted investment banks such as Lehman to hold higher-quality rated bonds. The only problem was that there was not a uniform standard. In response, the SEC created the designation National Recognized

Statistical Rating Organization (NRSRO) and immediately grandfathered in the Fabulous Three—Moody's, Standard & Poor's, and Fitch. These firms evaluated the likelihood of bond repayment and provided a ratings opinion. Through time, other bond rating firms received this lucrative designation, but with industry mergers only the Fabulous Three remained by 2000. In 2001 the sudden collapse of Enron shed light on the weakness of the rating process and the danger of "group think." All three of these firms kept a high rating on Enron until five days before its bankruptcy. In response to public outrage and congressional hearings, the SEC began to open up the NRSRO designation to greater competition. New bond rating firms were added to the approved list in 2003, 2005, and 2007.

Currently, there are ten independent NRSRO-approved bond rating companies. However, on Wall Street, if you want a corporate bond or an exotically structured product rated, Moody's and Standard & Poor's—and Fitch to a lesser extent—remain the preferred raters of choice.

PARTNERSHIP STRUCTURE

Up until the 1980s, much like Lehman, most investment banks were privately owned partnerships, and it was the partners' money at risk. Partnership size and the personal resources of members determined the amount of available capital, and predilection toward risk determined the level of risk taken. As the size of corporate transactions increased, investment banks that were not well capitalized were at a distinct disadvantage. Most broker-dealers took on the mantra "expand or die." This approach demanded larger balance sheets and the ability to put greater amounts of firm capital at risk. The old partnership structure increasingly was viewed as a constraint.

In 1971 NYSE lifted its member restriction, allowing broker-dealers to be publicly owned. In a rush to raise capital, investment banks began to go public (Lehman held off until 1994). The decision to go public solved one problem and created several new ones. In gaining access to greater quantities of capital, investment bankers could expand risk-taking activities. No longer was risk taking limited to the capital size of a few hundred partners. Shareholders and bondholders could be tapped to supply capital, allowing investment banks to make ever-larger bets. Under the old partnership structure, employees were tightly linked to the firm. Partnership stakes were illiquid, had long vesting periods, and could be difficult to cash out until retirement. This kept job-hopping to a minimum. Once investment banks went public, partnership stakes became liquid, and greater reporting requirements increased the likelihood that star performers could be poached. This in turn gave support to the compensation schemes created to entice and retain top talent. By the 1980s the theory quickly emerged that it was necessary to pay oversized bonuses to attract and keep oversized performers.

Finally, in going public, investment banks also subjected their franchises to increased uncertainties related to the market. A firm's stock price was now publicly traded and tracked daily. It was the market's referendum on the company's financial health. In a turbulent and unforgiving market, the perception of weakness could quickly create the reality of weakness as sellers outnumbered buyers.

THE FALL OF THE GLASS-STEAGALL ACT

The demise of the Glass-Steagall Act did not happen overnight but was the result of successful lobbying efforts waged by commercial banks over thirty years. Starting in the 1960s commercial banks began to lobby Congress to permit them to enter the lucrative municipal bond underwriting business. By the 1970s several retail brokerage companies encroached on banking services by offering money-market accounts paying interest, allowing check writing, and issuing credit or debit cards. In December 1986, spurred by a request from Bankers Trust, the Fed reinterpreted Section 20 of the Glass-Steagall Act.[13]

Historically, the act had barred commercial banks from engaging in securities underwriting. Showing leniency, the Fed decided to adopt a 5 percent rule, allowing commercial banks to engage in investment banking activities as long as such activities did not exceed 5 percent of gross revenues. This reinterpretation of Section 20 allowed banks to engage in underwriting, an activity prohibited since the Great Depression.

Glass-Steagall restrictions were further loosened in spring 1987. Responding to a request from J.P. Morgan, Citicorp, and Bankers Trust, the Fed agreed to allow these firms to expand underwriting activities to include commercial paper, municipal revenue bonds, and mortgage-backed securities. This was approved even though Fed Chairman Paul Volcker, who felt such activities would allow banks to lower their credit standards, opposed it. By March 1987 the Fed sent a signal to the banking industry that it would be open to changing the 5 percent rule as long as underwriting activities did not exceed 10 percent of a commercial bank's gross revenue. Further help in dismantling the act came in March 1987 with the appointment of Alan Greenspan, a former director of J.P. Morgan, to Fed chairman. A strong advocate of greater deregulation, Greenspan believed expanding banking risk-taking activities would help commercial banks better compete with foreign rival banks.

In January 1989 yet another assault on the Glass-Steagall Act occurred when J.P. Morgan, Bankers Trust, Chase Manhattan Bank, and Citicorp petitioned the Fed to expand the scope of underwriting further to include bonds and stocks. This request, which the Fed approved, was a clear attempt by commercial banks to strategically reenter investment banking in a much larger fashion. And in late 1989, after much lobbying from the commercial banking industry, the Fed acquiesced, increasing the 5 percent limit to 10 percent. By 1990, J.P. Morgan became the first bank to receive Fed permission to underwrite securities as long as this activity did not exceed the new 10 percent of revenue limit. In December 1996, in a decisive blow to the Glass-Steagall Act, with support of Chairman Greenspan, the Fed permitted bank-holding companies to own investment banks and pushed the underwriting revenue limit up to 25 percent. This aggressive move made Glass-Steagall virtually obsolete with the exception that banks were still not permitted to own insurance companies. By August 1997, the Fed indicated that the risk posed by underwriting appeared to be manageable and suggested that banks should have the right to acquire securities firms. In response to this pronouncement, Bankers Trust (now a part of Deutsche Bank) acquired Alex Brown & Company, becoming the first U.S. commercial bank to buy a securities firm.

CITICORP: THE FINAL SLEDGEHAMMER TO THE GLASS-STEAGALL ACT

On April 6, 1998, the announced merger of banking behemoth Citicorp and financial conglomerate Travelers Group initiated the final blow to the Glass-Steagall Act. The merger wed the largest U.S. corporate bank with a diverse collection of financial interests ranging from investment banking (Salomon Brothers); retail brokerage (Smith Barney); and property/casualty, life, and annuity underwriting (Travelers). The global reach of this new financial superstore spanned 140 countries and approximately twelve thousand offices.

This merger quickly tested the strength of the Glass-Steagall Act. In direct conflict with the purpose of the original act, the merger created a company that would engage in securities underwriting, insurance underwriting, and commercial banking. For Citicorp, this meant that it had to divest all of its nonconforming business activities unless it was able to get the act repealed.

At the time, there were many modern global finance skeptics who questioned the wisdom of the Glass-Steagall Act. Was Depression-era legislation still needed? The newly formed Citigroup lobbied government officials and bank regulators, and on September 23, 1998, the Fed completed its review and approved the Citicorp-Travelers merger. On November 12, 1999, under a Democratic administration and a Republican-sponsored bill, the Gramm-Leach-Bliley Act was passed allowing bank-holding companies to own financial companies such as investment banks. With the repeal of the Glass-Steagall Act, the Depression-era wall between these two distinct banking lines was completely torn down, and the "universal" risk-taking banking model received a government stamp of approval. Investment banks such as Lehman would now be thrust into direct competition with commercial banks, and the negative consequences of the repeal would not be fully felt for another decade.

Other regulatory changes were also unfolding. In 1988 the Basel Committee on Banking Supervision, an international organization of central bankers, issued the first set of minimum capitals standards. In the decade that followed it was clear that banking activities were becoming more complex, and tougher standards were in order. In June 2004 these revised standards, referred to as Basel II, were published and then officially accepted in 2006. Under these guidelines, bank assets are risk-weighted and adequate capital is divided into Tier I (most liquid) and Tier II (less liquid). The quality of bank capital is also important. The more liquid and less encumbered capital is, the more readily available it is to cushion against unexpected financial losses. Tier I capital—cash, reserves, and common equity—is the highest quality. Banks strengthen capital base by raising new capital and adding to retained earnings. The more banks pay out in dividends and bonuses, the less they have available to build up capital. Under Basel II a well-capitalized bank will have a total capital cushion of 10 percent of assets or greater. An adequately capitalized bank will have 8 percent or more, and banks with anything less are deemed undercapitalized. American regulators including the Fed, FDIC, and OCC continued to express caution about moving too quickly to completely adopt these higher standards. A decade had gone by since Glass-Steagall's repeal, yet tighter capital requirements to counterbalance increased risk taking were never implemented. Lehman competed against banks that were increasingly unconstrained. To stay competitive, Lehman also increased its risk-taking activities.

Chapter 5

How the Investment Banking Money Machine Works

nvestment banks—before, during, and after the Glass-Steagall Act—have thrived on risk. Narrowly defined, *risk* is the chance of losing money. Traditional fee-driven services such as underwriting and advisory work involve some risk taking while daily trading activities that put firm capital at risk create a much greater risk-and-return profile. Without taking risk, there is no financial reward for an investment bank. To gain return requires taking risk, and to gain even greater return requires taking even greater risk. This simple business principle is valid in virtually all profit-driven industries and could be called the golden rule of investing. Capital and leverage are the tools used to pan for gold. What separates successful investment banks from those that fail is the ability to pursue risk-taking opportunities without overdosing on them. Firms support risk taking based on organizational structure, capital size, and risk philosophy. If a sensible, risk-balanced culture prevails, an investment bank can be a profitable money machine, but an insensible risk-balanced culture leads to disaster, as Lehman discovered.

ROLE OF CAPITAL MARKETS

Capital markets are the financial arena in which investment banks attempt to raise money for clients and, in the process, make profits for themselves.

This multitrillion-dollar money store is where borrowers and lenders convene through a complex and fluid financial network. Trading activities involve equities, fixed-income instruments, derivatives, commodities, and newly emerging products such as carbon emissions credits. Through the past decade, global investment banking profit peaked in 2007 at more than $80 billion in revenue. More than half of this income came from U.S. investment banking activities.

The capital markets are a combination of formal exchanges and over-the-counter markets that allow buyers and sellers to raise money, make investments, dispose of assets, and obtain return. Products traded allow market players to redistribute risk from those who want to mitigate it to those who want to assume it. For investment banks, the capital markets are also a ready source of funding used to support daily business operations. As discussed in Chapter 4, the main suppliers of funds are households (i.e., individuals), and the main borrowers are corporations and governments. Investment banks sit in this intersection, mediating the flow of assets. Part of this mediation entails collecting information on the needs of issuers (sellers of assets) and investors (buyers of assets) and then using this information in structuring and selling products that satisfy both groups.

The development of mortgage-backed securities is an example of a client-driven product. Investment bankers can concoct new products, but customer demand is required to turn these products into profit. To perform these market functions, investment banks must be licensed broker-dealers and are subject to Securities and Exchange Commission (SEC) and Financial Industry Regulatory Authority (FINRA) regulation and oversight. The extent of regulation and level of enforcement sets the environment in which banks engage in risk-taking activities. Investment banks are an integral part of the plumbing of the financial system. When the capital markets function, much of what they do is invisible to the average person, but when cracked or broken the consequences can be disastrous.

Given that the flow of money is the lifeblood of the economy, investment bankers also assume an important gatekeeping role. If capital evaporates from the markets, there are significant financial implications for both businesses and individuals. Without money for lending and spending—the pump of the economy—entrepreneurs and growing companies have a difficult time securing much-needed capital. Simultaneously, it becomes increasingly difficult for lenders to find acceptable investment opportunities. Bad investment choices, particularly those that stray from adequate risk-adjusted returns, inflict significant financial harm if done in large enough quantities. This can culminate in economic decline as measured by lower gross domestic product (GDP), increased corporate bankruptcies, job loss, and government deficits.

The capital markets are heavily influenced by the monetary policies of central banks such as the Federal Reserve (Fed)[1] and the European Central Bank (ECB). These central banks are primarily responsible for maintaining the stability of the money supply for certain nations or groups of nation-states.[2] Central banks influence short-term interest rates through their decision-making and open market activities, and changes in these interest rates in turn drive economic activity. Measurements of policy success include low inflation, high employment, and steady year-on-year GDP growth. A central bank's ability to influence economic growth and the strength of the economy (e.g., cost of capital, inflation, and employment levels) directly impacts investment bank profitability.

In a down business cycle, investment banks tend to earn less in trading, underwriting, and advisory fees than in an up cycle. A central bank that targets a lower interest rate policy (cheap money) spurs greater borrowing while higher interest rates put downward pressure on borrowing. In the global money store, as the cost of products measured by interest rates goes up, the amount purchased by customers declines. Expected returns coupled with perceived risk contribute to how market participants make investment choices—is it better to invest in an unproven start-up company or a well-established utility company? What is a better fixed-income investment: government bonds, emerging-market debt, or mortgage-backed securities?

Capital markets literally redistribute risk from one set of parties to another depending on each party's risk tolerance level, and these markets only work correctly when money flows to its highest and best use.[3] In other words, when capital markets are working correctly, start-up companies, growing companies, and already well-established companies can obtain adequate funds at a fair market-derived price. The level of perceived risk (e.g., default, liquidity, market, quality of management, etc.) determines the cost of capital. Risk is measured either through internally developed scoring models, analysis completed by Wall Street analysts, and/or through credit rating agencies such as Moody's, Standard & Poor's, and Fitch (the Fabulous Three). In general, third-party rating agencies assign credit scores that are transparent, understood, and widely used in the marketplace. Historically, the Fabulous Three have provided credit ratings that the market perceives as similar to a Good Housekeeping Seal of approval. A company that has a "BBB" rating would have a higher cost of capital than one that has an "A" rating because it has been deemed at higher risk of defaulting on its bond issuances.

When credit ratings are accurate, they provide the market with the proper pricing signal. Ideally, capital markets would naturally operate efficiently, displaying a risk-related version of economist Adam Smith's invisible hand. In other words, when risk is apportioned correctly, investors would be rewarded and punished accordingly, and capital would then flow upward toward its highest and best use. However, when a large number of investors rely on faulty ratings and take too much risk relative to the level of compensation, investment capital can be quickly destroyed.

COMPENSATION SCHEME

The most valuable assets of investment banks are the employees who walk in and out of the firm every day. Those who decide to pursue a stress-filled and demanding investment-banking career do so because they want to make money. Investment banks are constantly searching for ways to increase firm revenue, stock price, and, consequently, employees' personal wealth. Firm compensation schemes reflect these facts. Compensation is a critical tool for motivating and retaining employees. Average bonus systems are designed to produce average returns, but aggressive plans are expected to produce aggressive returns. Typically investment banks set aside 50 percent of gross annual profit for compensation. Payouts are a combination of cash and stocks, and unlike commercial banks, stock grants are provided even at more junior levels in investment banks.

Investment banks also create compensation structures that place the importance of overall firm financial performance over that of individual units in an attempt to manage excessive risk taking. Lehman, for example, had a formulaic bonus approach that included unit performance but only as part of the larger firm profitability. In theory, such plans are designed to reward strong performance but reduce the incentive for any one unit to take excessive risk.

FUNDING AND LEVERAGE

The investment bank money machine is tied to the cost of capital and leverage the bank uses when it puts its capital to work in the markets. Traditionally, investment banks have funded their capital needs through a combination of short-term and long-term funding sources while considering how to balance cost and stability when funding debt. Increasingly, investment banks have relied on the lower-cost repurchase agreement market (or repo) and commercial paper market to meet their funding needs and have focused less on funding stability. A firm that can borrow at the repo market's lower overnight rates can plow this borrowed capital back into business activities, thereby generating higher profits. Longer-term sources of capital, such as bonds, provide stability but also increase the cost of financing, putting downward pressure on profits. By the 1990s the repo market was the funding source of choice for Wall Street's largest investment banks.

To grow, investment banks apply leverage to pump up balance sheet assets—stocks, bonds, real estate, commodities, derivative securities, or loans made—and also profits. *Leverage* refers to borrowing funds to invest in pursuit of greater profits than could be had with a firm's own capital and reflects how much debt a firm is comfortable with as it pursues profit. The amount of leverage a firm takes is a risk management decision made by board and senior management and helps define the firm's risk tolerance. For investment banks, leverage is commonly measured as the ratio of debt to equity. Historically this industry ratio was slightly under 20 to 1, but prior to the financial collapse of 2008, it increased to more than 30 to 1.

Once debt is raised, these funds are plowed back into the investment bank money machine in an attempt to reap greater profits. Investment banks look at a menu of potential transactions. A well-managed investment bank understands that these investment choices come with a set of unique risks and dangers. The leverage relationship investment banks employ in seeking profits is straightforward. In good times, higher leverage generates higher profit, and in bad times, leverage can kill. For example, a 5 percent return on $1 billion of assets is $50 million. However, if an investment firm decides to add $1 billion in borrowing, excluding interest cost, the same 5 percent return magically doubles to $100 million. In this example, profits were not increased by better investments but by greater leverage risk. In a down market or when a bad bet is placed, losses sustained by leveraged-based strategies can prove disastrous by the same multiplier, quickly eroding firm capital.

The use of leverage or debt is dangerous enough, but when used with derivative products that are inherently risky the combination can be deadly because the profit and loss swings can be even more dramatic. Despite this risk, leverage appeals to senior managers because it can be the fastest way to increase a firm's return on equity (ROE). Many investment banks have aggressive ROE targets that historically have averaged 20 percent or higher on an annualized basis. When Citicorp announced its historic merger with Travelers Insurance in 1998, achieving a ROE of 20 percent was a core goal. For Lehman, a similar ROE target was set.

ORGANIZATIONAL STRUCTURE

Full-line investment banks such as Lehman have traditionally been organized around three distinct pillars: risk taking, risk measurement, and operational controls. Although these pillars are not always equal, they need to be balanced if a firm is to be successful and stay in business. Using the vernacular of Wall Street, the institutions are divided into three activities: front office (trading, investment banking, research, and investment management); middle office (daily risk measurement, management, and reporting on risk-taking activities on a unit-, regional-, national-, and firm-wide basis); and back office (accounting, bookkeeping, trade confirmation, wire room, audit, compliance, and financial reporting). How these three distinct areas interact and the level of importance the firm places on each pillar help to determine the organizational risk-taking and control culture.

A firm faces a built-in conflict between the managers and traders who are paid to take risk and the risk managers who are paid to prevent excessive losses from occurring. And while traders earn sizable bonuses when they make money, risk managers do *not* get paid similar bonuses when they prevent the firm from losing money. Traders have an asymmetric payoff on the upside, which encourages greater risk taking, while the risk managers have an asymmetric bias on the downside to avoid a blowup that could cost them their jobs. It is not uncommon for the middle and back offices to be viewed as cost centers only standing in the way of the firm making additional profit. The level of importance an investment bank places on the middle office can be measured by the salaries paid, roles created, career opportunities, budget allocated, systems developed, and level of expertise the firm is able to attract and retain.

In addition to the organizational distinction between risk taking and risk measurement, investment banks are also separated by a "Chinese wall." This so-called structure is erected between the investment banking division and the trading division to prevent the flow of information that could result in insider trading. This important control ensures that investment banks maintain a strong ethical and fiduciary duty to their clients. The desire of some employees to realize quick profits by trading on merger or other insider information has often gotten investment banks into legal trouble.

Investment banks' profit-driven activities are typically organized into four distinct categories: (1) trading, research, underwriting, and sales in equities, fixed income, commodities, derivatives, and other emerging products; (2) mergers and acquisitions as well as other advisory work; (3) merchant banking activities—investing firm capital; and (4) asset management services. Within this framework, investment banks tend to generate revenue from seven primary sources: trading income, underwriting revenue, interest earned in providing margin loans, asset management fees, commissions from agency transactions, securities-related income from mergers and acquisitions, and dividends and interest from investment accounts. Investment banks also earn advisory fees for rendering fairness opinions. Such work typically occurs as part of firm buyouts. The investment bank is paid for opining on whether a transaction is fairly valued and if it is in the best interest of shareholders. This opinion is then used by company directors and executives to carry out their fiduciary duty.

Investment banks that rely heavily on revenue derived from advisory services, such as mergers and acquisitions, focus on building and maintaining a complex network of external contacts between themselves and their two main customers—sellers and buyers of assets. The quality of contacts and global reach of this network can determine the strength of the firm in generating current and future business. The investment banking industry remains unique because of the loose linkage between when value is provided to customers and when the firm earns the fees.[4] As part of cementing strong client relationships, investment banks provide a constant stream of market information, updates, opinions, and ideas in the hopes of generating future business. This business model puts immense pressure on deal flow and in finding consistently new ways to increase revenue. Investment banks make money not by cutting costs but by doing more deals, selling more products, and making more trades. A strong risk management and control structure is important to balance risk taking with the potential implications of putting excessive capital at risk. Profitability can also vary widely by product line with some low-margin products provided to clients as a means to open the door for future high-margin sales. Business disruption can occur rapidly when market events, political events, mergers, or other activities change the external business contacts required to run the company.

Investment banks tend to have flexible organizational structures so that employees, departments, and divisions can respond quickly to deal flows and sudden changes in market opportunities. This job-shop approach might require the resources of several departments working together for several months for one deal while the next deal might need the resources of completely different departments. This flexible atmosphere can also pose problems because employees are free to pursue customers or develop trade products that might not be in the best long-term interest of the firm,[5] which is why organizationally imposed risk controls are an important counterbalance.

FEE STRUCTURE

The investment banking money machine has two major components that drive earnings—fee income and profits from putting firm capital at risk. Traditionally, investment banks have made more of their money providing fee-driven services such as underwriting, advisory (e.g., mergers and acquisitions), and money management. In the last two decades, trading-related activities at the bulge-bracket firms generated a larger share of earnings. Up until the early 1970s, underwriting fees varied widely from institution to institution. A client raising capital could be charged a fee of 5 to 15 percent or more for the same transaction. Increased competition and a weak economy put downward pressure on acceptable fees. Lehman helped to standardize fees by introducing a 5-4-3-2-1 rate structure widely referred to as the "Lehman Formula." This tiered formula was transparent, easy to understand, and quickly adopted. Using this formula, an investment bank raising $100 million for a client would charge 5 percent on the first $1 million, 4 percent on the second million, 3 percent on the third, 2 percent on the fourth, and 1 percent on the dollar amount above $4 million. Based on this simplistic rate structure, such a transaction would generate $1.1 million in fee income. More recently, banks have adopted variations of the original Lehman Formula. Some use a "Double Lehman" method, applying the same percentage fee but doubling the dollar amount on which the calculation is based.

In addition to cash, investment banks seek payment in equity, mostly in the form of warrants. In a typical private placement transaction, compensation can range from 5 to 10 percent of the shares sold. Warrants generally have an exercise price equal to or slightly greater than the price of the security sold, and maturities can range from less than one to more than ten years.

Investment banks also generate substantial fee income for advising on mergers and acquisitions. Many factors determine the fee charged, including deal size, complexity, and resources needed. The sale of a smaller company can generate fees of 3 to 10 percent. This aspect of investment banking can be very lucrative and very risky. To reduce the risk of a deal falling through, multimillion-dollar termination fees are not uncommon.

COMPETITION

Industry competition influences investment bank behavior in its business lines, level of profitability, and willingness to take on added risk. Competition is the reference (good or bad) used to determine adequacy of profitability, risk taking, leverage, and the level of capital necessary to cushion against unexpected losses. If not harnessed correctly, competition can create pressure for firms to keep up with a competitor, even when that competitor is not a model citizen. Similar-sized investment banks tend to compete in the same areas and distinguish themselves based on the resources (human and economic capital) they bring to bear in meeting client needs and in their ability to craft new products and services.

With this in mind, it makes sense that employees and business contacts are important components of an investment bank's money machine. The uniqueness of each deal, the expertise required to close a transaction, and the unpredictability of when a deal will present itself means that a lot of firm capital is tied up in retaining talent. But talent is mobile. A sudden decline in deal flow can substantially hinder a firm's ability to retain top talent because employees may see better opportunities elsewhere or be poached by competing firms. At the same time, a rival firm can be an integral business partner. This is especially the case in securities offerings, which tend to be syndicated through multiple firms. Relationships with other investment banks contribute to a firm's perceived strength because firms share customers and negotiate with each other over mergers and acquisitions. But the strength of an investment firm's contacts and employees are not the only valuable asset. Of paramount importance is the size of its capital.

CAPITAL SIZE MATTERS

If bank earnings were predictable and balance sheet assets stable, banks would not need capital. In such a world, banks would receive financial reward without risk. In reality, banks take risks that sometimes are imprudent or unpredictable. As a result, capital is needed to cushion against unexpected financial losses. In theory, the larger the capital position is, the larger the level of acceptable bank risk taking is. In contrast to commercial banks, investment banks measure their financial position not by asset size but by capital size. As a result, the level of capital needed drives an institution's activities. Investment banks are not held to Basel II–type minimum capital standards. What comprises a strong and sound capital position varies by type of business activities chosen. For example, boutique firms, such as Lazard Frères, Greenhill & Company, Evercore Partners, and Rothschild, use a corporate advisory fee–based model and need much less capital than a full-line firm such as Lehman, with its more capital-intensive activities including trading, underwriting, and lending. In *Investment Banking*, financial writer Robert Kuhn states that "[c]apital is perhaps the most vital of an investment bank's vital statistics."[6] The reason for this is simple—capital size determines the extent of risky activities that can be undertaken. It only makes sense that firms with more capital can afford to take larger risks while smaller firms are forced to take smaller ones. Capital determines the size of a firm's boat, how far it can venture off shore, and in what adverse conditions it can remain afloat.

Capital size is also a competitive weapon in generating new business and searching for emerging opportunities. Without significant capital, a firm's ability to underwrite—to buy and turn around and sell an issue into the marketplace—is severely hampered. Similarly, financing client transactions (e.g., bridge loans) or trading large blocks of stock requires additional capital. Developing and marketing structured derivative products also obliges firms to put its own credit at risk, which means that firm capital has to be large enough to support such risk taking. Capital levels can also be influenced by what trading counterparties deem as adequate capital. Many firms will not assume a net trade position that exceeds 1 percent of a given trading counterparty's capital. But, when dealing with an important trading partner, an investment firm might increase capital in an attempt to foster more business.

While not having enough capital is a problem, having too much can also have negative consequences, especially from a shareholder's perspective. As discussed, in investment banking, ROE is a key investment performance measurement. If a firm does not have enough ways to use capital to generate income, ROE suffers. Since investment banks such as Lehman were historically private partnerships, the size of the wealth of the partnership determined the size of firm capital. If a firm wanted to obtain more capital, it had to balance the benefits of adding more partners versus dividing earnings and control up into more pieces. In this older structure, partners put their own money at risk and for the most part were not able to get the capital out until they left the firm or retired. These partnerships operated on much less capital but also took much less risk. They also made much less profit.

Adequate capital size is also influenced by credit rating agencies such as Moody's and Standard & Poor's because their corporate credit ratings, in part, are based on the size of capital. In general, the larger the capital base, the stronger the credit rating and the cheaper it is for investment banks to borrow funds (both short- and long-term debt) and conduct day-to-day business. For the largest investment banks, having a coveted bond rating of A or higher allows them to underwrite more derivative contracts, including the buying and selling of credit default swaps.[7] Recall that larger capital size also increases the chances that a firm will move up in the industry league table rankings.

In 1988 the top six Wall Street firms had capital ranging from $9.7 billion (Merrill Lynch) to approximately $2.5 billion (Morgan Stanley). Lehman's capital strength was second only to Merrill Lynch, with consolidated year-end capital totaling $8.2 billion. In the 1990s, this same group would need three times as much capital to stay competitive, and they would need five times these levels by 2008. Amazingly, this was still inadequate capital to support the level of aggressive risk taken by these top investment firms. There is no market standard for what is adequate capital. In some respects, it can be reduced to a judgment call made by the board of directors, senior management, third-party rating agencies, and independent financial analysts. What is clear is that greater risk taking needs to be supported by greater capital.

RISK TOLERANCE

An investment bank's senior executives and board of directors define the firm's risk tolerance. Collectively, these individual risk preferences reflect the risk-taking ethos of the firm. The level of risk tolerance shows up in the size of trading bets, how concentrated these bets are, and the size of acceptable financial losses before such activities are shut down. Is a firm willing to risk millions or billions of dollars in the pursuit of profit? Questions such as this should be asked and answered by directors, vetted by the firm's Risk Management Committee, and reflected in specific policies, procedures, and control limits of the firm.[8] Risk tolerance can also be expressed in the amount of earnings fluctuation, measured in earnings per share, that is allowed as part of daily business activities. For many firms, a deviation of 2 to 3 cents per share below Wall Street quarterly estimates would likely cause a reevaluation of the risk-taking activities that hurt firm earnings.

On an individual level, capital market participants understand the direct link between risk and return and tend to exhibit risk-adverse behavior. These investors are seeking risk-adjusted returns—they will take additional risk only if they are compensated for it. Lenders and borrowers drive this risk-and-return trade-off. When the balance is thrown out of kilter, it can cause a speculative bubble, which is best described as trade in products or assets with considerably inflated values. The boom cycle that follows a bubble can lead to investors overdosing on risk—the very irrational exuberance that former Federal Reserve Board Chairman Alan Greenspan famously described in 1996 in reference to the dot.com stock market bubble. The bursting of the bubble results in a period of falling asset values and financial hardship.

CASTE SYSTEM

One reason for the constant increase in capital among the top investment banks is the importance placed on each firm's status—the pecking order that allows the biggest to get the best deals and make the largest profit. Every investment bank's reputation is carefully managed and closely observed by rivals. By the 1980s the massive industry consolidation had weeded out weaker investment banks. Banks fell into a distinct four-tier hierarchy: bulge-bracket, major-bracket, regional, and boutique firms. Lehman was at the top of this caste system, referred to as a "bulge-bracket" firm.[9]

Firms at the top of the hierarchy tended to focus on servicing large-cap companies with more than $10 billion in revenues and mid-cap companies with revenue of $2 billion or more.[10] Although Lehman was considered a bulge-bracket firm, it was not able to secure a position at the top of the investment banking pyramid. For example, it was not at the top of the closely watched and status-heavy league table rankings. In 1988, according to the league tables compiled by *Institutional Investor*, the top six bulge-bracket firms in total securities underwriting in descending order were Merrill Lynch, Goldman Sachs, Salomon Brothers, First Boston, Shearson Lehman Hutton, and Morgan Stanley.[11] These firms handled the majority of transactions on Wall Street.

On September 22, 2008, due to widespread speculation that Goldman Sachs and Morgan Stanley would be acquired by commercial banks, whose ability to take deposits would provide them a reliable source of funds, both firms requested banking-holding company status.[12] This move, approved by the Federal Reserve Bank, signaled the end of the last two remaining Wall Street bulge-bracket investment banks.[13] Today, all surviving investment firms have banking charters and most operate under the universal banking model discussed in Chapter 4. In fact, of the top twenty full-line investment banks in 1988, only Goldman Sachs and Morgan Stanley continue to operate under their same name on a stand-alone basis. The remaining firms have been merged, purged, or sold off in pieces with little or no independent name recognition remaining.

Investment banking has never been a static industry. Profitability is determined by level of risk taking, leverage, financing cost, regulation, competition, and economic growth. In pursuit of profit, firms need to put capital at risk and *should* evolve. They also must continue to play an important role as intermediaries in markets, ensuring that capital flows to its best use. Investment banking can be a money machine, but if not closely tended to, it's a machine capable of breaking itself under the weight of dangerously high levels of leverage and risk.

Chapter 6

The Roller-Coaster 1980s

n unprecedented fashion, the 1980s demonstrated how investment banks could become money machines or money pits. The decade could be divided into two separate periods: the first few years were marked by high inflation, recession, and industry consolidation; the second half, except for two stock market dives, was more investment banking friendly. The recession at the start of the decade exposed weaker firms and accelerated industry consolidation. Aggressive Federal Reserve (Fed) policy eventually tamed inflation, fueled a bull market, and ushered in an era of junk bonds, leveraged buyouts (LBOs), hostile takeovers, insider-trading scandals, and the savings and loan (S&L) crisis.

Government policy paved the way for moral hazard risk and a "too big to fail" doctrine. Investment banking lost its veneer as a gentleman's sport and instead came to symbolize Wall Street's oversized risk taking and greed, capturing the fascination of Americans. Several national bestselling books and an Academy Award–winning movie were produced, all reflecting on this greed. The self-absorption of the so-called "Me Decade" of the 1970s had morphed into the unbridled materialism of the 1980s yuppies. Nowhere did this trend seem more evident than on Wall Street, where cigar-smoking bankers wearing red suspenders were being driven around in stretch limousines. By the end of the decade, the investment banking industry had a significant public relations problem. For Lehman, in particular, this decade included internal warfare and a raging bull market that helped redefine the firm.

INFLATION, RECESSION, AND INDUSTRY CONSOLIDATION

The late 1970s and early 1980s were a turbulent time in the U.S. market. In response to the energy crisis of 1979, the two-headed economic demon of stagflation—a simultaneous increase in inflation and unemployment rates—reared its ugly head. By 1980, annual inflation was more than 13 percent and unemployment rates exceeded 7 percent. In response to high inflation, the Fed, under Chairman Paul Volcker, acted aggressively to tighten monetary policy.[1] As a result, by 1981, the prime rate—the interest rate at which large corporations borrow—skyrocketed to more than 20 percent. While Fed policy worked in quelling inflation, it also pushed the U.S. economy into a deep sixteen-month recession with the national unemployment rate topping 10 percent by December 1982.

Profitable only a year earlier, Lehman was feeling the economic downturn as investment banking fees and trading revenue plummeted. On the national stage, the growing economic downturn also resulted in political upheaval as Democratic President Jimmy Carter was decisively voted out office in 1980. His Republican replacement, Ronald Reagan, the former Hollywood actor and California governor, would be in office for most of the decade (1981–1989). Reagan won on campaign promises to lower taxes and reduce government. Sticking to these promises, Reagan enacted significant tax cuts for the wealthy, slashed social programs, and beefed up military spending.

Reaganomics was based on the belief that tax cuts increased the incentive to work harder and longer, generated more savings and investments, and spurred greater economic growth. His administration also focused on reducing government regulation of the economy. The Reagan revolution ushered in a laissez-faire era on Wall Street, a legacy that would last long after his administration. Future Fed Chairman Alan Greenspan, appointed by Reagan in 1987, carried the laissez-faire torch until he left the Fed in 2006. Greenspan believed financial companies had self-interest in controlling their level of risk taking and could self-regulate accordingly. Such a regulation-light approach defined bank regulation into the twenty-first century. This model of deregulation was wrong, with Greenspan admitting so to Congress in 2008: "Those of us who have looked to the self-interest of lending institutions to protect shareholders' equity, myself included, are in a state of shocked disbelief."[2] This lack of oversight encouraged the increased amount of risk that Wall Street firms would take.

Competitive pressure and globalization of the securities industry led to a wave of consolidation as small and large broker-dealers merged, even bringing nontraditional buyers into the industry. An example occurred in April 1981 when American Express announced a $915 million plan to purchase Shearson Loeb Rhoades, the second largest brokerage firm on Wall Street. Only three years later American Express would also swallow Lehman Brothers. In this era, bigger was better. Several of the larger private firms were eventually pressured by market forces to go public. Morgan Stanley, one of Lehman's major competitors, went public in 1986, raising much needed capital and improving its competitive financial position. In 1987, Shearson Lehman sold 40 percent ownership and boosted capital by more than $700 million. Consolidation continued in the industry. By December 1987 E. F. Hutton & Company, an eighty-three-year-old brokerage company weakened by fraud and multimillion-dollar trading losses, agreed to join the American Express family in a $1 billion deal, creating the second largest firm on Wall Street. The new company was called Shearson Lehman Hutton, Inc.

To further add to the woes of a weak economy, investment banks were confronted with regulatory change that significantly reduced their underwriting revenues. In 1983 the Securities and Exchange Commission (SEC) adopted Rule 415, or "shelf registration" as it is commonly known. For a company wanting to issue new securities, this rule change was ideal because it added flexibility. New securities could be registered today and then shelved for up to two years, which gave companies more control when entering the market and allowed them to wait for favorable terms. This rule change reduced the workload and need for investment banks and their accompanying fees. While investment banks such as Lehman initially resisted shelf registration, it was well received by corporations and still exists.

SALE OF LEHMAN

The year 1983 marked an escalation in hostility between the investment banking and the trading factions at Lehman. The breaking point occurred when the trading-focused Lewis Glucksman successfully pushed out former CEO Pete Peterson, who left to found private equity giant Blackstone—eventually a direct competitor to Lehman. All was not well at Lehman. A significant drop in company revenue and management turmoil made Lehman ripe for a takeover. As Lehman's financial health deteriorated and Glucksman's inability to lead became apparent, Peterson's supporters lobbied American Express to buy the company.[3] By spring 1984 Lehman was sold off to American Express in firesale fashion. A deep-pocketed parent with big plans replaced the small-firm structure with less than fifty partners. The fiercely independent Dick Fuld, who was closely aligned in the Glucksman camp, would later say that April 10, 1984—the day when Lehman's seventeen-member board voted to sell the company to American Express and establish Shearson Lehman Brothers—was the "darkest day of his career" (with the exception of September 15, 2008).

The sale to American Express meant that a 134-year-old private partnership was no more. To add insult to injury, American Express paid a paltry $380 million, far less than what Lehman had estimated it was worth only one year earlier. As part of the buyout, Peter Cohen of Shearson took the reins from Glucksman. In protest, Fuld assembled a large group of traders and other key employees. He planned on staging a defection to rival Paine Webber or Dean Witter Reynolds. More than four hundred employees were willing to walk on his command.[4] But Fuld was never able to reach favorable terms with either firm. Remaining at Shearson Lehman, he was made vice chairman and a voting member of the board. By 1984 trading accounted for 21 percent of Shearson Lehman's revenue while investment banking accounted for only 19 percent.

TOO BIG TO FAIL DOCTRINE AND MORAL HAZARD RISKS

With the creation of the Federal Deposit Insurance Corporation (FDIC) in 1933, the U.S. government was successful in restoring market confidence and mitigating the threat of bank runs, which had forced thousand of banks into bankruptcy. The FDIC allowed for an orderly unwind of failed banks that overdosed on risk without destruction to the economy. For the next fifty years, commercial banks and their depositors enjoyed a period of calm. The FDIC mandate was narrow: protect small investor deposits. The 1929 Crash and subsequent Great Depression had shaped government policy and personally influenced executives to be more conservative when taking risks. Prior to the 1980s, being a banker was considered boring—the epitome of the man in the blue pinstriped suit. But that conservative nature would soon change.

The recession of the early 1980s, a sudden drop in energy prices, and risky lending practices in America's oil patch finally caught up to Continental Illinois Bank (Continental), at the time, the seventh largest bank in the United States. By May 1984 there was a full run on the bank, and large depositors withdrew more than $10 billion. Using the rationale that Continental's size and prominent position as a correspondent bank to many smaller banks in an already fragile economy made its survival crucial, the government responded by designating Continental "too big to fail" and proceeded to pump in more than $4 billion to keep the bank from collapsing. The Fed justified its strong participation in the rescue by citing the threat of systemic risk—the idea that the failure of one company could trigger a cascade of additional failures that might have a devastating impact on the entire economy. In theory, it was a save the "one" strategy to protect the "many." Though the government had no hard data to substantiate a claim of systemic risk, it moved quickly to the rescue.

Expanding its narrow legal mandate of protecting depositors, the FDIC recapitalized Continental from its own coffers. The FDIC decided that even careless bank customers—those with deposits greater than the $100,000 insured limit—would be protected. The government went out of its way to demonstrate that some banks and investors, even those that engaged in risky behavior, would be bailed out if necessary. Such governmental intervention set a potentially dangerous precedent.

Depositors were sent the wrong message: they no longer needed to practice due diligence before putting their money in banks. All banks are not equal, but the government action suggested that depositors and investors did not need to differentiate between the good and the bad. The seeds of moral hazard— the idea that a government policy of bailouts will encourage excessive risk taking—had been planted. This "too big to fail" doctrine would be invoked in decades to follow. Unfortunately, no firm guidelines or policy statements have ever been presented by any regulatory agency. It has never been clear which banks are too big to fail until they are actually bailed out. In 2008 Lehman incorrectly assumed that it was one of the banks the government deemed too vital to the economy to let fail.

JUNK BONDS

One of the hallmarks of the 1980s was the expanded involvement of investment banks in junk-bond financing. Many firms saw this emerging market as a way to extract large profits. Junk bonds, also called high-yield bonds, are rated by a credit rating agency and designated as noninvestment grade due to their inherently high default risk. Standard & Poor's uses the rating designation of below BBB- while Moody's uses the rating of below Baa3. Often referred to as "fallen angels," corporations with a noninvestment-grade credit rating found it more difficult to raise capital, so they resorted to issuing junk bonds to raise money for their operations. Given the high level of risk, most banks and investors tended to avoid this backwater of Wall Street throughout the 1970s.

As regulatory oversight slipped throughout the 1980s, Michael Milken, an undeterred bond trader from Drexel Burnham Lambert (Drexel), was drawn to this thinly traded market. Contrary to the golden rule of investing, Milken believed that low-grade bonds could offer high returns without greater risk. He found that empirically junk bonds outperformed investment-grade corporate bonds.[5] The key was to buy enough of these risky bonds to construct a diversified portfolio that could reduce the impact if any one bond defaulted. He also understood that investors would not buy into this scheme unless he could increase trading volume and create market liquidity. Milken was a good trader and even a better salesman, so he had no problem convincing Drexel that it should specialize in junk bonds. To make his case, he supplied his managers and the market with meticulous research and videos supporting his point.[6] Through aggressive marketing and a strong sales force, Drexel quickly became the leading underwriter of junk bonds for small to medium-size companies such as MCI, Turner Broadcasting, and Harley Davidson, all of which had previously been shut out of Wall Street's money machine. So successful were Milken's forays that he became known as the "Junk Bond King."

Not only were junk bonds a way for weaker companies to gain access to previously unavailable capital, but they also provided a new funding tool for corporate raiders. Armed with capital raised by issuing junk bonds, these raiders built a formidable war chest. Junk bonds were increasingly used in LBOs and hostile corporate takeovers, providing the financial underpinnings of much of the takeover mania of the 1980s. Carl Icahn, Robert Bass, Victor Posner, Kirk Kerkorian, T. Boone Pickens, and Ron Perelman became household names. Junk bonds unlocked capital that contributed to greenmailing, the practice of purchasing a large enough stake in a company to threaten a takeover and cause the company's management to buy back its shares at a premium. The raider would get paid a significant sum of money to go away even when he or she potentially had no intention of purchasing the targeted company in the first place (*greenback* + *blackmail* = *greenmail*). In response to public outcry, corporate raiders claimed they were providing an important shareholder service by keeping bloated companies and management on their toes. However, by the close of the decade, many of the firms that were targeted for buyouts, including those that were not successfully acquired, were saddled with excessive debt, forced to make significant payroll cuts, and filed for bankruptcy.[7]

By the mid-1980s Drexel was doing a brisk business in underwriting and trading junk bonds. Fees for underwriting junk bonds were three to four times higher than for higher-quality corporate bonds. Trading margins (bid-offer spreads) were also larger for the less liquid junk bonds, approximately four times more for a bond with five years to maturity. At the height of the buyout craze, junk bonds were approaching a $200 billion per year industry, and

Drexel was a market leader, controlling 60 to 70 percent of the deal flow. Drexel became the fifth largest investment bank in the country, employing more than eleven thousand people, and went from obscurity to bulge-bracket status overnight. This did not go unnoticed by other Wall Street firms. Milken further shocked Wall Street by receiving a $550 million bonus for the 1986 business year. The use of junk bonds to finance LBOs increased dramatically. In 1983, there were no such deals; by 1986, 18 percent of LBOs were financed through bonds. By 1988 the number had grown to more than 44 percent. This growth was explosive. Most other investment banks, including Goldman Sachs, Merrill Lynch, Morgan Stanley, Salomon Brothers, Kidder Peabody, and even the smaller Dillon Read, started scanning Wall Street for the next junk-bond opportunity. A large deal could earn up to $50 million in fees and make a firm's quarterly earnings.[8] To many investment houses that had experienced a recession-induced drop in retail-brokerage revenues, junk bonds and the additional business they could generate were manna from heaven. Pressure to do bigger and more lucrative deals took precedence over the ability to find good, high-quality deals. By the late 1980s the amount of available capital raised through junk bonds swamped available opportunities, and a larger openness to risk permeated Wall Street and its deal-making activities. Both of these trends would recur, leading up to the Great Credit Crisis of 2008.

SAVINGS AND LOAN CRISIS

A savings and loan association (S&L), also known as a thrift, is a financial institution specializing in accepting deposits and making loans, particularly mortgages. By the mid-1980s, with regulation of S&Ls relaxed, many of these institutions were looking for new ways to increase earnings, and to do so, they were willing to take on more risk. Traditionally, S&Ls relied on the interest rate spread—the difference between the cost of cheaper deposits and the income from loans issued to make their profit. To compete for deposits in the competitive marketplace, many S&Ls began offering higher deposit interest rates, and, to make up for this increase in cost, they looked for ways to enhance earnings. Junk bonds offering higher yields seemed like a good answer. Initially, only a few S&Ls purchased junk bonds, but the success of these risk-taking pioneers encouraged others to follow. Across the country S&Ls purchased larger and larger amounts of junk bonds, many buying them from Drexel and keeping the bonds on their investment books.

Even before the junk-bond market hit the skids by the late 1980s, excessive risk taking by S&Ls in residential and commercial loans was apparent.

Several large S&Ls failed, including giants Lincoln and Centrust. Junk bonds in isolation did not cause the S&L crisis, but they were gasoline on the fire. Junk bonds unlocked a giant safe full of money. Over-issuance of junk bonds by investment banks combined with an underestimation of the inherent risks spelled financial disaster for many investors. Eventually, junk-bond issuers started to choke on the size of debt. As the economy began to turn south, defaults increased, and S&Ls were stuck with worthless assets on their balance sheets, causing them to collapse. By 1988, at the height of the S&L crisis, bank failures hit a post–Depression era high of more than 230, representing about $50 billion in assets. While the S&L crisis and subsequent $293 billion government bailout were much smaller relative to the Great Credit Crisis of 2008, this period led to the first-ever operating loss for the FDIC, losses that continued until 1991.

By 1988 the SEC had Milken and his dubious business practices in its crosshairs. Eventually indicted and convicted of securities fraud and insider trading, Milken was fined $600 million and sentenced to ten years in jail.[9] Drexel was also charged with securities fraud and fined $650 million. These legal issues put a black cloud over the industry. By June 1989, Integrated Resources, a junk-bond-financed LBO, defaulted on $1 billion in short-term debt. This was followed by defaults by Southland and others, providing more anxiety to an increasingly jittery stock market. And as a bookend to the decade, with junk bonds out of favor and with a large inventory of risky bonds on their books, Drexel, the fifth largest investment bank in the country, was forced into bankruptcy in 1990.

The fall of Drexel did not signal the end of junk bonds. To the contrary, Drexel demonstrated that junk-bond underwriting and trading had a place in the market and could be very lucrative if firms and investors were willing to take on the high risk levels, albeit in moderation. Given the infancy of this industry, junk bonds showed great resiliency. With the dominant player gone, many investment banks looked at this as an opportunity to gear up and prepare for when the market turned back around. Unlike Goldman Sachs, Merrill Lynch, Morgan Stanley, Salomon Brothers, and Kidder Peabody, Lehman had a very small footprint in junk bonds in the 1980s. However, by 1994, with CEO Dick Fuld's blessing, Shearson Lehman finally bowed to competitive pressures and jumped headfirst into junk bonds, signifying an underlying change in the firm's approach to risk.

In addition to straight junk bonds, the 1980s also brought about another bond-related innovation: mortgage-backed derivative securities. By the end of the decade, Drexel had become successful in creating the first high-yield collateralized mortgage obligation (CMO). Ironically, this instrument was originally envisioned as a means to mitigate, not magnify, risk. But it would not be until the 1990s that CMOs and, later, collateralized debt obligations (CDOs) would be commonplace on Wall Street. Shearson Lehman would eventually bet its success on such derivative instruments. As a fixed-income house, mortgage-backed securities were a natural extension of the firm's core competency. The creation and rapid expansion of this market as well as Lehman's involvement is discussed in Chapter 9.

POP GOES THE INVESTMENT BANKING CULTURE

The 1980s were marked by a public fascination with investment bankers—the vast wealth they generated and their sometimes unethical behavior. In 1987, *Wall Street* became a box-office sensation. Gordon Gekko, the film's main character, never let ethics stand in the way of profit. His "Greed Is Good" speech came to symbolize this decade on Wall Street. Shearson Lehman's investment banker J. Tomilson (Tom) Hill III, a prominent figure in the 1980s corporate takeover mania, was even called one of the inspirations for Gekko.[10]

Unflattering portrayals of investment bankers made national bestsellers, including the novel *The Bonfire of the Vanities* (1987), with main character Sherman McCoy as a multimillionaire bond trader and adulterer; *Predators' Ball* (1988), about the dubious investment bank Drexel; *Liar's Poker* (1989), about the excessive risk-taking culture at Salomon Brothers; and *Barbarians at the Gate* (1990), which portrayed Shearson Lehman as the hapless investment bank that let incompetence and greed stand in the way of completing the biggest deal in history—the $25 billion merger of R.J. Reynolds Tobacco Company (RJR) and Nabisco, which was instead completed by the boutique firm Kohlberg Kravis Roberts & Company (KKR) with the assistance of Drexel. *Barbarians at the Gate* retold the story of the fallout of the RJR-Nabisco deal in which Peter Cohen, the head of Shearson Lehman, was ousted and Tom Hill, Shearson's well-heeled banker, achieved star status. Cohen's ensuing resignation determined the future of Lehman as Fuld and Hill soon shared co-CEO and president roles at Shearson Lehman.

STOCK MARKET GYRATIONS

The late 1980s were also punctuated by two stock market crashes, one big and one small, occurring in 1987 and 1989, respectively. In percentage terms, the crash on October 19, 1987, referred to as "Black Monday," resulted in the largest percentage drop in the Dow Jones Industrial Average (Dow) in a single day: 22.6 percent (508 points). More than $1 trillion in capital evaporated from the stock market. Many argued it was caused by newly employed trading techniques called program trading. In response, a market-based system was put in place to help build in controls and delays pertaining to large buy-and-sell orders. This market drop had a significant impact on Wall Street. Trade and deal flow, the industry's bread and butter, also declined, triggering the downsizing of approximately fifteen thousand financial industry–related jobs. Shearson Lehman was one of the firms affected. After this dramatic single-day drop, the market would not recover until 1989. Then on October 13, 1989, just when it appeared stability had returned, the Dow experienced a single-day drop of 6 percent. While not particularly large in percentage terms, the fall signified a limit to the long-running bull market. In the end, this drop would be only a pause in the bull market until the next decade.

This economic low-water mark in 1989 ushered in a recession and exposed the dangers of saying yes to investment bankers pedaling high-risk junk-bond financing. What had looked like a high-margin business segment only two years earlier was now in turmoil. The premise was that junk bonds could be sold, but in reality, the stock market gyrations, coupled with the legal issues hanging over Drexel and a looming recession, made such bridge loan financing much higher risk, leading many investment firms to suffer major losses. In particular, Shearson Lehman under the guidance of Peter Cohen had aggressively ramped up its investment banking activities by the second half of the 1980s, and, initially, it appeared the firm was making inroads and profitably expanding. However, by 1988, Shearson Lehman lost an estimated $250 million in fees by missing out on the RJR-Nabisco deal. Not capturing this one-time earnings bonanza exposed the weakness in Shearson Lehman's investment banking franchise, compounding its drop in earnings for the year. Losses for 1989 would eventually total $1 billion and help jolt American Express into rethinking the benefits of owning Shearson Lehman. The trading side of the house was still making money. If there was one bright spot during this roller-coaster decade, it was that Shearson Lehman's fixed-income area proved it could generate high levels of profits, albeit accompanied by measured amounts of risk.

Chapter 7

The 1990s: Rebuilding Years

To an outsider, Shearson Lehman might have appeared as if it had made the right strategic moves. It was part of American Express, a deep-pocketed parent. It had significantly enhanced its capital position, expanded its retail brokerage footprint, and by 1988 had even picked up the venerable E. F. Hutton brokerage firm at a discounted price. American Express had a global financial supermarket strategy, and Shearson Lehman was central to it. The second half of the go-go 1980s had been a gold rush for investment banking. Unfortunately, Shearson Lehman's aggressive foray into this arena proved financially disappointing. For Lehman, the decade of the 1990s was marked by executive infighting, more focus on core competencies, elimination of deadwood, and a build-out of the franchise. On becoming Lehman's CEO, Dick Fuld took great pains to create a monarchy and strengthen his power base. In doing so, a clear leadership vacuum below him emerged.

EARLY 1990S

In 1990, Shearson Lehman shocked Wall Street by reporting losses of approximately $1 billion from transactions related to junk bonds, real estate transactions, and failed investment-banking activities. To American Express, the promised synergies for which they had waited a decade never materialized. Shearson Lehman was also struggling to protect its own bond rating from being downgraded. Peter Cohen, Shearson Lehman's wheeler-dealer chairman, was forced out in February and replaced by the more conservative American Express CFO, Howard L. Clark. In March, in an attempt to stabilize the firm, American Express announced it would buy all outstanding Shearson Lehman shares. As part of a broader senior management reshuffling, Fuld, the trader, and Tom Hill, the highly regarded investment banker, would assume co-CEO roles. Jointly they also held the titles of co-president and co–chief operating officer (COO). Fuld and Hill focused on the institutional side of the business (trading and investment banking), and Jonathan Linen, an American Express credit card executive, took responsibility for the retail side.

By July 1990 the nation was into a recession. Sluggish gross domestic product (GDP) and increasing unemployment rates that hit 7.8 percent persisted until late 1992. Unlike previous recessions, this one hit white-collar jobs hardest, particularly in the financial sector. Under Clark, Shearson Lehman laid off more than two thousand employees firm-wide. Fuld and Hill took out the meat cleaver and hacked into their divisions, firing 20 percent of the bankers and consolidating departments, including combining mergers and acquisitions with corporate finance. From the stock market peak, prior to Black Monday (October 19, 1987), Shearson Lehman's workforce reductions totaled more than one thousand employees. Morale at Shearson Lehman was low, and its parent was not faring any better.

By September 1992, with losses still mounting, American Express's board forced longstanding CEO James Robinson to resign. Robinson's abrupt departure also marked the end of the firm's attempt to become a global financial supermarket. American Express needed to get back to its core business. By February 1993, Harvey Golub, a former McKinsey & Co. partner, replaced Robinson and became Mr. Fix-It. As a sign of a change in corporate direction, American Express sold The Boston Company, a Shearson money management subsidiary, for $1.45 billion. This sale brought Shearson Lehman's previously wobbly bond rating closer to an A, making it more attractive for acquisition and signaling that it was for sale. To Golub, Shearson Lehman and its highly paid bankers and traders were an unnecessary drain on revenue. As part of the senior banker incentive program, American Express was required to set aside millions of dollars in deferred compensation regardless of an up or down market. Keeping Shearson Lehman was like throwing good money after bad, and Mr. Fix-It was ready to end the tomfoolery.

To Fuld, the recent corporate about-face was an opportunity to gain freedom and restore the Lehman family name. Many in his camp felt that having American Express as a parent was like a ten-year prison sentence. While it was true that America Express provided safe harbor in a time of financial need, it came at a cost. Adding Shearson to the front of Lehman's name and slapping E. F. Hutton at the end had soiled Lehman's marquee reputation. It was now up to Fuld and his core team to restore the family honor. As part of the Shearson–American Express family, Lehman had become a significant player with sizeable retail and wholesale equity market penetration. However, even after aggressive attempts, Shearson Lehman still was not a major power in investment banking. Stated simply, Shearson Lehman was not a Goldman Sachs, Morgan Stanley, Merrill Lynch, or even a First Boston.

SENIOR MANAGEMENT CHANGE

Beginning with Cohen's departure, former fixed-income traders increasingly dominated Shearson Lehman's senior management ranks. Tension between investment banking and trading factions again intensified. By early March 1993 co-CEO Hill, the firm's most senior-ranking investment banker, was pushed out, consolidating Fuld's power base and marginalizing the firm's investment banking area.[1] Many of the bankers thought of themselves as second-class citizens because Shearson Lehman's competitive strength primarily rested in fixed income, which had a commanding and profitable bond business. In November 1993, American Express CEO Harvey Golub made the consolidation of Fuld's power base official, naming him sole CEO of Shearson Lehman and appointing T. Christopher (Chris) Pettit as president and COO, the firm's second most powerful position. In separating these two duties, the company reduced the likelihood of too much power being concentrated in the hands of a single person. In theory, each would be a check on the other. Similar to when the firm was founded, there would be a Mr. Inside and a Mr. Outside, both working to ensure a balance between risk and return. Their ambition and competitiveness would help Fuld and Pettit keep each other on their toes.

Pettit had joined Lehman in 1977 and in the early years worked with Fuld on the trading floor (both were Glucksman protégés). But Pettit was the opposite of Fuld in many ways. Pettit was the outgoing former bond salesman while Fuld was the introverted former bond trader. Pettit was charismatic, a people person, and an accomplished public speaker, a rally-the-troops type of leader. At company meetings and outings, Fuld and Pettit would often speak side by side, and it was clear Pettit was the better presenter. At company Christmas parties, Pettit was usually asked to give the annual address. At one such gathering, he regaled the troops with a story about the right people needed to rebuild Lehman. He asked whether it should be people from Wharton Business School who want to be accountants or those who want to be rock stars. On perfect cue, he energized the crowd by shouting back: "I don't know about you, but I want to work with rock stars. . . . How about you?"

Fuld was more a risk taker, the taskmaster, a numbers guy who commanded but also demanded respect. What Pettit and Fuld shared in common was that they both were extremely competitive—at work and in sports. Pettit, a West Point graduate, was a college All-American lacrosse player and leading scorer for his team. Fuld was a gym fanatic and an accomplished squash player. He was a U.S. Amateur Seniors Squash Champion and had won a gold medal in the 1997 Maccabiah Games in Israel. Initially, Fuld and Pettit worked well together and maintained a close friendship. With Hill out of the way, the taciturn Fuld assumed the Mr. Inside role of focusing on the numbers and firm strategy, while in perfect cadence Pettit assumed the broader Mr. Outside role of being the public face of Lehman. Unlike Peterson and Glucksman, Fuld and Pettit respected each other and worked well together.

At the parent company, other major changes were afoot. American Express decided to finally cut its losses and sell Shearson Lehman. The divestiture was to be completed in two phases: first, the sale of Shearson Lehman's retail brokerage operations to Smith Barney in 1993 and, second, the spin-off of the remaining company to American Express at the end of May 1994.[2] The name of the spin-off company was Lehman Brothers Holdings, Inc. (Lehman), headquartered in New York City at 3 World Financial Center. The newly issued stock traded publicly under the symbol LEH. Although Lehman's stock had a book value of more than $25 a share, it started trading at less than $20 and eventually fell to $13 only a few months later. This created much discontentment with those senior employees who had been strongly encouraged to purchase shares at book value before the initial public offering. Within a short period, they had lost almost half their investment. Adding to this frustration, Lehman leased office space from its former parent at a rate deemed considerably above the going market rate. The parent had sold the firm, but it still had a hand in Lehman's pocket. To keep what he called the "Mother Ship" intact, Fuld would have to rebuild Lehman back to profitability.

REBUILDING LEHMAN

After the spin-off, Lehman was a much smaller company than it had been only a year earlier. As the firm's pieces were sold, significant headcount went to Smith Barney, diminishing Lehman's standing in the wholesale equities sales and trading area. In 1991 and 1992 Lehman was at the top of the industry league tables for equity research and trading. However, by the end of 1993, with equity analysts departing, Lehman's prominence in this area had rapidly declined. Lehman's 1994 league table rankings showed that it had dropped out of the top tier with a lowly ninth-place ranking. The *New York Times* went so far as to refer to Lehman as a one-trick bond shop.[3] Bad news kept getting worse as the firm's return on equity declined to a meager 3 percent, and the stock continued to decline. Lower rankings, subpar returns, and lower stock prices were more proof Lehman needed a complete makeover.

Fuld's first order of duty was to gain greater revenue diversification and fill gaps in Lehman's business model. Similar to Bobbie Lehman, he saw the need to diversify income. This gap was met through entering the higher-risk and higher-return junk-bond market. Despite the fall of "Junk Bond King" Michael Milken and the tarnished reputation of junk bonds, their fundamentals remained sound enough, and more important, the potential rewards of the high-yield bonds were very alluring. Lehman had not been an early participant in the high-yield bond party, but an opportunity to build out the firm's high-yield debt business occurred in 1994 after Kidder, Peabody & Company (Kidder) sustained destabilizing trading losses from collateralized mortgage obligations (CMOs) and other risky products. Phantom profits booked by trader Joe Jett, combined with more than $1 billion in other trading losses, compelled parent General Electric to sell off Kidder to Paine Webber.

For three years, Tom Bernard had been the hotshot running Kidder's high-yield bond group, but now he was without a job. Seeing an opportunity to fill a strategic gap, Lehman hired Bernard and virtually his entire junk-bond trading desk.[4] To the dismay of many existing Lehman employees, Bernard's team arrived in 1994 with exclusive pay packages and a newer, riskier approach to business. Several fixed-income employees were so upset, they left. Initially, Bernard's new high-yield group produced solid revenues for Lehman. But by 1998 the profitability had fallen, tarnishing some of Bernard's luster. He switched positions, managing the firm's Global Credit business, before eventually leaving the firm in 2002.

Fuld's second order of business was bringing Lehman's cost structure in line. Robert Genirs, Lehman's CFO and controller, assumed the position of cost-cutting czar. An internal memo to the more than 9,200 firm employees announced his appointment and indicated that no cost was too small, including supplies such as pencils. In 1993 cost cutting started slowly but noticeably. On some floors at the Lehman headquarters in Lower Manhattan, air-conditioning was turned off at 7 P.M. instead of the standard 8 P.M. The lenient limousine voucher policy that some employees used to cart friends and family around town was curtailed. Under the new environment, there would be no more deep-pocketed parent to pick up the tab. Lehman would have to get leaner.

Changing behavior was not only important to meet the new demands of public shareholders, but it was also important for Lehman to convince the rating agencies that it deserved at least an A long-term credit rating. Fuld promised the rating agencies he would act decisively. It would take more than cutting pencils, air-conditioning, or travel vouchers. On September 8, 1994, he delivered on his promise with a first wave of layoffs, 3 percent of employees. Shortly thereafter, the free employee lunches Lehman had made available in the tradition of the old Wall Street partnerships were eliminated. One year later, another more aggressive wave of layoffs occurred. By the end of 1995, Lehman emerged leaner and meaner with less than 7,800 employees. The changes worked. All the key credit rating agencies assigned Lehman a coveted A rating. Fuld had proved he could get the job done.

LEHMAN'S OTHER BUSINESS LINES

Initially, Lehman's Emerging Market Group (EMG) focused on trading and underwriting bonds in rapidly developing countries. Not shying away from taking risk, EMG's trading strategy included betting on dollar-denominated Mexican debt called *tesobonos*. At the market peak, these debt positions equaled the firm's entire capital.[5] This concentrated position generated profit until the significant market disruption caused by the Mexican financial crisis began in December 1994. As the Mexican peso collapsed against the dollar, *tesobonos*—whose interest payments were indexed to the dollar—also plummeted in value. When Dick Fuld was told of the level of exposure and mounting losses, he was shocked. Fortunately for Lehman, the IMF, and the Clinton administration's Treasury Undersecretary Robert Rubin quickly constructed a sweeping financial rescue plan. This helped to stabilize the Mexican market by 1995, making Lehman one of the many beneficiaries. Lehman also received help internally. Luck would have it that around the same time, a Lehman trader in the London office was accumulating a significant short position, assuming that the value of the Mexican peso would drop. Rumors even circulated that Fuld received a panic call from Mexico's foreign minister pleading that Lehman not short his country's currency. As the peso dropped in value, profits from this single trade position soared, reducing the losses that the EMG had sustained. Lehman had dodged another bullet, but the Mexican crisis should have demonstrated to Fuld that Lehman needed a better handle on risk management.

In 1995 Lehman installed Brian Zipp, a former mortgage manager, as the new EMG head. He quickly cleaned house by firing numerous people and transforming the new group into a more formidable competitor, particularly in the emerging-market derivatives area. But compared to revenue-generating areas across the firm, EMG was providing less than stellar returns on capital. By 1998 Lehman decided that EMG would never be a material part of the firm's revenue stream, and it was subsequently downsized.

During this period, Lehman also tried to bolster its activities in the asset management business. The sale of smaller retail accounts to Smith Barney freed up Lehman to focus on growing its higher net worth investment management business. Unlike the emerging-market desk, investment management business demanded much less staffing. Yet, after building this new asset management division to more than two hundred employees, Lehman reversed course and eliminated the entire business line. Management determined that the return on equity was not high enough to support these lower-risk activities. Many of these employees had contracts with termination clauses that had to be bought out—an expensive way to venture in and out of a business line, but this was how Lehman tested the waters until it became comfortable in its new shell.

CUTTING NONCORE BUSINESSES

By 1996 Lehman began to take a fine pencil to profitability, eliminating numerous noncore businesses. Over time, Lehman had ventured into various commodities businesses, trading oil-based crack spreads, gold, heavy metals, and electricity. The firm even hired a gold research maven. Sporting a long white beard, this "maven" made price forecasts on CNBC and looked every bit the part of a gold wizard. Around this same time, Lehman also ventured into the energy trading business, investing in Boston-based trading company Citizens Lehman Power LLC.[6] To traders, these commodities provided higher price volatility, uncertainty, and risk as well as the possibility of higher profits. However, compared to the fixed-income side of the house, these businesses contributed mere decimal points to Lehman's earnings. Many of these ancillary commodity-trading activities were viewed as a distraction from Lehman's true focal point.

BUILDING OUT FIXED INCOME

Lehman's bread and butter—what paid the bills and bonuses—remained fixed-income trading, sales, and research. Despite efforts to diversify, this was Lehman's core competency and had essentially defined the firm since the 1980s. Increasingly, Lehman built its business model around customer flow trading and the information flow emanating from it. This was a lower-risk strategy that still allowed Lehman to gain respectable returns. Stated simply, Lehman made money by meeting customers' financial needs and by trading information gleaned from maintaining these relationships. Lehman sat at the headwaters of thousands of trades each day and could peer in and pick and choose profitable trends it found in this onslaught of information. Lehman began to expand its focus to serving institutional clients and wealthy individuals. Investment banking provided a list of issuers, supplying a steady stream of new equity and debt issues, and laying the foundation for derivatives trading with corporate customers.

Lehman's flow trading strategy put firm capital at risk but not at levels that could blow up the entire firm. Flow trading was different from the riskier proprietary trading model employed by such competitors as Salomon or Goldman Sachs. In flow trading, a firm wanted to know what its biggest and brightest clients were doing, while in proprietary trading, the knowledge of client trading was usually viewed as a distraction from a firm's internal strategies. Proprietary trading also required larger amounts of capital and a willingness to put more at risk.

In rival firms, proprietary trading desks were located away from the fixed-income or equity trading floor to avoid being biased by the information derived from the customers. By the mid-1990s, firm-driven proprietary trading desks demanded physical separation, relying on independently developed trading models that completely ignored the information from flow trading. Today, true proprietary trading firms are called hedge funds. In the 1990s Lehman resisted the competitive pressure to morph into a hedge fund, but by the next decade, the firm would finally succumb to this pressure.

The risk of a complete desk and earnings exodus was the main reason Lehman, at least initially, had no interest in allowing proprietary trading activities to grow too large. Take Salomon, for example. By 1990 the lion's share of Salomon's earnings during the past decade had come from proprietary trading while other areas such as the flow desk, trading, sales, or traditional investment banking activities contributed very little to overall profitability. The complete walling off of the proprietary trading desk was why John Meriwether and his trading group from Salomon was able to quickly leave the firm and set up shop as the hedge fund Long-Term Capital Management in 1994. The danger Fuld saw was not trading losses, but rather the risk of trader defection and one business area getting too big for its britches.

BUILDING OUT EQUITIES AND INVESTMENT BANKING

Although Fuld had a personal preference for fixed-income trading, his broader objective was to build a world-class investment bank. He understood that having a diversified revenue stream was important to long-term success and independence. While it was a given that Lehman was a top bond house, to reach top-tier investment banking status required building out the equity trading and investment banking capabilities. This was particularly true if Lehman were to attempt to compete with its much bigger, well-diversified rivals. As a publicly traded company that issued a lot of debt, Lehman had to satisfy the concerns of both investors and the credit rating agencies. Lehman needed to demonstrate that it could manage the revenue side as well as the cost side of the business. The final main objective was to create a stronger global presence.

By the summer of 1992, Jack Rivkin, the highly regarded head of equities, abruptly resigned. As his replacement, Paul Williams, formally the head of fixed-income research, was tapped by Chris Pettit to rebuild the equity business even though he had no trading experience in equities. In an August 1, 1995, article, *Institutional Investor* summed up the consensus on the Street by questioning whether Lehman could recapture its research franchise.[7] When it came to such important decision making, Dick Fuld and Chris Pettit were both known to let loyalty trump competence—a potentially dangerous flaw. For them, loyalty was earned by putting time in on the fixed-income trading floor.

PETTIT'S FALL FROM POWER

With the constant internal turmoil, Lehman often seemed more like a dysfunctional family than a top-tier investment bank back on the rise. Senior-level infighting and intrigue persisted throughout the mid-1990s. President and COO Chris Pettit's outgoing personality made him very popular at Lehman. Even prior to becoming second in command, he had worked to place fixed-income people loyal to him in top operating spots throughout the firm, which obviously increased his internal power base. Tapping Paul Williams to head the entire equities operation was a prime example. Outright nepotism even played a hand when Pettit made his brother-in-law head of this area. During this same time, Pettit was allegedly having an affair with the head of fixed-income research. It became a source of rumors within the firm and across Wall Street. In May 1994 the head of fixed-income research resigned from Lehman. The cumulative effect of these events strained the Fuld-Pettit relationship—the general finally had doubts about his colonel.

In a bold power grab, Fuld stripped Pettit of his COO title and removed many of his handpicked executives in April 1996. Fuld next removed Williams. Not surprisingly, Fuld's own handpicked replacement for this position was a former bond trader and trusted ally, Joseph Gregory (although he did not assume the role of president and COO until six years later). Within six months, Pettit resigned. Only a month later he was killed in a freak snowmobile accident while vacationing in Maine. Lehman had lost its charismatic public face, Mr. Outside, for good. With Pettit gone, there were no more speeches at annual holiday parties to rally the troops of the Mother Ship. Fuld was on top without a potential successor, and Lehman became even more Fuldcentric.

KEEPING THE MONARCHY INTACT

The fallout with Pettit had a profound impact on Fuld.[8] Many thought Steve Lessing, the head of fixed-income sales and a consummate salesman, would be ideal as Pettit's replacement. But he was never promoted to the job. In fact, nobody was promoted. The unpleasant situation with Pettit taught Fuld an important lesson: the best way to preserve a monarchy is to not appoint a number two person. No doubt, the power struggle that cost Peterson and eventually his mentor, Glucksman, the top spot also influenced Fuld's thinking process. The president and COO slot—this important corporate checks and balances position—was not filled for six more years. Fuld's need for job security trumped the need for stronger corporate governance. He strengthened his control but weakened the company. Autonomy and risk taking were concentrated solely in Fuld's hands. Having no one who could be called an heir apparent, or even an extra set of eyes, became Fuld's strategy into the next decade.

Despite the internal turmoil, Lehman seemed to be getting its financial house in order. By the end of 1997, Lehman's stature in the industry league tables was up in trading, equities research, underwriting, and mergers and acquisitions. Year-on-year profits beat industry expectations. In three short years Lehman had survived the Mexican financial crisis and recalibrated its business model with great success. It was making money in all three core areas: fixed income, equity, and investment banking. Lehman was far removed from its Shearson–American Express days. No sooner was the firm ready to bask in its newfound success in rebuilding the franchise than storm clouds started to form.

Chapter 8

Lehman's Near-Death Experience

By 1998, Lehman had finally hit its financial stride after working through a turbulent market, sorting out management uncertainty, and building out its core business activities. Firm profitability was up, and Wall Street continued to stage a broad market rally. A relatively new hedge fund called Long-Term Capital Management (LTCM) borrowed heavily from investment firms across Wall Street, making billion-dollar bets using extremely high leverage to invest in esoteric derivative securities. But bets that in previous years had paid off eventually began producing unthinkable losses.

In the wake of LTCM's near collapse, the market responded by searching for others that would be next. Lehman quickly rose to the top of the list. Rumors spread across Wall Street, and a run on the House of Lehman ensued. Lehman CEO Dick Fuld had already demonstrated that he could navigate through market turmoil, but this was a much bigger challenge—now the firm was in the eye of the storm. Fuld's success in quelling the market stampede and methods used would be the blueprint for responding to the future crisis. The Federal Reserve (Fed) also stepped into the fray and orchestrated an eleventh-hour rescue of the fallen hedge fund, reinforcing the "too big to fail" doctrine first set out a decade earlier, and thereby strengthening the precedent that would come back to haunt Lehman in 2008.

A HEDGE FUND IS BORN

A hedge fund is an investment company that uses various investment techniques to generate above-market returns by pursuing numerous strategies, including long, short, or market neutral positions. The bulk of a hedge fund manager's compensation is linked to oversized returns, so leverage and other aggressive risk-taking approaches are not uncommon within the industry. Hedge funds have been on Wall Street since the 1940s but didn't gain popularity until the 1990s. One of the largest and best-known hedge funds of this decade was LTCM, started in 1994 by John Meriwether, the famed bond arbitrage trader from Salomon Brothers. Over the decade prior to his creation of LTCM, Meriwether and his bond arbitrage group had been the source for most of Salomon's earnings.

Not only did LTCM include many former traders from Salomon, it also collected a dream team of financial minds, including such notables as David Mullins, the well-respected former vice chairman of the Federal Reserve System, and future Nobel Prize winners Robert Merton and Myron Scholes. Two-thirds of the partners had either gone to Massachusetts Institute of Technology (MIT) or had taught there. From the moment it opened its doors in Greenwich, Connecticut, LTCM was greeted with much market fanfare, and few on Wall Street doubted whether it would make financial history. Indeed, the men behind LTCM were dubbed the new "masters of the universe."

The hedge fund's formula for success included arbitraging the difference in pricing between nearly equivalent securities through the use of mathematically driven models. In theory, LTCM would profit by buying undervalued securities and selling overvalued ones, locking in the profit by hedging out the risk. To achieve this foolproof profit formula, Meriwether assembled mathematicians, academicians, and traders. He also demanded loyalty and a high degree of secrecy. When asked how LTCM worked, partner Scholes described it as one large vacuum cleaner sucking up nickels from around the world.

Central to LTCM's arbitrage-based trading strategy was placing bets on relationships between a broad array of investments across global markets, including the relationship of government bonds with differing maturities to themselves and that of corporate bonds. Many of these trades were placed in higher-risk emerging markets. In addition, LTCM entered into convergence trades where it bet that bond spreads between two securities or derivatives would narrow and converge over time.[1] In a typical trade, LTCM would go long (buy) in risky, illiquid, and complex derivative securities and short (sell) in safe U.S. Treasury securities.

To investors the bond spread is an important risk barometer measuring the chance of default. The larger the spread between two bond instruments, the greater the perceived risk. In times of market stress, investors tend to sell risky bonds and seek the safety of lower-risk government bonds. Such a flight to quality increases the spread. Trading spreads involved making risky bets on the price behavior of these two types of bonds. For this strategy to be successful, markets and the relationship between bonds need to behave in a predictable manner.

An integral part of the LTCM trading strategy was the use of leverage. It knew that placing bets on incremental price movements and not leveraging capital would only produce average returns. To generate double-digit returns required using substantial amounts of debt. Ultimately, LTCM would borrow more than $120 billion, posting only minimum collateral. The sizes of LTCM's positions were comparable to Lehman, Salomon, and other investment banks but were lacking the benefits of a diversified stream of fee income. Leverage also posed another problem—it was a double-edged sword. For a given movement in bond prices, LTCM could make or lose significant amounts of money. This was where the mathematical models came into play. To minimize the chance of loss, LTCM attempted to hedge out risk and gain diversification by placing thousands of bets in positions spread around the globe. The firm believed that diversification would reduce correlation—the chance that all bets would come up losses at the same time. Central to this approach was a belief that models could and would mimic investor behavior. In the simplest of terms, LTCM believed that its models were precisely right.

With its star-studded team, LTCM was able to quickly raise more than $1.2 billion in capital. Many of the leaders of Wall Street had studied under Scholes at Stanford University or Merton at MIT and felt honored to be given the opportunity to invest in this new model-based trading company.[2] Partners also put up $100 million of their own money. Minimum investments in LTCM started at $10 million, and investors were not allowed to withdraw money for up to three years, not to mention the sizable management fees. Investors paid a fee of 25 percent of all profits earned on top of an annual 2 percent management fee. From inception, the LTCM models generated exceptional returns with apparently little risk. The firm rewarded its investors with a compound annualized return of almost 40 percent through 1997.

With no losses and consistently high returns, it appeared that LTCM had created an unstoppable money machine. The market appeared to be behaving as LTCM's models predicted it would. In four short years, partner equity had increased to more than $2 billion. On Wall Street, LTCM's profitable trading strategies were quickly replicated. Although LTCM attempted to spread out its trade execution so not to disclose its strategies, its positions were large enough that the market quickly pieced together the magic formula. By the mid-1990s, it was commonplace for investment banks, including Lehman, to set up and run separate bond arbitrage desks. Although on a smaller scale, these new trading groups met with success, forcing down LTCM's profit margins. Ironically, increased competition reduced the trading spreads that had attracted LTCM in the first place.

A FATAL RISK-MANAGEMENT DECISION

At the end of 1997, LTCM appeared to be well capitalized. It had balance sheet assets of about $130 billion, supported by $7.5 billion in capital. But, during that same year, LTCM made a significantly flawed risk-management decision in response to declining trading margins. It returned half the firm's capital to investors while retaining the same size of investments. The firm was taking the same level of risk but supported by half the amount of capital. This decision made the fund much riskier in a market downturn. In early 1997 LTCM had a leverage ratio (assets to equity) of greater than 18 to 1, but once a sizable amount of the firm's capital was returned, this leverage ratio shot up to 25 to 1. More leverage equals higher profit potential and more risk.

Adding to this uncertainty, political events in 1997 began to make global markets edgy. Initially these market events seemed isolated from the rarified world in Greenwich, Connecticut, and went little noticed. But, bit by bit, they became the spark that set off the financial turmoil that would undermine LTCM's solvency. These seemingly improbable events first surfaced in Southeast Asia, where market chaos pushed out the long-standing president of Indonesia, resulting in an economic crisis that swept across Asia and caused many prominent banks to fail.

The shockwave from these bank failures gained momentum and eventually reached Japan, Korea, and Russia. In the wake of this financial storm, Asian currencies began to collapse, and global stock markets began falling. By May 1998 currency speculators targeted the ruble, betting it would be the next currency to fall. In an effort to halt the flight of capital, Russia immediately tripled interest rates. Such a drastic action only reinforced the prevailing view that Russia was on the edge of a full-blown collapse. Other events also added to market uneasiness, including Iraq's refusal to allow a full weapons inspection, China's potential devaluation of its currency, the President Clinton–Monica Lewinsky affair, and the slowing of the U.S. economy. Many investors responded to growing market uncertainty by buying safety (government bonds) and selling risk (nongovernment bonds). The spread between safer government bonds and riskier nongovernment bonds widened even further, moving outside of historic norms and against LTCM's model-driven bets.

By July 1998, LTCM's trading losses increasingly eroded sparse capital. Suddenly LTCM had only $3.6 billion in capital to support a trading position in excess of $100 billion. Including the off-balance-sheet assets, the notional value of the exposure was $1.25 trillion. At this time, the firm's leverage ratio was closer to 30 to 1—the equivalent of a five-hundred-pound pumpkin being supported by a stick. Now even a slight adverse price movement of 3 percent, if not properly hedged, would wipe out the firm's remaining equity. The trading strategy that had worked so well under calm conditions was now breaking apart. Competitors had entered into similar trades and were now more interested in saving themselves than LTCM. In forced liquidation, as LTCM or their trading partners decided to sell, bond prices dropped even further.

TRADING STRATEGY

Long-Term Capital Management had invested heavily in Russia. With an economy that had recently embraced capitalistic ideals, Russia's newly issued government bonds seemed poised for significant financial growth. So LTCM entered into convergence trades utilizing derivative instruments called swaps—a financial instrument where the buyer and seller agree to swap cash flows based on a specific face value, rate, and time period. These swaps were bets on how U.S. Treasury bonds would move in relation to Russian bonds. LTCM gambled that the relationships would narrow and *not* move out of their historical norm.

But the improbable events that were unfolding in Asia, Russia, and the United States caused emerging-market bond spreads to widen—the very opposite of what LTCM and its models had predicted. The models that LTCM used were turning out to be precisely wrong. This trend was first noticeable in May 1998, when the firm recorded a loss of 6.7 percent.[3] For LTCM, this was a shocking turn of events. During the previous four years, the firm was able to provide consistent returns and avoid material losses. This loss trend continued into June. Suddenly LTCM no longer had the Midas touch and instead was losing mountains of money. For July its trading losses totaled more than $500 million. Then on August 17 more unexpected bad news occurred. Russia dropped a financial bomb that would seal LTCM's fate and cause Lehman to fight for its survival. The Russian government declared a debt moratorium and defaulted on a massive amount of local debt—$13.5 billion worth of its bonds. This action immediately put into question the willingness of the Russian government to repay its even larger external debt to foreign institutions.

Russian bonds that had traded at 80 cents to the dollar now traded as low as 4 cents to the dollar. By August 20, global investors were selling these already faltering bonds like hotcakes. By August 21, the yield on safer mortgage bonds climbed to 121 basis points, up from 107 only a week earlier. At the same time, yields on riskier bonds increased to 276 basis points, up from 269. While a move of 7 to 14 basis points might not seem large, when adding in the amount of leverage used by LTCM and the size of derivative positions, these price movements were financially devastating.[4]

In an attempt to get out of the way of the crumbling LTCM, a stampede of worried investors continued driving bond prices down even further. As a large holder of Russian debt, LTCM was squarely at the center of this financial calamity. The firm's mathematical models continued to indicate that the losses would be manageable, remaining under $45 million for a given trading day, but the market continued to think differently. There were several times in August when LTCM lost more than $100 million in a single day, and, toward the end of the month, the firm lost in excess of $550 million in a single day. There was no longer just investor flight to quality. It had turned into a massive flight out of bonds. By the end of August, LTCM had lost half of the capital it had at the start of the year. The firm's leverage ratio ballooned from 30 to 1 to 45 to 1. By September, this leverage ratio would reach the astronomically risky level of 55 to 1. Later LTCM management would argue that the firm was exposed to involuntary increases in leverage that were outside its control and caused by market forces as asset prices were pushed down.

KEY LESSONS LEARNED

During September 1998, LTCM and others should have learned several important lessons. First, the models and assumptions LTCM heavily relied on were capable of gross miscalculation. Like an umbrella pulled away when it rains, the diversification anticipated from the thousands of trades was nowhere to be found. The stressed market had behaved as LTCM least expected. Second, leverage can kill. The more leveraged a firm is, the more important it is to maintain investors' confidence. If this confidence is lost, a run on the firm will ensue. Third, if leverage is employed, it should be used to hold more liquid positions that can be sold rapidly in times of market stress. Fourth, risk measurement models can understate actual risk. Last, the trading model employed by LTCM worked well under Salomon Brothers' diverse business lines. However, as a stand-alone mono-line hedge fund, LTCM did not have the benefits of other lines of revenue. The firm was vulnerable should the arbitrage trading strategy fail.

One of the largest hedge funds in the world was teetering on the edge of bankruptcy and causing other hedge funds with exposure to also become financially stressed. High Risk Opportunity Fund, run by III Offshore Advisors, was forced to close its doors. Ellington Capital, run by a former Lehman employee, almost did not survive. The losses associated with LTCM were not isolated. Many large banks that had helped Russia make the transition to capitalism, including First Boston, Credit Suisse, and Republic Bank of New York, reported surprisingly large losses. Rumors even circulated that on a mark-to-market basis, the gigantic U.S. government–sponsored mortgage agencies, Freddie Mac and Fannie Mae, were also insolvent. It was a time of severe market uncertainty.

LEHMAN—THE WEAK LINK?

In response to the LTCM debacle, the market was now running not just from emerging-market debt but also from perceived risk wherever it was found. Investors were looking for firms that had any hedge fund exposure. Which would be the next firm to fall? Numerous prominent firms on Wall Street had LTCM exposure—most of them more than Lehman. On paper Lehman looked financially sound. Yet by the third week in August 1998, market rumors quickly circulated, and Lehman was singled out as the weak link that might be insolvent.

For Fuld and his firm, these rumors were puzzling. Although Lehman had provided some short-term funding to LTCM through its repo desk, the lending was backed by good collateral. Lehman's unsecured exposure to all hedge funds, including LTCM and emerging-market debt, was less than 1 percent of its total capital.[5] And LTCM's leverage ratio was two times that of Lehman's 20 to 1 and was growing by the day. From inception, LTCM had actually snubbed Lehman as a smallish investment bank, giving more business to rivals such as Goldman Sachs, Morgan Stanley, and Merrill Lynch. These firms had greater than three times the credit exposure to LTCM. Not only had these other major investment banks enabled LTCM to borrow billions of dollars, they had also invested in the firm. At Merrill, more than 120 executives had invested approximately $22 million in LTCM as part of their deferred compensation plan.[6]

In stark contrast, Lehman had not made similar loans or investments. They had exercised sound risk management judgment by keeping exposure low and tightening the credit standard on LTCM before the significant August events unfolded. Moreover, Lehman was not a major player in Russian bonds. It was only when LTCM was on the ropes that it came to Lehman for assistance. On September 14, 1998, LTCM approached Jeff Vanderbeek, head of Lehman's fixed-income group, and asked if he could raise money through the firm's private equity group.[7] In reality, LTCM was asking Lehman to help sort out its financial mess while the broader market increasingly viewed Lehman as the next to fall. This notion infuriated Fuld. Lehman was a sound company. It even had an A long-term corporate credit rating from Standard & Poor's. Not surprisingly, Lehman chose to distance itself from LTCM and declined to assist in this fund-raising scheme.

On Wall Street, rumors tend to emanate from trading floors, and even rumors not grounded in facts can turn the capital faucet off in a matter of minutes. Moreover, investment firms such as Lehman borrow on a short-term basis, meaning that increased costs of borrowing can pose major challenges in running the day-to-day business. Obviously, the bond market meltdown had created increased volatility for all broker-dealers. But, throughout the 1990s, under Fuld's guidance, Lehman had positioned itself as a bigger force in the bond market without having the benefit of diversification into other business lines. The market thought Lehman was a single-trick pony. Fixed-income trading and sales had paid the bills in the past and continued to keep the lights on. Unlike Morgan Stanley, Merrill Lynch, or Goldman Sachs, each of which received more of its revenue from non-fixed-income activities, Lehman stood out as a broker-dealer with a fixed-income addiction. As the bond market crisis grew, investors speculated about potential losses on Lehman's books. Moreover, Lehman bought and sold bonds from many trading partners that might have direct exposure to LTCM. In a sense, the market was justifiably penalizing Lehman for being perceived as one big, undiversified bond shop in a turbulent bond market.

By September 2, 1998, when John Meriwether confirmed that LTCM had lost big, the market rumors continued to hound Lehman. Meriwether issued a letter that did not mince words: LTCM trading losses were down 44 percent for the month of August and 52 percent for the year. Widely circulated on Wall Street, this letter was quickly picked up by the media. There was now a clear run to the door as investors attempted to sell all investments that even resembled those of LTCM. These losses were staggering for a firm that only six months earlier had been one of the biggest and most respected hedge funds in the world. To the market, the size of the losses reported was just additional proof that there must be other firms in trouble. In rapid fashion, the market began to act on its fears, selling Lehman bonds and stocks. Lehman bonds dropped to as low as 60 cents on the dollar, and the firm's bonds, as measured by yield, began to trade more like junk bonds than A credit-rated bonds. Above $42 in July, Lehman stock was at $12 a share by October, a 70 percent drop, erasing billions in firm value.

The market's dramatic re-pricing of Lehman's securities put many of its trading counterparts on edge. As protection against the growing storm, credit limits across the industry were reduced and margin calls became the norm. Morgan Stanley was one of the first counterparties to land a destabilizing blow to Lehman. As a trading partner, Morgan Stanley decided to cancel a foreign exchange trade claiming credit concerns. As discussed, an investment bank's ability to access credit in the market is driven by the market's perception of creditworthiness. To a trading firm, capital and access to it are its lifeblood. Once capital lines are restricted, trading grinds to a halt. As a former trader, Fuld understood he had to confront the market and quell the rumor mill before it became a self-fulfilling prophecy. He had to place a swift blow to the irrational market's solar plexus. But the question was how best to do so.

FULD TO THE RESCUE

The bell had rung, and it was time for Lehman's CEO to come out swinging. Lehman was being hit with rumors and innuendo that, for all Fuld knew, could have been planted by one or more rival firms wanting to profit at Lehman's expense. Was archrival Goldman Sachs at it again? Fuld needed to quickly demonstrate to the market that Lehman was financially sound and big enough to withstand the market waves created by the Russian default and subsequent LTCM fallout. Fuld rapidly devised a response that was, in effect, a communications battle that enveloped the firm: internally with employees and externally with investors.

The internal campaign was launched by going directly to the more than eight thousand Lehman employees. Fuld sent the message personally, physically getting out of his office and rallying the troops. In September 1998 he surprised the Boston office by arriving on the trading floor, looking each employee in the eye and conveying that everything would be fine. Boston was a smaller branch in the Lehman family, but the head of Lehman—not some executive underling—walked the floor, shook hands, and spread the convincing message. Lehman was literally at war with the market. At the time, Fuld was fifty-four years old, but years of rigorous gym workouts had kept his six-foot frame trim and made him appear much younger. Employees saw Fuld as Lehman's fit captain who could beat the market rumors into submission. With the employees behind him, Fuld had an army of mouthpieces who could send a convincing, and harmonious, message to the Street.

The second front of the communication battle targeted Lehman investors. With the help of his top lieutenants (CFO; head of fixed income, equities, investment banking; and head of global risk management), Fuld created a war-room atmosphere. Fuld made house calls to Wall Street analysts, investment shops, mutual funds, and other institutional investors. He opened Lehman's books. Many large customers such as Fidelity and Charles Schwab walked in and received Fuld's personal attention. In parallel, much effort was made to persuade large holders of Lehman bonds and stocks to retain ownership. This group was particularly important. If not convinced that Lehman was solvent, investors dumping their holdings would drive prices down further, giving additional credibility to rumors. There was also an effort to use the recent improvements in the risk management control as evidence that Lehman had a firm handle on things.

On October 5, 1998, Lehman filed an 8-K with the Securities and Exchange Commission. This filing is used by companies only to report significant and material events. In an unusual but effective move, Lehman revealed confidential trading positions, clearly demonstrating that it had little direct exposure to LTCM, other hedge funds, and emerging markets. The full counterattack with Fuld at the helm succeeded. Slowly the word on Wall Street turned: Lehman was financially sound and would live to trade another day.

FED TO THE RESCUE

By early September 1998, the Federal Reserve Bank of New York (Fed) determined that the systemic risk associated with a LTCM failure could cause major Wall Street firms to seize up and stop functioning. The Fed concluded, as it had fourteen years earlier when it led the rescue of Continental Illinois Bank, that LTCM was "too big to fail." Now the financial stakes were seen as even higher. The Fed feared that if LTCM defaulted on its trade obligations, many Wall Street banks would hold the other side of worthless derivative contracts. These banks would be forced to sell the collateral supporting these contracts, which could push market prices down further, triggering even greater instability.

The Fed appeared to understand that of the thousands of LTCM trades outstanding, many were entered into with non-pared trading partners, in part to reduce the market's ability to decipher trading strategies and positions. Now these risky trades could not be quickly identified, pared up, and off-set. In bankruptcy, this meant such trading partners would have to fend for themselves and not have the ability to net out exposures. It was estimated that the biggest counterparties to LTCM—Merrill Lynch, Morgan Stanley, Salomon, and Goldman Sachs—would lose as much as $2.8 billion. Of the approximately seventeen banks with the most LTCM exposure, the losses were predicted between $3 billion and $5 billion. In isolation, divided among these firms, the losses would be sustainable even at $300 million each. However, the Fed was concerned that the financial impact of such losses would have a knock-on effect, leading to darker consequences for the entire financial system.[8] By the second week in September, LTCM had only $1.5 billion left in equity, a decline of 50 percent since August. With a plummeting equity value, the fund's leverage ratio now exceeded the lofty heights of 100 to 1. This meant that a 1 percent adverse movement in price would wipe out the firm. In essence, LTCM was insolvent.

By the third week in September, the Fed organized a series of meetings with the major financial firms that had the largest credit exposure to LTCM. The goal was to hammer out a rescue package. In attendance were many of Wall Street's elite bankers, including John Thain and John Corzine, Goldman Sachs; Phillip Purcell, Morgan Stanley Dean Witter; Thomas Labrecque, Chase; James Cayne, Bear Stearns; Sandy Weill, Citigroup; Jamie Dimon and Deryck Maughan, Salomon Smith Barney; Allen Wheat, Credit Suisse First Boston; Herb Allison and Dave Komansky, Merrill Lynch; and Dick Fuld, Lehman. Fifty people crammed into the New York Fed's ornate wood-paneled conference room.

The initial plan proposed that sixteen banks would put up $250 million each, or a total of $4 billion. Given Lehman's minimum direct exposure to LTCM, Fuld objected because he felt banks should post money based on actual exposure. In response, Goldman's Thain responded that doing so would be too complicated and that they were running out of time to strike a rescue plan.[9] By late September, it was becoming harder to keep bankers in agreement on how to handle the LTCM crisis. Some firms threatened to cut off trading and clearing services. Bear Stearns' Cayne, a card-playing tough-guy banker, threatened to stop clearing trades. Such a move would have put

LTCM out of business. In fact, Bear Stearns eventually did stop clearing for LTCM and, more important, decided not to participate in the final rescue plan even though it had credit exposure to LTCM and had earned more than $30 million in associated trade-clearing fees. This unwillingness to help would come back to haunt Bear Stearns when it found itself in similar straits ten years later.

After a final week of different rescue plan permutations, including an offer from a group led by investor Warren Buffett that LTCM rejected,[10] the Fed was finally able to convince fourteen banks to pony up $3.65 billion. A private rescue solution was reached. On the day of the bailout in late September 1998 the leverage ratio was 300 to 1. Most banks paid $300 million each to rescue LTCM. Given Lehman's smaller exposure, it was able to win concessions and only paid $100 million into the rescue plan. All of these banks helped out of self-interest. None came to the rescue because the Fed held their feet to the fire.

AND LIKE THAT, CRISIS OVER

With the help of the Fed-organized rescue plan, complete market disruption was avoided. At the time, the Fed received accolades for its swift action in saving a sinking firm from pulling down the rest of the financial market. Systemic risk was averted. By the end of September, Lehman bonds and stock prices were on their way back up. The two-month storm that hit Lehman completely subsided when another unexpected market event occurred. Julian Robertson, the head of Tiger Management and a noted value investor, threw in the towel. He had been sitting on a multibillion-dollar foreign bond position, which had taken a significant hit as a result of the LTCM crisis. Simultaneously, he had a misplaced yen currency bet that had large mark-to-market losses. Capitulating on October 7, 1998, Tiger Management sold more than one hundred thousand German bond futures contracts. Once this trade was executed, in the snap of a finger, bond prices around the world moved up by 20 to 30 basis points and spreads began to finally fall. This was the equivalent of the sun coming out after a tornado, announcing the storm was over. As a result of Tiger's actions, Lehman stock bottomed out on October 7, 1998, at $12.37. As if the LTCM crisis were only a dream, by June 1999 Lehman stock was back up to more than $40 per share, and its bonds were trading once again at a pre-LTCM crisis level. Fuld's strategy of quelling the Wall Street rumor mill had worked, and it appeared Lehman had won.

By the end of the 1990s, derivative-related trading implosions were becoming commonplace. Along with LTCM, Orange County, Bankers Trust, Barings Bank, Metallgesellschaft, and Sumitomo Bank all suffered debilitating trading losses. Given these collapses, were the creation and use of derivatives a positive addition to the financial markets or not? The debate had two camps. Some thought derivatives were the best thing since the Walkman; others thought they were dynamite in the wrong hands. Warren Buffett would later suggest that derivatives were weapons of mass destruction. The LTCM situation certainly provided ammunition to such sentiments. It was different from other derivative blowups due to the sheer size of its trillion-dollar, highly leveraged trading portfolio.

By orchestrating a LTCM rescue and using systemic risk as its rationale, the Fed contributed to a growing sense of moral hazard. Saving this ill-conceived hedge fund allowed excessive risk taking to not be fully punished, but it might have also saved the world markets from plummeting. Anyone doubting the veracity of systemic risk only needs to observe the series of events that led to the unraveling of LTCM. Clearly, the panic caused by the failure of a company like LTCM could have potentially sent shockwaves through the financial world. Criticizing the Fed is too easy and perhaps misguided. First, the Fed did not simply dip into the U.S. Treasury (as it would a decade later)—it jawboned banks into coughing up the money. Second, if only the risk takers (management, shareholders, and bondholders) could be punished without collateral damage, then the Fed's job would be straightforward: let them suffer. But if the economic health of average people with 401(k)s and pensions is potentially in danger, then the dilemma becomes stickier. More frustrating than the decision to save LTCM was the Fed's continued reluctance afterward to define clearly which firms or industries might pose systemic risk, where potential problem areas might be for such firms, and what precautions should be taken to avoid future meltdowns of "too big to fail" firms. The Fed did not encourage companies to reassess or reduce their risk-taking behavior. Regardless of the Fed's or the government's reaction, the LTCM crisis offered several lessons for Lehman.

Near-death experiences tend to change personal behavior and influence the thinking process. Lehman gained both experience and a false sense of comfort by dodging the LTCM bullet, with some unintended consequences. Fuld may have pulled a rabbit out of the hat and saved the firm, but he did so by battling market rumors that were categorically false. What if the market rumors circulating held some truth? Would it even be appropriate for Fuld to apply the same approach to save the firm? How would opening the books help if all you have to show investors and employees is a book full of concentrated real estate bets, debt, and worthless or risky derivatives? What if Lehman—similar to LTCM—made misplaced bets using massive amounts of leverage and markets did not cooperate? Under these scenarios, it would be much harder to go toe-to-toe with the market and make the case that Lehman was solvent. In the future, it would take more than fancy footwork for Fuld and his lieutenants to save Lehman.

Chapter 9

Innovation, Imitation, and Increased Risk

On Wall Street, rival firms quickly imitate competitors' profitable innovations. Since it is difficult to patent financial products, the innovator's advantage is short-lived. Once a new product comes out, it is fairly easy to replicate. In fact, many times it is *more* profitable to replicate than invent a product because the imitator avoids product development costs. However, when new trading products or models are employed before risks can be properly assessed, there can be unintended financial consequences. This was one of many lessons learned from the collapse of Long-Term Capital Management (LTCM).

A key function of investment banks is to effectively price and manage risk. Developing new products does not negate this responsibility. The multitrillion-dollar mortgage-backed securities market is an example of Wall Street financial engineering. Success with such manufactured products led to other imitators that created even more products. Eventually mortgage derivatives became one of the market's largest asset classes. When innovation becomes this profitable, it accelerates risk taking and heightens risk to participants system-wide. Lehman was a central link in this risk-taking chain. By increasing its involvement in the derivatives market, Lehman's financial future was shaped by the creation, expansion, and assumption of the risks associated with these securities.

Like switching from gunpowder to dynamite, in a controlled environment and used in the right proportion, derivatives can be useful. In a portfolio, they can provide an effective hedge against risk or be applied as a speculative instrument to enhance risk. In the simplest of terms, derivatives do *facilitate* the redistribution of risk and, when apportioned correctly, keep money flowing to the highest and best use. But derivatives are usually highly leveraged, just like the trading strategies at LTCM were. When misused, derivatives can blow up and cause financial harm.

In the early 1980s, Lehman was not yet a player in the residential mortgage–backed securities (RMBS) market. Salomon Brothers, First Boston, and government-created mortgage providers were the innovators—the industry leaders—that dominated this budding market. Over time, imitators emerged and competition intensified. By 2004 Lehman rose to the top of the heap, becoming the market's largest underwriter of mortgage-backed securities. Prior to the advent of the RMBS market, a mortgage lender kept good and bad loans on its books. Banks lived with thirty-year loan decisions—good or bad—as the loans ran their courses. But RMBS allowed lenders to package and sell their loans, severing the accountability between those who created the risk and those who assumed it. Banks and other lenders could pass the risk down the line to further removed and often less-informed investors.

GROWTH OF THE AGENCY MORTGAGE MARKET

Although investment banks helped invent mortgage-backed securities, without the federal government's assistance, these instruments would not have come into existence. The mortgage-backed securities market can trace its roots to three government entities. In 1934, at the height of the Great Depression, Congress passed the National Housing Act, creating the Federal Housing Administration and initiating twenty-five- to thirty-year residential mortgages. A critical element of this legislation was making mortgage funding readily available. To achieve this goal, the government protected lenders against credit default. For the first time, home ownership was promoted as government policy. Government felt that home ownership meant shelter, not greater financial risk.

At the time of the National Housing Act, a significant portion of loans were provided by the nation's more than nine thousand savings and loan associations (S&Ls). In 1938 Congress amended the act to create the Federal National Mortgage Association (Fannie Mae). This government-sponsored enterprise (GSE) helped more Americans gain access to capital for purchasing a home. This industry, intertwined with the American dream of home ownership, formed a powerful "apple pie" lobby. To further support home ownership, the government established a third organization—the Government National Mortgage Association (Ginnie Mae) in 1968.

Ginnie Mae immediately began guaranteeing the mortgages of less affluent borrowers who qualified for either a Federal Housing Administration or a Veterans Administration loan. Each of these mortgage loans had to meet tight, congressionally set credit guidelines. Loans could be given for single or multi-family homes up to a stated dollar limit, which was periodically adjusted to reflect changes in national prices. Mortgages that met these standards were called "conventional conforming" loans. These loans were designed for Middle America; lending caps kept the rich from using this program to finance mansions. Unlike Fannie Mae, Ginnie Mae was owned by the federal government and operated by the Department of Housing and Urban Development (HUD). Fannie Mae was privatized in 1969 in an effort to limit budget deficits during the Vietnam War.

To further promote mortgage lending, Congress gave birth to a sibling GSE, Federal Home Loan Mortgage Corporation (Freddie Mac), in 1970. Fannie Mae and Freddie Mac were chartered by Congress but owned by public shareholders. In contrast, Ginnie Mae was *explicitly* backed by the full faith and credit of the federal government. In essence, Ginnie Mae was the federal government. The strongest credit in the land earned the strongest credit rating: AAA.[1] The sterling credit rating for GSEs was a competitive advantage because borrowing costs were lower than for banks, S&Ls, and other lenders. The secretary of HUD was responsible for ensuring that GSEs fulfilled their lending mission. An independent office of HUD, the Office of Federal Housing Enterprise (OFHEO) Oversight, performed safety and soundness reviews to ensure GSEs had enough capital and were operating soundly. Over time, the scope of mortgage products developed expanded dramatically, but regulatory controls and OFHEO oversight did not keep pace.

MISSION ACCOMPLISHED

These government-related agencies achieved their goal. After World War II, home ownership in America increased steadily from approximately 55 percent to almost 69 percent, according to the U.S. Census Bureau. This rate soared above that of other industrial nations such as Germany, where home ownership was approximately 43 percent. From 1950 to 1980, the volume of outstanding U.S. mortgage loans increased from $55 billion to a staggering

$1.2 trillion.[2] Further reinforcing the idea that it was every American's destiny to own a home, Congress passed the Community Reinvestment Act (CRA) in 1977. This federal law encouraged banks and S&Ls to meet the needs of all segments of their communities, including low- and moderate-income neighborhoods. The CRA has undergone several revisions, most notably the one included in the Gramm-Leach-Bliley Act of 1999 that was responsible for tearing down the walls built by the Glass-Steagall Act. Language was added in 1999 to ensure that giant banks created through mergers would be subject to CRA compliance. On signing the act, President Bill Clinton stated that it "establishes the principles that, as we expand the powers of banks, we will expand the reach of the [Community Reinvestment] Act."[3] The Federal Reserve (Fed) oversees the majority of commercial banks to ensure CRA compliance. Under the George W. Bush administration, a policy of greater home ownership continued. By 2008, the residential mortgage market had grown to more than $14 trillion, and Fannie Mae and Freddie Mae insured directly or indirectly in excess of $6 trillion of mortgages. The American Dream had been realized through government-mandated policy, but credit risk to the entire system had increased.

THE PROBLEM WITH MORTGAGES

Mortgages are secured by collateral that can be repossessed if the contract is defaulted on. Real estate lending has not always been lucrative for investment banks. Traditionally, lending margins were average and it was a labor-intensive business. Individual residential mortgages in particular posed a challenge for Wall Street. They represented separate pieces of paper held by individual lenders across the country with different credit standards. Most loans were for fifteen to thirty years and were based on a fixed rate of interest. Lenders were constrained by their own balance sheets. Once a loan was made, a new one could not be added until an older one matured or new deposits (capital) were obtained. Mortgages were boring securities that could not be traded. Unless mortgages could be pooled together in a portfolio, they would never look, feel, or act like a bond. Using Wall Street parlance, individual mortgage loans had too much hair on them.

The government first demonstrated how to shave mortgages. In 1970, Ginnie Mae began exploring ways to increase available funding for mortgages. Securitization, the process of turning separate cash-flow receivables into a security that could be bought and sold, was identified as a solution. Ginnie Mae wrapped its gold-plated credit rating around a pool of mortgages to alleviate investor fears and began packaging and selling these new securities. On March 1, 1970, Ginnie Mae successfully issued $2 million of mortgage-backed securities—the first time these securities had ever been offered anywhere. This initial product innovation allowed for guaranteed payments of interest and principal to pass through to a group of investors. Though primitive, this was a significant breakthrough. Freddie Mac and Fannie Mae soon issued their own similar mortgage pass-through securities. This early mortgage security had one major flaw—it failed to provide a discrete time period in which an investor could expect to be paid. Unlike a non-callable government or corporate bond, the pass-through securities were subject to *prepayment risk*—the borrower could pay off a mortgage early or refinance when rates fell, which meant the investor would not get the income it anticipated.

Seeing a unique profit opportunity, in 1977 Salomon Brothers became the innovator, creator, and seller of the first mortgage-backed security not issued by the government. Salomon Brothers pooled loans made by Bank of America, put them into bonds, and persuaded insurance companies to buy them.[4] These novel securities still carried significant prepayment risk and were only legal in three states.[5] The Securities and Exchange Commission required documentation, and the IRS expressed an interest in taxing these hybrid structures. By 1978, anticipating an upsurge of activity, several investment banks set up mortgage departments, but there was little business. Without eliminating prepayment risk, investors were not interested in these non-tradable, illiquid mortgages. These financial products were viewed as a backwater of fixed income, the spot relegated to those who couldn't cut it in corporate and government bonds. According to Michael Lewis in *Liar's Poker*, "The prevailing wisdom was that mortgages were not for Wall Street."[6] Residential mortgage–backed securities would not gain Lehman's attention until the 1980s. The bomb was built but not fully detonated until two decades later.

WALL STREET INNOVATION: COLLATERALIZED MORTGAGE OBLIGATIONS

In June 1983, Salomon Brothers and Freddie Mac solved the decade-old problem that had eluded firms and kept investors from buying mortgage-backed securities: isolating and redistributing the prepayment risk. Working together, they transferred cash flows into a new entity, separating them into time-sequenced tranches, or tiers. These different levels with various risk characteristics were then sold to investors. In their simplest form, collateralized mortgage obligations (CMOs) might have three tranches defined by payment priority. Later, in their more complex form, CMOs could have up to fifty tranches. Investors chose their level of prepayment risk, with the understanding that the top tranches (lower risk) would have first entitlement to income generated from the pool of mortgages backed by the security. In other words, the senior levels received priority repayment but offered a lower yield. The middle tranches offered a higher yield while the bottom, or "kitchen-sink," tranches—the riskiest—offered the highest yield and had the greatest prepayment risk. The lynchpin to all CMO deals was the ability of investment bankers to sell the bottom tranche. Large institutional investors greeted CMOs with open arms because they provided prepayment protection and extended the average life of bond investments.

Collateralized mortgage obligations added a twist to the earlier pass-through securities. Their complicated tranching structures—based on Ginnie Mae, Fannie Mae, or Freddie Mac mortgages—had to comply with strict loan limit requirements. They had either an explicit or implicit government credit backing. These agency CMOs even carried top AAA ratings from bond rating agencies because credit risk remained minuscule. With yields higher than U.S. Treasury or corporate bonds, investors began to turn to agency CMOs as an investment substitute. Lenders were also eager to get the mortgage loans off their books so they could realize profits (or take their losses), gain liquidity, and issue new loans. Investment bankers astutely realized that investors would be willing to pay more for customized repackaged loans than the original value lenders placed on these non-securitized loans. The cash flows did not change, but the products did. This was financial alchemy, and CMOs began to act like tradable bonds. This success inevitably led to the expansion of the non-agency CMO market.

GROWTH OF THE PRIVATE-LABEL MARKET

Mortgages that did not have government credit backing—called private-label or non-agency CMOs—generated significantly higher credit risk. They were backed by nonconforming loans that fell outside of the government's underwriting guidelines. This could be due to the size of the loan, the level of the down payment, or simply the borrower's poor credit. To reduce this inherent risk, non-agency CMOs were credit-enhanced through cash-flow subordination (more tranches) or private insurance. Once non-agency CMOs were made, the pieces were sold in the global marketplace. Fees could exceed tens of millions of dollars to the underwriting bank, quite an incentive for investment bankers to "push all product" out the door, and many early customers were banks.

Like a menu in a fancy restaurant, these private-label CMOs allowed customers to pick and choose according to their risk preferences. Some dishes decelerated prepayment risk while others actually accelerated it. Many of these early customers were large commercial banks. Why were some investors willing to order such risky dishes? Congress and credit rating agencies played an important role. In 1984, Congress passed the Secondary Mortgage Market Enhancement Act, which increased the number of CMO customers by allowing national banks to purchase and hold these private-label mortgage securities on their books. This law also called on credit rating agencies to rate these mortgage pools. Those bonds that got top ratings, signifying that investors should be confident of repayment, were easily sold. This was a turning point because mortgage securities sold were no longer limited to those directly or indirectly backed by the U.S. government.

Prior to the Secondary Mortgage Market Enhancement Act, Lewis Ranieri,[7] an influential investment banker from Salomon Brothers, stated before Congress, "We believe that the rating services do offer substantial investor protection."[8] This independent credit rating agency seal of approval provided comfort to a swelling investor base. Provided these ratings were accurate, investors were adequately protected.

As part of the CMO securitization process, once a new legal entity was created to hold the assets, a separate credit rating was assigned. As long as high ratings were assigned to securitized mortgage pools, investment banks were able to sell these to eagerly waiting buyers. For many of these non-agency transactions, Standard & Poor's and Moody's assigned an AA credit rating or higher. Ratings were driven off of internally built models, using historical data, and based on the underlying asset pools of mortgages that each CMO held. Credit rating agencies had the benefit of existing models that, if modified correctly, could adequately rate the latest Wall Street innovations. All tranches—senior, middle, and bottom—were evaluated. These high credit ratings for CMOs held significant market weight, especially because the higher yields of the riskier tranches heightened investor appetite. As CMOs gained greater acceptance among investors, they became the investment of choice.

Under the Reagan administration, the CMO market received yet another boost with the Tax Reform Act of 1986, which created the Real Estate Mortgage Investment Conduit (REMIC). Key to this legislation was the simplification of CMO tax treatment, increasing the number of interested investors. Today, almost all CMOs are still issued in REMIC form.

ASSET-BACKED SECURITIES

Early innovation spurred more innovation and imitation, fueling the growth of the mortgage-linked bond market. By 1985 expertise gleaned from structuring CMOs mutated into creating other credit derivatives, many of which Lehman later adopted as part of its aggressive risk-taking strategy. One of these innovations was the rise of asset-backed securities (ABS). In 1985, Sperry Lease Finance Corporation, with the help of First Boston, issued the first of these securities, raising $146 million. Similar to mortgages, leases have a defined cash flow stream. As part of this structure, Sperry sold its rights to lease receivables to a separate legal entity or trust. Interest in this entity, referred to as a special purpose vehicle (SPV), was then sold to investors. Analogous to CMOs, ABS represented an ownership in an underlying pool of assets securitized by an issuer. These payment streams were legally separated from the originator and used to back bond repayments. The logic appeared sound. If the originator went bankrupt, the assets would still be there to make payment. Early financial successes in this market motivated banks to find other asset classes that could be securitized. Auto loans, credit card receivables, manufactured housing loans, student loans, and even movie industry receipts were soon being sliced and diced into ABS and sold to investors.

MUSICAL CHAIRS

In the RMBS and ABS markets, investment banks served as underwriters—the intermediaries between issuers and investors. They also provided warehousing loans that supported the lending activities of mortgage providers, including regulated banks and mortgage companies. Investment banks influenced credit underwriting standards, the filter used to decide who gets a loan and who does not. Lenders who wanted to sell their mortgage pools needed to stay within set guidelines. Typically, banks and mortgage companies evaluated a borrower's ability to pay, obtaining a credit score and staying within a stated loan-to-value ratio. Credit scores were provided by third-party vendors, including Experian, Transunion, and Equifax. These agencies apply a credit scoring method—referred to as FICO—that provides a lending benchmark. A FICO score of 660 or higher out of 850 indicated a prime credit borrower. Over time as competition intensified, what constituted a strong FICO score varied. For many investment banks, including Lehman, the prevailing thought was that weak credit scores should not stand in the way of strong profits. However, as long as credit rating agencies continued to assign mortgage pools high credit ratings, and investment banks had willing buyers, there was little incentive for anyone to worry about declining credit standards.

As part of the underwriting role, investment banks also assumed a degree of inventory risk related to buying a bond, slicing it up, and reselling it to investors. The risk was related to the CMO structure. For example, in CMOs, to mitigate prepayment risk, certain tranches were crafted to reduce risk while others took on the leftover (less desirable) risk. At the right price and yield, investors were willing to hold their nose and buy the riskier tranches. Yet these mortgage- and asset-backed securities created a new problem: what if unfavorable market events happened before a banker had finished manufacturing or selling all the tranches? It would be the capital market's equivalent of musical chairs. If the music stopped and you were stuck holding the toxic, bottom tranches, you were financially in trouble.

It did not take long for investment banks to experience the risks associated with these new financial innovations. After winding down its initial attempt in RMBS, Merrill Lynch took a second bite at the apple. As soon as it jumped back in, it ran into trouble. In April 1987, Howard Rubin, their 36-year-old star bond trader, shocked Wall Street with a trading loss of $377 million, tied to riskier pieces of a CMO. Rubin had sold the less risky piece of a bond security but was left holding the higher-risk principal piece. When interest rates skyrocketed and many individuals defaulted on their loans that made up the low tranche, Merrill Lynch was left with the loss. In the wrong hands, CMOs could be financial dynamite. At the time, this was the single largest trading loss ever experienced by a Wall Street bank. Yet it could be chalked up as Lehman's first lesson not learned.

RISE OF COLLATERALIZED DEBT OBLIGATIONS

Despite the growing risks posed by CMOs, they were the forerunner for even more complex products. The next product evolution was collateralized debt obligations (CDOs). Where CMOs redistributed prepayment risk, CDOs redistributed credit risk. The birth and growth of the CDO market can be traced back to Drexel Burnham Lambert and Kidder Peabody and their pioneering use of junk bonds. TriCapital Ltd. was the first issuer to use a CDO structure, raising $420 million in July 1988.[9] In only five years, investment bankers were able to convince investors that moving from the safety of AAA-rated bonds to junk was a safe investment. By 1989, $3 billion in CDOs were manufactured and sold. In less than a decade, CDOs began to replace CMOs as Wall Street's investment of choice.

Later these instruments mutated again. Lehman and other investment banks began concocting CDOs that no longer needed to be supported by physical assets. Investors reaching for yield were willing to buy bonds that were not backed by hard assets. These instruments were backed by credit default swaps (CDS), a form of insurance against the chance of bond default. In the case of CDS, a buyer would identify a bond it wanted protection on and pay a premium up front, typically for a five-year term. In exchange, the CDS seller made a financial payment if the identified bond defaulted. Unlike physical assets that could be felt, CDS were more esoteric. Their value hinged on the perceived ability of the CDS seller to honor its obligation. As long as the firms selling CDS remained financially healthy, no collateral was required by the counterparty.

LOOMING DERIVATIVES RISK DISCOUNTED

Under the Clinton administration, despite recommendations to the contrary from Brooksley Born, then head of the Commodity Futures Trade Commission, strong banking industry lobbying efforts prevailed, allowing the rapidly growing CDS market to remain unregulated. As early as 1998, Born argued that OTC derivatives such as CDS should be regulated because they "could pose grave risks to the American public."[10] In 2000, with the blessing of many policymakers including Treasury Secretary Larry Summers, the Commodity Futures Modernization Act was passed. Not putting CDS under greater regulatory scrutiny or on a standardized exchange allowed sellers to take risk without having to set aside capital to cover their bets. "Off exchange" meant these instruments were not formally reported or tracked. Less than a decade later, the market would prove that this policy decision was a catastrophic mistake.

These derivatives were not traded on a standardized exchange but on the lightly regulated over-the-counter (OTC) market. Major investment and commercial banks made up the bulk of the trading, with more than 80 percent of the business controlled by just sixteen firms. Lehman was a top-five buyer and seller of CDS. Another dominant market underwriter of CDS was AAA-rated American Insurance Group (AIG). Remarkably, in less than two decades, the CDS market became a $60 trillion market. But what if even one of the largest providers of CDS was no longer creditworthy and unable to honor the CDS contract? The loss in market confidence and the sudden need to post collateral could cause a severe liquidity crisis. How would such an event impact this market? Lehman and the small group of other major Wall Street firms had amplified credit risk to each other in case of such an event. If a firm had credit problems, the value of products it manufactured and held on its books (e.g., CDOs and CDS) would plummet.

A WIN-WIN-WIN SITUATION?

The innovation process on Wall Street continued to morph as investment bankers turned their attention to the commercial real estate market. Securitization of this market segment received a significant boost during the S&L crisis and the creation of the Resolution Trust Company (RTC) in 1989. This governmental agency warehoused bad loans from failed S&Ls. As a result, the government was sitting on a multibillion-dollar pot of assets and was a willing seller creating the perfect opportunity for securitization. The U.S. commercial real estate market, while one-third the size of the residential market, was still several trillion dollars in size. Lehman jumped in and bought large quantities of discounted RTC commercial loans, securitized them, and quickly profited. These early successes only whetted Lehman's appetite for churning out more commercial mortgage-backed securities (CMBS).

By 1992, the jumbo mortgage market also began to take hold. In cities across the country—especially Boston, New York, and San Francisco—it was not uncommon to find even a modest-size home falling outside the conventional conforming loan limits set by Fannie Mae and Freddie Mac. This non-agency market had risk, but it was perceived to be low because jumbo loans were given to wealthy people who could afford million-dollar homes. Initially, underwriting standards were stringent, defaults were low, and only large commercial banks typically made these loans.

Identifying the profit potential, Lehman was one of the first investment banks to come out with a jumbo mortgage default probability model. Though rudimentary, this development put Lehman at the forefront of a budding segment. Jumbo mortgages, which previously sat dormant on bank balance sheets, were now being securitized similar to agency credits. The market greeted jumbo mortgage securitization with great enthusiasm, as various stakeholder concerns were solved. Lenders liked being able to collect the upfront loan fees, and securitization freed up capital so other high-quality loans could be made. Investors liked securitization because jumbo mortgages provided higher yields than usual for an AA default rating. Investment bankers liked underwriting these mortgage securities because they provided substantial upfront fees. It seemed like a win-win-win situation.

As bankers searched for new ways to enhance earnings, they continued to crawl further down the credit quality scale. Soon, Alt-A mortgage loans were determined strong enough to support securitization. This category of credit was weaker than the jumbo segment and included borrowers who might be self-employed, relied on unpredictable income sources, or were non-resident aliens. The loan-to-value ratio might exceed 90 percent or lack primary mortgage insurance. As the mortgage derivatives market mushroomed, investment banks and certain mortgage companies took on more and more credit risk and started securitizing subprime loans.

"Subprime," a term used repeatedly by the media since the crisis, is similar to non-agency mortgages that did not adhere to the government's guidelines: a low sizable loan, a low down payment, weak borrower credit, and so on. Though there is no standard definition of subprime loans, they are generally understood to be the riskiest of consumer loans. Subprime loans had always been a niche market relegated to a handful of specialty lenders who were willing to assume the greater likelihood of credit default. In the early 1990s, this was a small market segment making up less than 5 percent of home loans. By the end of the decade, securitization, government financial support, and a seal of approval from the credit rating agencies had magically legitimized investment in subprime mortgages. Unfortunately, there was only one problem: investment banks had not fulfilled their important market role of effectively pricing and managing risk. Product innovation and the race for profit had trumped strong risk management. In this atmosphere, at least initially, credit risk was allowed to grow and go little noticed.

In less than a decade, with the help of Wall Street innovators and a flood of imitators, the mortgage derivatives market was born. It was now up to the market and bank risk managers to test the strength of these new products. In a strong economy there tends to be little default along the full spectrum of mortgage loans—CDOs, ABS, jumbos, Alt-A, subprime, and so on. But these mortgage-related products were still relatively new and lacked a long, observable track record. Many investment banks understood that they were behind the risk management curve and began a catch-up strategy. Models and quantitative techniques that could capture and measure the uncertainties of derivative-based risk taking were essential. In this environment, more resources—human and financial capital—needed to be allocated to properly evaluate risk. Unseasoned models contained many assumptions that had not yet been tested. What would happen if the economy turned down, especially affecting the less creditworthy, subprime borrowers?

Lehman increasingly hitched its financial well-being to this risky wagon. By 1994 a Federal Reserve–led run up of interest rates allowed CMOs to claim their first victim. Storied investment bank Kidder Peabody lost hundreds of millions of dollars in trading related to mortgage-backed securities, forcing the sale of the firm to Paine Webber. The advent and rapid growth of the mortgage-backed securities market provided Lehman with another clear warning—mortgage derivatives were not child's play and strong risk management was essential.

Chapter 10

Lehman's Risk Management

With greater risk taking comes greater responsibility for evaluating and controlling the risk. Risk in investment banking is as natural as air—without it, investment banks can't breathe. If firms never experience financial losses, they probably need to increase their levels of risk. Such firms could be underutilizing capital. Like a gambler who sits at a craps table, profits from winning bets must outweigh the losses; if not, the gambler is out of business. Extensive modeling is used to measure risk taking. Firms that balance the tug-of-war between risk and return avoid making costly mistakes and, in the long run, are more profitable. Well-run banks make risk management a central part of their cultures. Board of directors and executive-level risk committees also play a critical role. But it's not always easy to adhere to strong risk management principles, especially during a bull market like the one fueled by mortgage- and asset-backed securities. Often on Wall Street, as profits swell, risk management is viewed as a constraint on profit—a dangerous sentiment.

Through the years, Lehman witnessed firsthand what happened when banks did a poor job of managing risk: Shearson's ability to purchase rival E. F. Hutton at a fire-sale price (1987); Merrill Lynch's $377 million CMO-related trading loss (1987); Kidder Peabody's rushed sale to Paine Webber after millions in trading losses, some of which were related to mortgage-backed securities (1994); and Long-Term Capital Management's (LTCM) meltdown in derivative securities (1998). Many of these bets were placed using overly optimistic assumptions. These warnings were costly, and the industry took notice. In response, financial firms began building out risk management capabilities, set up as independent business functions. In the past, "sector specialists," usually former traders sitting at desks, monitored trading by checking on positions and making sure nothing foolish happened. But the ever-increasing complexity of the over-the-counter (OTC) derivatives market, in which investment banks heavily traded, as well as the growing credit derivatives business, created a necessity for independent valuation, position compilation, and risk evaluation. Risk measurements such as simple duration—the price sensitivity to a change in interest rates—no longer adequately captured the more complex risks linked to option-dependent products. Using leverage with these instruments only amplified the risk.

Rating agencies, regulators, analysts, and investors increasingly demanded that sophisticated bets be backed by sophisticated risk-measurement techniques. Professional organizations such as the Global Association of Risk Professionals (GARP) sprouted up.[1] Magazines and analytic software companies catering to the growing profession were also started. On Wall Street, risk management became a buzzword. The industry bar was raised. Many banks understood that building out an independent risk function provided an additional set of eyes and ears and could improve overall decision making. Trading limits by product type, size, and maturity were instituted. Traders were also assigned dollar stop-loss limits to place a defined cap on losses. If a trader were to breach a dollar loss limit, say $2 million in a single day, these loss positions would automatically be closed out. Strong risk management could also provide a competitive advantage, especially if peer firms failed to made adequate investments in people and capital.

LEHMAN FINDS RISK-MANAGEMENT RELIGION

Lehman was preparing to be spun off from American Express in 1993. During its tenure under American Express, it had basically managed risk by placing bets and then having any financial losses absorbed by its deep-pocketed parent. Risk management and reporting systems were not viewed on a firm-wide basis nor were they considered as important as they should have been. Instead, risk was handled on an ad hoc, product-by-product basis as was common throughout the industry. Risk managers would sit on the trading floor and focus on mortgage trading or government bond trading. At that time, if asked what the firm-wide risk was, a product-specific risk manager might have responded by saying, "How the hell should I know?"

Lehman traders took on risk with each trade every day. At day's end, these bets showed up on the firm's profit and loss (P&L) statement as either profit or loss. This provided immediate feedback on whether risk was appropriately managed or not. The head trader was charged with managing an overall book, or portfolio, and had primary say when to cut losses and take the chips off the table. Successful traders got bigger bonuses and more firm capital to play with. If an area lost too much money, its traders were asked to sit out for the remainder of the year. Those with consistently negative P&L got fired. Under the Shearson banner by 1993, Lehman made more money from fixed-income trading and sales than from investment banking activities, a trend that continued into the next decade. By 2004, capital markets activity, including trading and sales, represented 66 percent of the firm's revenue; investment banking represented only 20 percent of revenue. This bias toward putting firm capital at risk as profits grew provided some level of confidence that the traders must have understood risk management. Lehman also relied on the fact that it had avoided major trader blowups or scandals, unlike rival firms that were forced to close or merge. In the early 2000s, the risk-taking culture at Lehman was still primarily based on hitting line drives; home run hitters were appreciated but not required.

Under the American Express umbrella, mergers resulted in a hodgepodge of dissimilar financial reporting systems. Historically, different trade data were stored on different systems that did not talk to each other. Data was stored on mainframe computers the size of a Mack truck. These disparate systems made it challenging to gain comprehensive, timely, and accurate risk management reports. The 1994 spinoff provided Lehman with the needed kick in the pants to develop a comprehensive and effective risk management policy. To operate as a profitable stand-alone bank, Lehman needed access to cheap capital. Under American Express, Lehman enjoyed the benefits of an A rating. But as a stand-alone, without a strong credit rating, trading partners were less willing to do business with the firm. The credit rating agencies were the gatekeeper to obtaining this critical benchmark. Lehman needed to show the credit rating agencies it understood risk and also had the systems and infrastructure to adequately measure and control it. As part of this process, the credit rating agencies provided a shadow rating, a blueprint of what type of capital structure Lehman would need in order to gain an A rating. This iterative process, involving the use of the agency models, was a common way of backing into what was required to obtain a certain rating.

At one particular bond-rating meeting with Standard & Poor's (S&P), CEO Dick Fuld claimed that Lehman had strong risk-management capabilities. As proof, he referred to the highly publicized Salomon Brothers' trading scandal of 1991, boasting that Lehman, unlike Salomon, had solid firm-wide risk reporting. The Salomon scandal had broken on a Friday, and it was true that Fuld had a summary risk report on his desk the next business day. What Fuld failed to mention at the meeting with S&P was that to have the information on his desk by Monday morning, an army of employees had to work straight from Friday's close to Monday. This data had to be extracted in a cumbersome manner from mainframe computer printouts and put into a legible format. In other words, Lehman's risk reporting was a manual process fraught with human error. In essence, there was no firm-wide risk reporting system.

Lehman's antiquated financial reporting infrastructure could not measure the more sophisticated risks it was taking. No longer did Lehman just have plain vanilla U.S. Treasury and corporate bond risk, which was the world Fuld understood. Lehman was now subject to non-linear risks that behaved in a less predictable fashion. These less predictable risks took on fancy names such as *inverse floaters*, *reset options*, and *knock-out options*. Derivatives entailed the use of leverage that added to price swings. Lehman's increased trading of mortgage-backed securities (MBS), asset-backed securities (ABS), and over-the-counter (OTC) derivatives particularly drove the need for greater risk measurement and reporting sophistication. The complexity of these products and the often multi-year term of many OTC derivatives increased the back-office requirements in servicing and tracking the various cash flows.

Lehman's rivals were also beefing up their risk management capabilities. J.P. Morgan called its firm-wide risk report the 4:15—the time each day this single sheet of paper needed to be on the desks of senior management. In response, Fuld aggressively began to hire the best and brightest from top graduate schools. In 1993 and 1994, several M.B.A.s and Ph.D.s with strong science and math backgrounds were snatched up to improve Lehman's analytic capabilities. To meet new standards, secure a solid credit rating, and keep up with rivals, Lehman needed to get a better handle on risk.

BUILDING OUT THE RISK MANAGEMENT DEPARTMENT

In 1993 Chris Pettit, Lehman's president and COO, appointed his chief of staff, James Vinci, to head the newly formed risk management function. Vinci's mandate was simple: formalize the firm's risk management capabilities on a centralized platform. Moving to a risk platform and away from stand-alone computers or spreadsheets would ensure firm-wide risk reporting could take shape. System development can be very difficult, time-consuming, and lagging because traders and bankers are continually creating new products. Pettit quickly moved to build a state-of-the-art risk management platform. He hired information technology personnel and mathematicians to do the quantitative risk evaluation. Ray Li, a Wharton finance Ph.D., was hired as head of the market risk quantitative and model validation group. Erwin Martens, a Canadian national and former ice hockey pro, was hired from Credit Swiss in Zurich to head fixed-income risk management.

Up until this time, Lehman's risk managers tended to have trading backgrounds rather than the quantitative skill set now needed as the firm transitioned into a more centralized and model-based risk approach. To satisfy credit rating agency requests and to complete the Securities and Exchange Commission–mandated initial public offering (IPO) prospectus, Lehman leaned on the firm's intellectual firepower: the Ph.D.s located in research. This was a change in mind-set. Traders were used to crowing about their individual trading books, regarding themselves as independent profit centers. An enterprise-wide approach to risk taking countered this trading fiefdom view of life. Eventually Lehman was successful in demonstrating to the credit rating agencies, particularly S&P and Moody's, that it understood its risk positions, but the coveted A rating didn't last long. Only one month after the May 1994 IPO, with a faltering economy and as part of a wider industry reassessment, Lehman's rating was downgraded to BBB+, a significant blow to many at Lehman who thought they were on stronger financial footing. It would take several years before Lehman could convince the rating agencies it was worthy of the coveted A rating. In the interim, Lehman's cost of capital increased.

Making risk management a central part of Lehman culture required that risk not only be reported up through this newly formed department but also closely linked to the board of directors (board) and the company's executive levels. If risk was to be effectively managed, it had to be seen, understood, and controlled at the most senior levels of the organization. To make sure that Lehman risk management got a proper audience, a board-level risk management committee was formed and met at least twice a year. In addition, a formal executive-level risk management committee, led by the head of risk management, was established. This committee, along with the board, set and monitored the firm's risk-taking profile and appetite. Fuld was an active member of this committee. At Lehman it appeared that the right steps were being taken to build a first-rate risk management structure.

In 1996 Lehman's risk management department got an unexpected upgrade. Fuld successfully pushed out rival president and COO Chris Pettit, and with him went close ally and head of risk management Jim Vinci. To replace Vinci, Fuld hired Maureen Miskovic, a former treasurer for Morgan Stanley Europe, as chief risk officer (CRO). Miskovic represented a new trend on Wall Street: the rise of CROs. Separated out, this role no longer fell under the duties of the treasurer. The risk management function at Lehman would report up through CFO Jeff Vanderbeek and eventually to Fuld.[2] In creating a CRO position, Lehman appeared to be taking risk seriously, at least on paper. From the start, Miskovic was less concerned about the risk of a single collateralized debt obligation or ABS trade and more concerned about the firm-wide risk associated with all trade positions combined. Under Miskovic, the department was built out even more. As a sign of how serious Lehman took risk management, in its 1999 annual report, Miskovic summed up the firm's risk philosophy as follows:

> At Lehman Brothers we believe risk management is distinctly different from crisis management. We have clear processes and procedures to support the Guardianship role undertaken by risk management. We define guardianship as identifying, measuring, monitoring and reporting risk. To support this, the Firm has made, and continues to make, a significant investment in technology and people. However, risk management can succeed only if risk management is perceived to be an important part of culture—as is the case at Lehman Brothers.[3]

The firm even adopted the phrase "demonstrating smart risk management" as a core operating principle. To remind employees, Lehman printed this on company swag, including Rubik's cubes, which was then distributed globally. Sitting on employee desks for all to see, how could it not be evident that Lehman was now focused on risk management?

CRO Miskovic understood the persuasion of numbers, and under her stewardship the use of quantitative market risk measurements including Value-at-Risk (VaR) increased dramatically. The advent of stronger computer-processing capability at lower costs also helped usher in stronger quantitative risk modeling. Value-at-Risk reported firm risk positions to top management and the board. This was important as Lehman's trading activities increased and the size and type of the portfolio expanded. A statistically based tool, VaR estimates how much a trading book or entire portfolio could lose over a given time frame and is communicated in terms of dollars of potential loss. Typically, investment banks estimate and report VaR daily. To a trading company, risk forecasting models are as vital as a weather radio on a boat. The model, when accurate, provides insights into what to expect in the future. If risk appears to be growing to uncomfortable levels, it might trigger a preemptive risk reduction strategy to avert financial disaster.

In compliance with SEC rules since the late 1990s, banks are required to provide investors with VaR reporting in which trading portfolio positions (e.g., CDOs and ABS) are measured against an adverse change in market value. In 1999 the Basel Committee on Banking Supervision, an influential international policy-making body, endorsed the use of VaR, recommending that banks use this measure to set and meet capital requirements.[4] For a trading-focused bank, success is measured by the daily P&L; VaR is the corollary measurement. What if a trader gained $1 million in a trade—but risked $2 million in the process? Value-at-Risk is an attempt to measure this risk-return trade-off. Industry standards include measuring VaR on a one-day basis, using a 95 percent confidence interval. Simply stated, a $40 million VaR is the maximum amount that the firm should lose in a single trading day with 95 percent probability. In other words, it could lose more than $40 million on 5 percent of all trading days, or one out of every twenty days. The appropriate size of VaR is determined by senior management, the board of directors, and the head of risk management. By mid-2000, Lehman ran this size of VaR.

The upgrading of Lehman's risk management function gained additional traction. In 1999 Madelyn Antoncic, a former mortgage trader from Goldman Sachs with a Ph.D. in economics from New York University (NYU), was hired to assist Miskovic. Antoncic's risk management experience spanned Goldman Sachs, Barclays Bank, and the Federal Reserve Bank of New York. She was a top-notch risk professional, a highly trained quantitative analyst who had extensive experience involving the risks of the more complicated products that Lehman had begun to structure, trade, and sell—principally mortgage-backed and asset-backed securities. By 2000 Miskovic left her post and was replaced by Antoncic, her logical successor.[5] From the start it was clear that Antoncic's strong risk background could help bridge Fuld's understanding of the more complex instruments that were becoming the firm's bread and butter. Like Miskovic, Antoncic thrived in her new position. Value-at-Risk and many other risk calculations were completed daily and reported firm-wide. System improvements and better models created a more centralized risk-management structure. Traders, business units, and product lines were given VaR limits and required to follow them. Noncompliance required explanation, and violators were reprimanded. Finally Lehman had its own 4:15 risk report.

VALUE-AT-RISK FLAWS

In spite of its usefulness, VaR does not always capture the full extent of risk. One major flaw of the model is that it is a good-weather estimate. Value-at-Risk is most accurate during calm markets and least accurate during turbulent markets. It assumes that volatility, the change in trade position market price, is more a constant than an uncertain variable. Using the example above, 5 percent of the time, single-day losses could exceed $40 million. This is the *minimum* expected to be lost in one out of every twenty days. Value-at-Risk is based on the assumption that returns are normally distributed, or a bell-shaped distribution of returns. If returns follow the normal distribution, the expected losses at the 95 percent confidence interval would be 1.25 times larger than the minimum loss, about $50 million in this example. In reality, rare and worst-case events—financial disasters—tend to be much larger than the normal distribution suggests. These loss events have been well documented on trading floors and in numerous academic studies with colorful names such as *fat-tail, kurtosis*, and *black swan*.

Good risk managers understand the shortfalls of VaR and get around this problem by applying different risk measurements such as stress tests and "what-if" scenario analysis. Doing so gives a broader snapshot of potential risk. While many industries have remained insulated from unexpected risk, investment banking, trading, and sales have not. Using the standard 95 percent parameter, given that there are approximately 250 trading days in a year, Lehman was expected to experience trading losses outside of these bounds twelve to thirteen times a year. Unfortunately, *how much* higher the losses could be was not well defined. Having this information would have provided more clarity on when and by how much Lehman's risk levels should have been reduced or capital added.

Mark Twain was fond of saying there are three kinds of lies—lies, damned lies, and statistics. In other words, statistics and those risk measurement models based on statistics can be used to bolster weak arguments. In 1998, LTCM had reported daily VaR of $45 million, yet in a single day in August and September of that same year, they lost more than $550 million. The VaR models they relied on were off the mark. The inherent flaws of VaR certainly impaired Lehman's ability to see the mortgage-based financial disaster growing on its books. Value-at-Risk would not capture the dollar size of the collapse—only the chance of collapse. For 2000 and 2001, Lehman's actual daily firm-wide VaR remained flat at approximately $14 million. For 2002 and 2003 daily VaR exposure increased to about $22 million, and in 2004 daily VaR increased to $30 million. By 2005 daily VaR shot up to $38 million. In 2006 VaR had increased to $55 million. This meant that on any single day, there was a 95 percent chance that losses could total up to $55 million, but there was a 5 percent chance that losses could be even greater. In 2006 there was only one trading day when losses exceeded $55 million. By 2007 daily VaR—how much Lehman was willing to risk in a single trading day—doubled, increasing to $124 million.[6] At these lofty risk levels, daily VaR exposure was twice that of Bear Stearns, one-quarter greater than Morgan Stanley, and almost equal to Goldman Sachs. The problem was Lehman had only half the amount of capital as Goldman Sachs to fall back on in times of financial trouble.[7]

Measured against Lehman's capital, which grew from $3.4 billion in 1994 to $22.5 billion in 2007, VaR was well under 1 percent of capital. It appeared that internal VaR models were accurate, and only a small percentage of firm capital was being put at risk. According to VaR, Lehman was safe and sound. But there was one trend that should not have gone unnoticed: Lehman's risk taking was increasing. In only four years firm VaR increased by more than 400 percent. Lehman was willing to risk an increasingly larger amount of capital on a daily basis in pursuit of profits. Compared to other bulge-bracket firms, Lehman was now swinging for the fence. Fuld and the board of directors had allowed the firm to dramatically change its risk tolerance.

The firm's VaR exposure doubled in less than three years, but profit during that same period more than tripled. Could it be that Lehman had created a money machine where greater returns could be generated from only a modest increase in risk? On a risk-adjusted basis, skyrocketing revenue suggested that actual risk taking had *declined*. From 2002 to 2006, net revenue increased from $6.2 billion to $17.6 billion. To the outside observer, it looked like Lehman had generated billions in profits, had achieved a record high return on equity of 23.4 percent, and was on its way to finally showing Goldman Sachs who was the boss. Falsely, it appeared that the investment made in strengthening the firm's risk management capabilities was beginning to pay off.

In 2006, CRO Antoncic received one of the industry's highest accolades, the prestigious *Risk Magazine* Risk Manager of the Year award. According to Wall Street, Lehman had finally created a top-notch risk management department. But if the strength of a risk management department is its ability to accurately report on risk *and* be heard, then Lehman's risk management department was a complete failure. Lehman reported in its 2006 annual report that it had approximately $9.4 billion in real estate investments. From a risk perspective, the department estimated that a 10 percent decline in real estate prices would generate only a $270 million loss. In hindsight this estimate was off not by millions but by billions of dollars.

To assume that real estate prices could drop by 10 percent in a given year as Lehman had done appeared to be conservative. However, from 2007 to 2008, in many markets across the country, real estate dropped by 15 percent to 20 percent. The previously reasonable assumption was not conservative enough. In addition, Lehman failed to monitor other equally important risks—liquidity, availability of funding, operational costs, and the likelihood of credit default. Over time, the real-life market stress test would provide a clearer picture: Lehman was actually risking billions of dollars in an attempt to make more billions. Reported VaR showed that risk taking was escalating, but it grossly understated the true risk associated with a growing portfolio of mortgage-linked bonds and real estate loans. The board and the executive-level risk management committee had access to these reports. Either by design or sheer ignorance, Lehman's growing risk was not addressed.

Because of the gross underestimation of Lehman's risk exposure, daily losses increased tenfold in 2007 and 2008. The major flaw was the one just described: VaR was only a good-weather risk estimate. Lehman's inability to measure and accurately capture the potential for high-dollar losses meant that rare events could shatter the illusion of risk control. In times of stress, the global financial markets often behave differently than what can be captured in a quantitatively driven market. The losses sustained by LTCM in 1998 should have been a clear sign that overreliance on models was dangerous. While VaR captured what can happen on a sunny trading day, in the middle of a financial storm it was of diminished value. The products VaR was measuring for Lehman—RMBS, CMBS, other types of ABS, and CDOs—were highly leveraged good-weather instruments. A flawed modeling approach was being used to measure products with flaws, a combination that proved lethal. David Einhorn, president of hedge fund Greenlight Capital and well-known short-seller of Lehman, has suggested that VaR is like "an airbag that works all the time, except when you have a car accident."[8]

OTHER WARNING SIGNALS IGNORED

Inherent flaws in VaR or a lack of using other broader risk measurement techniques cannot fully explain Lehman's inability to measure its growing risk. Surely, some of the highly educated and experienced number crunchers at

Lehman were able to see past VaR and believed that the excessive credit risk in mortgage- and asset-backed securities needed serious hedging. Lehman employed the risk manager of the year. Other risk warnings were evident, including escalating leverage ratios, as discussed previously. The size of bets placed on real estate relative to firm capital continued to swell. A growing portfolio of derivatives had to have more credit risk. Did the board and members of the executive-level risk management committee not see this growing risk trend?

Reports that have surfaced from the inner workings at Lehman so far indicate that top-level management refused to heed such warnings and continued to bet that the real estate market, in particular, would continue generating booming profits. At a 2007 risk management committee meeting, Antoncic, the most senior risk officer, was reportedly marginalized by Fuld. At this particular meeting she was asked to leave the room while firm risk was being discussed.[9] As the head of this key committee, such a request was highly unusual and a clear sign that the risk management infrastructure so carefully put into place during the past decade was now valued in title only.

By 2007, risks associated with Lehman's overindulgence in mortgage-backed securities (MBS) were widely apparent. Antoncic not only had experience managing such risk but also had extensive experience in trading it. It was surprising then that her skills were not better utilized. Later Antoncic was quoted at an industry conference in New York stating that hedging of the residential mortgage–backed securities (RMBS) risk was frowned upon at Lehman because top executives thought it reduced profits too much.[10] By September 2007 Antoncic was officially reassigned to a newly created role as head of Financial Market Policy Relations. Lehman did not want the market blowback from a high-level firing, but this was a clear demotion. Antoncic no longer reported to Fuld, nor did she have a material say in how Lehman managed its radioactive RMBS risk. Her replacement was CFO Chris O'Meara. O'Meara met two important requirements: he was Fuld-friendly and had no formal training in risk management—a dangerous combination and hardly an adequate counterbalance against oversized risk taking.

Chapter 11

The Real Estate Bet
and the Race to the Bottom

Lehman had a toe in the real estate market since the 1990s, but it was during the first decade of the twenty-first century that it became the largest mortgage-backed underwriter on Wall Street. Lehman thrust itself into the residential and commercial real estate business through its securitization activities, providing warehouse loans to mortgage originators and participating directly in numerous commercial real estate deals. Lehman became a mortgage origination machine. These activities were a single bet on rising real estate prices and strong investor demand. At a minimum, it appeared that residential mortgage–backed securities (RMBS) and asset-backed securities (ABS) were backed by valuable real estate, making them safer than stocks. Those securitized pools rated AAA were "money good" (i.e., safe).

To muscle its way to the top, Lehman followed the rest of the residential and commercial mortgage originators by accepting lower credit standards. To stay competitive and enhance earnings, Lehman significantly increased its leverage ratio. It expanded its mortgage origination platform and the amount of mortgage derivatives held, and magnified the company's financial risk. It also ratcheted up commercial real estate lending and leveraged loan activities. Initially this aggressive strategy paid off. Profits in the billions of dollars flowed directly to the bottom line, and the stock hit new highs. But by late 2006 cracks in this strategy emerged. Default rates on mortgages escalated. The leveraged real estate boom screeched to a halt, and Lehman was stuck holding billions of dollars in junk loans on its books. Oversized bets had turned Lehman into an overloaded elephant walking on thin ice.

GLOBAL CREDIT BUBBLE

In response to the bursting of the dot.com bubble, high oil prices, and the terrorist attacks of 9/11, in late 2001 the Federal Reserve (Fed), under Chairman Alan Greenspan, began reducing interest rates to lows not seen since John F. Kennedy was president. The exceedingly low interest rates were intended to encourage consumer spending and prop up a fragile economy. When adjusting for inflation, the true cost of borrowing became negative. This was an adrenaline boost to the market. Cheap credit and lax lending standards allowed more people to borrow more money at lower rates. The ballooning ranks of eligible borrowers pushed up the demand for real estate, causing residential and commercial real estate prices to skyrocket. Between 1997 and 2006, the average home price in America increased by more than 120 percent. By 2005, 40 percent of homes purchased were either done on speculation or as a second home. Stated differently, a record number of homes were not purchased as primary residence—they were increasingly being treated as an asset to be bought and sold for profit. Eventually when the bottom dropped out of the housing market, many owners were not committed to staying and paying.

At the same time, another powerful trend was unfolding. During the early 2000s, residential construction plus consumer spending accounted for nearly 75 percent of gross domestic product (GDP) growth. The Fed's policies under Greenspan did not escape criticism. In its January 14, 2006, issue, the editorial board of *The Economist* wrote:

> [C]heap money has not spilled into traditional inflation, but into rising asset prices instead—first equities and now housing. . . . The problem is not the rising asset prices themselves but rather their effect on the economy. By borrowing against capital gains on their homes, households have been able to consume more than they earn. . . .
>
> When house-price rises flatten off, and therefore the room for further equity withdrawal dries up, consumer spending will stumble. . . . [I]t is hard to see how this can occur without a sharp slowdown in the economy.[1]

The Fed's accommodating interest rate policy had another unintended consequence: low rates forced U.S. Treasury bond investors—institutional investors, sovereign funds, and foreign governments—to look for alternative investments to earn higher returns. From 2000 to 2007, the global pool of money seeking fixed-income investments increased from $31 to $67 trillion. Much of this growth was fueled by economic progress in countries such as China and India as well as the oil-rich countries of the Middle East. Investors were hungry for safe, higher-return investments. Low rates made U.S. Treasuries less attractive and generously rated AAA mortgage-backed securities more attractive. The Fed had unlocked the door, and investor demand appeared insatiable.

With the high demand for residential and commercial real estate complemented by investor demand for mortgage-backed securities, credit standards applied by lenders inevitably declined. Lehman was not alone in this practice. Everybody got involved—commercial banks, investment banks, and non-regulated mortgage lenders. The motive was simple enough: those who failed to loosen their credit standards lost to the more aggressive lenders. The repeal of the Glass-Steagall Act in 1999 intensified the competition between investment banks and commercial banks, triggering a financial arms race. Firms such as Citigroup, Wachovia, and J.P. Morgan used the strengths of their larger balance sheets and ready access to an insured depositor base to support their investment banking divisions. Many commercial banks adopted a "pay-to-play" approach, bundling loan services as a way to increase fee income.

In turn, investment banks such as Lehman, Bear Stearns, Merrill Lynch, Goldman Sachs, and Morgan Stanley used leverage to increase their balance sheets and lending. Eventually, Lehman, Bear Stearns, and many other investment banks raced to build or acquired their own subprime origination and servicing arms. In addition, they provided independent non-bank mortgage lenders with capital, ensuring themselves an endless pipeline of residential and commercial loans for securitization. Eventually, riskier commercial bridge loans were offered as a way to compete against larger commercial banks. Many of these loans were in the billions. Such speculative loans were temporary until equity investors could be secured. If investors did not materialize, these loans became the riskiest portions of a deal as they were subordinated to first and second mortgage holders. If a property started to lose value, the bridge lender would feel the financial hit first. In a very short period of time, investment banks went from a lower-risk business model of advising, underwriting, and trading to increasing leverage and placing large concentrated bets on real estate. The problem was that these banks did not have the financial discipline or regulatory requirements to force them to reserve adequate capital to offset their increasing levels of risk taking. Nor was real estate—residential or commercial—a core competency.

From 2003 to 2006, in major U.S. metropolitan areas it was not uncommon for residential real estate prices to increase by 30 percent or more. On a national basis, real estate prices in 2004 and 2005 increased by more than 10 percent annually. A borrower did not have to own property in upscale areas to benefit. And though returns were unusually high, investors believed they were making safe investments because there was a perceived floor on how low prices could drop nationwide. Typically, real estate prices across the nation did not move in lockstep. Some pockets of the country might experience a dip while others remained flat or increased in value. During the savings and loan (S&L) crisis of the late 1980s, for example, real estate prices in Texas and New England showed significant declines, but there was no nationwide drop. The worst observed single-year decline in residential real estate prices was 5 percent, which occurred in the midst of the Great Depression in 1932. With the modern economy much more diversified and regulated, investors assumed a similar event could not happen again.

This worst-case scenario of a 5 percent price drop provided the floor widely used by lenders such as Lehman to evaluate the risk and return trade-off of real estate. In this lopsided coin toss, it was heads, "I win 10 percent" and in the rare event of tails, "I only lose 5 percent." Both Main Street and Wall Street were willing to take this bet. Residential real estate became an opportunity to get rich. Lower rates gave borrowers the ability to buy homes at a lower cost and to supersize into larger houses. The rising real estate values increased collateral cushion and reduced the chance of defaults. To lenders, this was additional proof that these loans were safe. Only when the loan size exceeds the value of the underlying collateral do defaults start to mount. Almost no one believed this condition, called negative equity, could happen in this supercharged real estate market. The commercial market was a bit different. Memories of the late-1980s S&L crisis, when prices plunged by a whopping 27 percent, lingered.

By the early to mid-2000s, as residential property values increased and interest rates declined, many borrowers refinanced their homes, withdrawing more money. As early as 2003, one out of every five households had refinanced. These withdrawals were used to cover mortgage payments, go on vacation, buy a new car, pay for a divorce lawyer, or cover college tuition. Increasingly, American borrowers were using their homes as personal ATMs and in the process increasing their overall debt. In the United States, unlike other industrialized countries, mortgage interest payments are tax deductible. This favorable tax treatment often increases the incentive to get deeper in debt. In 2005, the U.S. personal savings rate turned negative. Consumers began to actually spend more each year than they made. In this borrower-friendly atmosphere, by 2007 the amount of outstanding U.S. mortgage loans doubled to $14 trillion. Consumer debt as a percentage of income reached new highs. In the 1980s this indebtedness ratio remained under 70 percent, but by 2007 the ratio hit 133 percent.[2] Borrowing increased faster than income to support this swelling debt burden. Consumers were figuratively over their heads in debt. Lenders were satisfying the wants of their customers and not looking at the long-term consequences to their firms, the borrowers, or the economy. Risk regulators and legislators appeared to be oblivious too.

At the start of the decade, less than 50 percent of mortgage loans were packaged, rated, and resold as RMBS or ABS. By 2007, the majority of U.S. home mortgages were. The relationship between lender and borrower fundamentally changed. The lender no longer held a fifteen- or thirty-year mortgage on its books to maturity. The shift from a relationship to a transaction culture had occurred. Mortgage lenders adopted a factory mentality. Borrowers were now just numbers. They made the loans, quickly sold them to Wall Street, and repeated the process again. Zip code areas were used as a way to construct desirable mortgage pools. This trend was not unique to the United States. Simultaneously, this phenomenon was unfolding in China, the United Kingdom, France, Spain, Ireland, and Iceland. By the mid-2000s, it was not uncommon for a mortgage loan given in Texas to be packaged, rated, and sold to investors in China. Cheap money, weak underwriting standards, and rapid growth of securitization had created a global real estate bubble.

By the second quarter of 2006, mortgage origination volume at Lehman began to slow down. This rang true throughout the industry. Was this simply a brief pause, a slowdown, or the beginning of a full real estate crash? As investor Warren Buffett has suggested, you can see who's swimming naked only when the tide goes out. By the time the answer arrived, it was too late for the two most highly leveraged investment banks, which just happened to also be the two largest mortgage underwriters and traders: Bear Stearns and Lehman Brothers.

RESIDENTIAL MORTGAGE LOANS: THE GOOD, THE BAD, . . .

Once a loan is made it can take several years before a bank knows whether it has made a good or bad loan. On the first day a loan is made, a banker never makes a bad loan: a default cannot occur until payment stops. Historically, residential mortgage loans—non-subprime—had a long-term default rate of less than 2 percent. This is the average across the entire borrower credit spectrum. In other words, banks get this lending risk-return equation correct 98 percent of the time. This success rate might seem high, but commercial banks use a highly leveraged business model leaving very little room for error. Commercial banks tend to have an asset-to-equity leverage ratio of 20 to 1 or slightly higher. This means that a 2 percent decline in asset value can reduce equity value by half. As a cushion against default risk, commercial banks are required to maintain a minimum level of capital, the difference between assets and liabilities. Regulators also use capital as a measurement of bank solvency. The Basel II, a committee made up of global regulators, attempted to establish higher capital standards for banks. Regarding appropriate capitalization, many countries have embraced the Basel II standards discussed in Chapter 4, although the United States has not fully embraced them.

Even before the repeal of the Glass-Steagall Act, investment banks utilized much higher leverage ratios than regulated commercial banks, meaning they retained less capital to cushion against unexpected losses. It was not uncommon for investment banks to maintain leverage (the ratio of assets to shareholder equity) of 30 to 1 or higher. Compared to commercial banks, this ratio was 1.5 times greater. (By 2007, investment-bank leverage ratios would far exceed 30 to 1, and commercial banks would exceed 20 to 1.) Once investment banks jumped into the real estate lending and securitization business, these ratios began to skyrocket. It appeared to be a virtual money machine. Investment banks borrowed at historically low short-term rates and were able to use debt to pump up their balance sheets to compete in lending. As real estate values increased, the likelihood of default was reduced. Banks also manufactured and held investment portfolios of higher-yielding MBS. Investment bankers understood the basic equation: the higher the leverage, the bigger the balance sheet, the greater the securitization and lending, the higher the profit and bonus.

Henry Paulson, the chairman and CEO of Goldman Sachs in 2004, evidently understood this equation. That year, a strong industry lobbying effort with Paulson's ardent support succeeded in persuading the Securities and Exchange Commission (SEC) to weaken the leverage restrictions previously imposed on investment banks in favor of asset-class-driven capital require-ments. Goldman Sachs, Lehman, and others were quick to take advantage of this regulatory loosening. For 2003 Lehman had $11.9 billion in tangible equity and $308.5 billion of tangible assets, a ratio of approximately 26 to 1. By the start of 2008, Lehman's leverage ratio had mushroomed to 32 to 1. The firm had only $22.5 billion in tangible equity supporting $690 billion in tangible assets. Lehman had increased its leverage ratio to compete with larger commercial banking rivals but, in doing so, had left little cushion to absorb losses in a financial downturn. Bear Stearns had a similarly high leverage ratio. Even if the 2004 SEC amendment change did not "undo" leverage restric-tions, as the SEC claimed in 2009, the escalation of leverage ratios across the entire industry should have triggered stronger oversight. To the contrary, the SEC did not engage in material enforcement actions. Under the SEC's watch, the top five investment banks, particularly Lehman, Bear Stearns, and Merrill Lynch, grew riskier.

Lehman put itself in such a position that it *required* real estate to perform favorably to grow revenue and remain profitable. Once these mortgages were securitized, Lehman had little incentive to care about future defaults. Since defaults were usually rare during the first six months or so of a new loan, the main risk was that loan inventory would pile up. If the securitization machine slowed down, the firm could be seriously endangered. Loans purchased by Lehman, or loans held by the originators and financed by Lehman, could stay on the books longer than anticipated. Keeping the loans for too long meant Lehman would become subject to increased price and default risks. Ratings agencies might look at the stale inventory as a warning signal and lower a firm's credit ratings accordingly.

For lenders, the best way to protect against loan default has always been strong underwriting standards. Underwriting standards and adequate due dili-gence determine which borrowers have the privilege to get a loan. The weaker the credit filter, the more borrowers are allowed in and the higher the chance of loan default. Traditionally, the primary source of loan repayment is earned income. This is the current earnings stream a borrower needs to make timely payments. The secondary source of loan repayment is the collateral support-ing the loan (e.g., the real estate). An increase in housing prices, the value of collateral, protects the lender while a decline in housing prices increases the incentive for a borrower to default. In lending, there is a direct correlation between a decline in housing prices and an increase in loan defaults. When a bank makes a loan, it is placing a bet that, in the event of default, the col-lateral will be sufficient to pay off the loan. This is why, historically, prudent bank lending has required a maximum loan-to-value (LTV) of 80 percent. This ratio is important as it determines how much money the borrower has to put in and how much the lender will provide. Loan-to-value determines the level of risk sharing between the borrower and lender. For example, if a borrower wants to purchase a house worth $400,000, an 80 percent LTV ratio ($320,000/$400,000) requires a cash contribution of $80,000. This greater cushion allows for a market downturn whereby the lender may need to sell the collateral to pay off the loan. At 100 percent LTV, which is what many lenders were allowing during the bubble, there is no room for error.

. . . AND THE UGLY

Subprime is not a new lending category. Since the advent of banking, there have been borrowers with spotty credit histories who have defaulted on loans. Subprime as a targeted lending category began in the 1980s, but by the 1990s, it still represented less than 5 percent of the total mortgage market. Subprime lending was frequently shunned because of its obviously higher default risk compared to prime lending. Traditional lenders did not let dodgy borrowers anywhere near their money. It was a small, niche market left for fringe lenders with names like Household International or the Money Store and not well-respected commercial or investment banks. To compensate for the higher risk they were taking, fringe lenders provided loans with high interest rates. Though these weren't exactly Tony Soprano–type loans, borrowers certainly felt the bite.

Even in the 2000s, there was no universal definition of a subprime borrower. As lenders continued to ease their credit standards, the concept of subprime continued to evolve. Third-party vendors including Experian, Transunion, and Equifax provided individual borrower credit scores. These agencies apply a credit scoring method, referred to as FICO, that provides a lending benchmark. A FICO score of 660 or higher out of a possible 850 indicated a prime credit borrower. In early 2000, a subprime borrower had a FICO score of 660 or less. By 2005, many lenders dropped the required FICO score to 620, making it much easier to qualify for prime loans and making subprime lending a riskier business. Proof of income and assets were de-emphasized. Loans moved from full documentation to low documentation to no documentation.

One subprime mortgage product that gained wide acceptance was the no income, no job, no asset verification required (NINJA) mortgage. Informally, these loans were aptly referred to as "liar loans" because they encouraged borrowers to be less than honest in the loan application process. Many borrowers were honest, but the incentive-driven mortgage broker could falsify the borrower's reported financial information. Some lenders even resorted to predatory lending practices, taking advantage of unsophisticated borrowers and putting them into inappropriate products.

Subprime lenders also expanded the use of adjustable-rate mortgage (ARM) products. These products started with an extremely low interest rate, referred to as a teaser rate. Many times these interest rates were below prevailing rates and would reset to a higher rate in one, three, or five years. By 2005, 80 percent of subprime loans utilized ARMs. When confronted with concerns about "reset risk," a typical mortgage broker responded, "Don't worry about it—when that time comes, your house will be worth even more and you can refinance again, if needed." This reasoning created a false sense of borrower optimism: interest rates would remain low and house prices would continue to rise. Providing borrowers with a low introductory interest rate allowed more borrowers to qualify and ensured that more mortgages would be available to sell to Lehman and other Wall Street firms. Adjustable-rate mortgages also presented a larger systemic risk. Unlike prime borrowers, this was a group that had less financial cushion to withstand an interest rate spike. What if, when the ARMS reset, interest rates increased enough that borrowers could no longer afford the payments and were shut out from refinancing? The credit merry-go-round fueled by securitization would stop and loan defaults would escalate.[3]

GROWTH OF THE SUBPRIME MARKET

The 2000s were the decade of subprime borrowers. No longer was this a segment left to fringe lenders. The relaxing of credit lending standards by investment banks and commercial banks drove this about-face. Subprime did not become magically less risky; Wall Street just accepted this higher risk. Lehman, Bear Stearns, Merrill Lynch, Morgan Stanley, and Goldman Sachs provided the credibility and cash needed to fuel the race to the bottom. To ensure a constant stream of new loans that could be rapidly repackaged and sold, the Wall Street elite began to provide warehouse loans to mortgage lenders.[4]

Government intervention also helped to grease the skids. As part of a broader policy to free up capital for low- to moderate-income borrowers, Fannie Mae relaxed credit standards and became an aggressive buyer of subprime loans. This further helped to legitimize subprime as a viable business. At the time, charismatic CEO Franklin Raines led Fannie Mae. He later left under a cloud of controversy involving significant accounting irregularities relating to ABS and MBS held on Fannie Mae books. The problems that Fannie Mae experienced by 2006 were a warning sign that the subprime market was dangerous to a firm's financial health. But by then, it was too late. Subprime origination increased fivefold in just five years. For 2001 subprime origination was $190 billion with approximately half of these loans securitized. By 2003 this market had more than doubled in size with more than 60 percent of loans securitized. And by 2006 subprime origination was $600 billion with more than 75 percent securitized. From the start of the real estate boom in 2001 through 2006, subprime as a percentage of all home loans rose from 7 percent to 14 percent. The number of subprime borrowers didn't increase, the underwriting standards declined. Loans were now given to more people with bad credit.

Predatory lending and the use of aggressive lending tactics are not new phenomena, but the consequences can have broad financial implications as weak borrowers are approved for inappropriate loans. Many times subprime borrowers were the target of less than ethical, commission-driven mortgage lenders. For example, in the fall of 2006, a couple living in Dillon, South Carolina, found a four-bedroom, three-bath ranch home for sale. The borrowers met with Landmark Mortgage, a non-bank lender, and although their FICO score was low they secured a 30-year fixed-rate mortgage at a grossly inflated rate of 10.1 percent. The couple purchased the house for $123,000, and the mortgage was immediately sold to One Mortgage Corp., then a unit of H&R Block. This mortgage was packaged with others and became part of an $818 million Wall Street–created asset-backed security. Less than two years after the loan was made, a bank serving as the trustee for the mortgage-backed security began foreclosing on the home. That house in Dillon was not unique in this sort of lending practice—giving above-market-rate loans to people with poor credit was going on across America. What makes this house unique is that it was the boyhood home of Ben Bernanke, chairman of the Fed. His father had sold the house in the 1990s, and after changing hands several times it had ended up in foreclosure. In December 2008 a new couple bought the house at a much lower interest rate and for $83,000, 33 percent less than the purchase price two years before. Lax, and in some cases inappropriate, lending practices had overinflated real estate prices, and prices were now coming back down to earth. In this market, even the former home of one of the most powerful bankers in the world could not be spared from the housing bubble.

In the subprime arena, mortgage brokers—individual loan shops run by only a handful of people—were particularly active. Big mortgage originators such as Ameriquest, New Century Financial Corporation (New Century),

IndyMac, and Countrywide Financial Corporation (Countrywide) became significant prime and subprime lenders. The state of choice for this growing shadow banking system was California, where more than 40 percent of all mortgage lenders were headquartered. This location made perfect sense. Some of the highest real estate values in the country are in California. From 2000 to 2007, residential housing prices in major metropolitan areas increased annually by 15 percent. Mortgage lenders had created an art form of getting a growing number of people (prime and subprime borrowers) into increasingly expensive housing. These lenders exported their tricks of the trade across the country. In the larger securitization machine, these West Coast–based mortgage lenders supplied the raw materials that Lehman and other East Coast–based investment banks turned into securities for resale.

IMPLOSION OF THE MORTGAGE MARKET

With every asset bubble there is an eventual pop. Subprime was the pin that burst the broader housing credit bubble. Though subprime still only represented about 14 percent of the total mortgage market, the spillover effect on other products and markets was enormous. Real estate prices and delinquency rates tend to serve as a leading indictor of economic health. In a weakening economy, real estate prices tend to fall, and the riskiest borrowers in the lending chain usually show the earliest signs of trouble. In this case, subprime borrowers were the canary in the coal mine. By 2006 the delinquency rates of subprime borrowers increased to 7.5 percent from a 2003–2004 low of 2.4 percent. In comparison, for this same time period, prime and Alt-A delinquencies were only 0.17 percent and 1.4 percent, respectively.

Other market indictors also pointed to a bubble. The Case-Shiller home price index hit a historical high in March 2005 and began to decline in 2006. In May 2006 *Fortune* printed an article stating that the great housing bubble was starting to deflate. On September 13, 2006, the U.S. Senate Banking Committee held hearings on the housing bubble titled "The Housing Bubble and Its Implications for the Economy."[5]

By December 2006, mortgage originators, those on the front line of lending in an increasingly wobbly real estate market, were going rapidly out of business. Loan delinquencies and defaults had escalated, and real estate prices were falling. In a flip of a switch, lenders found they could no longer fund their day-to-day operations. Many banks, including Lehman, began to heavily discount the value of mortgages used as collateral to support warehouse loans. Investment banks were exercising prudent credit risk management but cutting off key business customers in the process. The lending faucet was being turned off, and out-of-favor mortgage lenders were scrambling to stay alive.

One of the early bankruptcies was Ownit Mortgage Solutions, of Agoura Hills, California. In January 2007 IndyMac, the large Pasadena, California, Alt-A lender, announced fourth-quarter write-offs of $7.6 million and reserved $9 million more to cover potential loan problems. It was not the size of these numbers that was disturbing—it was the fact industry leaders were starting to show losses. By February 2007 Mortgage Lenders Network USA, a top-fifteen subprime lender, closed its doors. A week later, ResMae Mortgage Corporation of Brea, California, was out of business. From that period on, a cascade of mortgage lenders, large and small, went bust. In March, New Century, the country's second largest subprime leader with more than 220 branches nationwide, disclosed that it had breached minimum financial ratios imposed by its warehouse lenders. By the next month, New Century—one of Lehman's clients—was bankrupt. On March 4, 2007, HSBC, Europe's largest bank, reported a $11 billion write-off to cover mounting losses from bad subprime loans and even higher-quality real estate loans. At the time, HSBC was a top subprime mortgage lender in the United States. One of the largest banks in the world with one of the largest subprime loan portfolios in the world was warning the market that this good business had turned bad.

The real estate bubble was starting to burst, yet Lehman continued to expand its real estate activities. At the time of these bombshell announcements, Lehman had more than $25 billion in prime, subprime, and similar residential mortgages on its books. These included loans in the process of being securitized and assets held as investments. Competitors were marking down these assets by 10 percent and more. This residential exposure was on top of an even larger position in commercial real estate–related securities. Lehman felt that subprime was adequately contained on its balance sheet. The Fed also agreed that subprime was isolated and would not become a contagion to the wider market. At a speech in Chicago on May 17, 2007, Ben Bernanke stated, "We do not expect significant spillovers from the subprime market to the rest of the economy or to the financial system."[6] In June 2007 Lehman indicated that subprime mortgages provided less than 3 percent of its revenue. This statement might have been factual, but it failed to address the risk posed by $25 billion of mortgage-linked securities festering on its books and the impact on its capital position. With a leverage ratio of more than 30 to 1, Lehman had very little room to maneuver. In June 2007, Bear Stearns (discussed in Chapter 12) abruptly closed two subprime-related hedge funds after the funds dropped in value by more than 90 percent. During the first six months of 2007, the financial markets had provided numerous signs of a subprime market turning from bad to worse.

For Lehman, Bear's announcement should have resonated. As the fifth largest investment bank, with a real estate business model similar to Lehman's, Bear was showing what could happen when a firm used excessive leverage and overdosed on subprime risk. As summer 2007 came to a close, Ameriquest was on life support. In August, Citigroup picked through the carnage and purchased Ameriquest's wholesale unit (Argent Mortgage) and servicing unit (AMC Mortgage Services). The rest of Ameriquest, formerly the largest sub-prime lender in the country, was immediately shut down. That same month, Countrywide, the $500 billion home loan giant with more than sixty thou-sand employees, shocked the market by drawing down its entire $11.5 billion credit line. This last-gasp effort to remain liquid was additional proof that the subprime and broader mortgage market was terminally ill. Shortly thereafter, Bank of America came to Countrywide's rescue, injecting $2 billion for a 16 percent stake in the company. Six months later in February 2008, Bank of America announced the purchase of the entire firm.

LEHMAN'S ROLE IN THE REAL ESTATE MARKET

Lehman was a pioneer, one of the first Wall Street firms to get into the busi-ness of mortgage origination. In 1997 Lehman bought an interest in Aurora Loan Services (Aurora), a Littleton, Colorado–based lender specializing in Alt-A loans. These loans were made to borrowers with credit ratings that fell between prime and subprime. Originally, the Alt-A target market represented buyers of houses in the few-million-dollar range in tony locations. In the 1990s many of these borrowers were California-based high-tech executives who received most of their compensation in unpredictable stock options rather than monthly salary. These borrowers did not conform to standard credit cri-teria. In 2000, to expand their mortgage pipeline, Lehman also purchased a small ownership stake in BNC Mortgage LLC (BNC), a West Coast subprime mortgage lender.

Lehman quickly became a force in the subprime market. By 2003 Leh-man was already ranked third in lending with 9 percent of the market and $18.2 billion in loans. The only two firms larger in terms of market share and volume were Ameriquest and New Century. Since 2002, Lehman had increased its lending in the subprime space by a whopping 71 percent. Leh-man's strategy matched what rival firms were doing. In herdlike fashion, Bear Stearns eventually purchased mortgage lender EMC Mortgages and Encore

Credit Corporation (October 2006), Morgan Stanley purchased Saxon Capital (August 2006), and Merrill Lynch purchased First Franklin Financial Corporation (September 2006). Commercial banks took a similar approach: HSBC purchased Fremont Capital and Household International (March 2003), and Deutsche Bank purchased Mortgage IT Holdings (July 2006) and Barclays Equifirst Corporation (April 2007).

As the nation continued its real estate boom, Lehman's timing was excellent in utilizing such a vertically integrated strategy. It had built a mortgage securitization platform and was squeezing profit along every step of the transaction life cycle—lending, securitizing, selling, and servicing. By 2003 Lehman gained complete ownership of Aurora and expanded its national footprint to more than two thousand employees. Industry research began to show that Alt-A mortgages over the first year of origination had a lower prepayment risk than higher-quality jumbo loans.[7] Such research, counter to investment theory, meant higher returns were attainable at lower risk levels, providing investors with added incentive to move into the more risky Alt-A market. From 2004 to 2006, the Alt-A market doubled in size to $400 billion. Aurora originated one-third of the mortgages Lehman securitized. At the top of the market, the only Alt-A originator bigger than Aurora was IndyMac. Then in 2004 Lehman squeezed even more profits from the lending chain by purchasing BNC in its entirety. BNC provided Lehman with approximately 20 percent of the mortgages that it securitized. By 2004 BNC and Aurora churned out $40 billion in subprime and Alt-A mortgages. By 2006 this dynamic duo was lending more than $4 billion per month, putting Lehman at the top of investment bank mortgage underwriters. In the Alt-A market and subprime market, Lehman was *the* significant participant.

LEHMAN'S TRANSFORMATION INTO A REAL ESTATE HEDGE FUND

The residential mortgage market wasn't the only way Lehman boosted profits. Lehman placed its commercial real estate bets through the Global Real Estate Group (GREG). Located in the Fixed Income Group within Capital Markets, GREG focused on underwriting and origination, securitization, warehouse lending, and bridge equity. Lehman's single most powerful real estate profiteer was Mark Walsh, the head of GREG. His rumpled Brooks Brothers suits and sometimes-awkward demeanor in larger groups was offset by his keen intellect and ability to print money. Walsh's rise to power was nothing short of meteoric. He arrived in 1988 and won Fuld's respect and trust during the commercial real estate bust and refinancing boom of the late 1980s and early 1990s. For the aggressive Walsh, timing was everything. The economy had hit a brick wall. Its sudden decline exposed the excessive lending practices of many of the nation's largest S&Ls. There was now a multibillion-dollar glut of bad commercial loans that the Resolution Trust Company (RTC) took over. Once on the RTC's books, the government was motivated to sell these mortgages, and Walsh saw this as a unique opportunity. Using his experience as a trained real estate attorney, he began buying and selling foreclosed properties. These early trades were risky and generated hundreds of millions of dollars in profit for Lehman. Fuld was pleased and rewarded Walsh with even greater loan authority. Lehman had found its home run hitter.

Another important trend was unfolding at this time. The MBS derivative market was now considered a mainstream (safe) investment. This opened up the door for applying securitization techniques to commercial real estate transactions. Under Walsh's leadership, by the late 1990s, Lehman developed a strong reputation in the rapidly growing commercial mortgage–backed securities (CMBS) market. By 2004, all GREG businesses were combined under Walsh. Similar to the residential markets, principal investments were increasingly financed through the firm's securitization unit. Lehman carved out its niche and became a pioneer in using securitization to lend to office building developers. Similar to RMBS, Lehman sliced up cash flows and repackaged them. Once rated, the least risky pieces might go to institutional investors and the riskier slices to hedge funds or other high-risk investors. To the delight of developers, this in turn increased the number of investors willing to throw money at deals either as debt or equity. No longer were developers held hostage to the demands of a few large commercial banks and life insurance companies. If they did not like commercial banker terms, they could now come to Lehman.

With a flood of cash available and real estate prices booming, Lehman's CMBS business took off. By 2000 Walsh was promoted to co-head of a new private equity group focused on real estate. Hitting the ground running, Walsh raised $1.6 billion from institutional and university endowments. This first fund earned an impressive return exceeding 30 percent. This approach was profitable but did not provide the large returns that a red-hot commercial real estate market had to offer. Lehman saw many of its developer clients getting rich and wanted in too. The industry capitalization rate (cap rate), which is calculated by taking a property's net operating income divided by the purchase price, was falling. The lower the cap rate, the more expensive property is to buy. It also meant property owners were making money hand over fist. In

2002 the cap rate in the United States averaged 9.25 percent. By 2007 competition for properties pushed some cap rates to as low as 5 percent. This meant a building that had cost $100 million five years earlier was now worth $200 million, a whopping 100 percent return. What created this financial alchemy? The rent did not increase, the location did not change, and the square footage remained the same. The only factor that changed was the market's perception of the value. The drop in cap rate to historic lows was proof there were more buyers chasing fewer deals. The country was in a real estate bubble.

Seeing the profit opportunities, Lehman increased its risk profile, moving away from a pure fee-driven business model to putting greater firm capital at risk. Lehman began lending out its balance sheet for a price. Earlier on, Lehman had several successful deals that gave the false impression it could earn money at no cost. An example occurred in 2003. Lehman worked with Beacon Capital Partners to purchase the John Hancock Tower, the tallest skyscraper in Boston. This prime property located in a real estate–constrained city sold for $910 million. As part of the transaction, Beacon Capital Partners financed $620 million. Lehman responded by providing a $200 million bridge equity line with a 6 percent commitment fee. In less than a month, the buyers were able to find permanent financing, the bridge loan was never funded, and Lehman walked away with $12 million. There was still more profit to be had. On the remaining $420 million, Lehman sliced up, securitized, and sold these CMBS to the market, collecting additional fees. Lehman had found the path to fast profits. This assumption was true as long as real estate prices went up, other lenders were willing to provide permanent financing, and the market remained hungry for CMBS. In 2006, Beacon Capital Partners flipped this property to Broadway Partners for a profit. On March 31, 2009, the John Hancock Tower was sold in a foreclosure auction for $660.6 million, half the amount it sold for only three years earlier.

Under the guidance of Walsh, real estate became Lehman's main growth engine. Though Walsh did not sit on Lehman's trading floor shouting out buy and sell orders while glued to a Bloomberg terminal, his real estate deals were as lethal as those of a rogue trader. Years of generating strong profit had allowed him to gain authority to place billion-dollar bets around the globe. From 2004 to 2006, these activities produced record earnings, increasing revenue at the capital markets division by 56 percent. This was more than double the growth rate of investment banking and asset management combined. At the peak of the real estate boom, the activities directly attributed to Walsh's areas generated more than 20 percent of Lehman's $4 billion in profits.[8] These profits helped bankroll the firm's growth in other key areas, including fixed-income trading.

As the largest mortgage-backed securities underwriter on the street, Lehman's balance sheet of global bets ballooned in excess of $89 billion, with commercial loans representing two-thirds of this exposure. Walsh was basically playing a real-life version of the board game Monopoly. True to the game, he eventually risked Lehman capital on a marquee Park Avenue property. The difference was that real money, not Monopoly money, was at stake. In 2005 Lehman lent $1.7 billion for the New York–based Tishman Speyer purchase of the MetLife Building on Park Avenue. In 2006 similar bridge equity was placed to support Beacon Capital Partners' purchase of News Corporation's headquarters on the Avenue of Americas.

Walsh also built up the firm's international real estate exposure. He went to Paris and purchased two prestigious office buildings for $2.8 billion. The market for this deal was small, and the seller was rival Goldman Sachs. Most of the ownership of this transaction was housed on Lehman's books, with some unloaded to investors in the private equity fund run by the firm. The firm's appetite for bigger and riskier deals continued to grow. Walsh's signing authority allowed him to pull the trigger. Developers realized this, and many deals beat a path to his door. By 2006 Walsh placed a single $2 billion bet on the McAllister Ranch. Lehman's commercial paper department would take exposure of $235 million. The project entailed carving out a high-end six-thousand-unit residential community on more than two thousand acres in dusty Bakersfield, east of Los Angeles. Lehman consummated this transaction at the peak of the market just prior to the start of the subprime credit crisis. This crisis would hit Southern California real estate, residential and commercial, particularly hard. In this single transaction, Lehman put 10 percent of its entire capital at risk, literally betting the "farm" on the ranch.

Unlike a trader's positions, which Lehman's risk management department measured on a daily basis, Walsh's positions were not measured daily nor compared to stated limits. Walsh, however, did have to gain approval for large deals through the management committee, which Fuld sat on. The size of Walsh's transactions also meant Lehman's board of directors were aware of them. But Walsh's strong profit record had basically earned him the right to operate by his own rules.

As a final opus of escalating firm risk taking, in October 2007 under Walsh's direction, Lehman banked Tishman Speyer's purchase of Archstone-Smith Trust, the owner of more than 360 large high-end apartment complexes, for

$22.2 billion. In a deal struck at the market peak, Lehman, in a joint partnership with Bank of America, put up more than $17 billion of first-mortgage debt and almost $5 billion in bridge equity financing. This was the largest real estate deal Lehman or the industry had ever done. In hindsight Lehman could have learned a few things about risk management from Tishman Speyer. In this deal, the developers only risked $250 million of their own money. Between the time the Archstone deal was first announced and was scheduled to close in October, the market cooled off. Lehman had an escape clause but decided to go through with the deal rather than risk paying the $1 billion breakup fee or damage its reputation. Once the deal closed, Walsh sold $8.9 billion of the debt to Fannie Mae and Freddie Mac and convinced Bank of America and Barclay to buy $2.4 billion of the bridge equity.[9] What remained on Lehman's books was more than $5 billion in a deal that increasingly smelled bad.

In one deal, Walsh had committed a remarkable 20 percent of the firm's equity capital. Against basic risk-management wisdom, he put an incredibly large portion of Lehman's eggs in one basket. As the nation's real estate market collapsed, Walsh and his team rushed to flush assets off of Lehman's books. Between November 2007 and February 2008, Lehman unloaded $2.8 billion of commercial real estate.[10] This still left more than $75 billion residential and commercial loans that were hard to value, including debt and equity in the risky McAllister Ranch and Archstone deals. Walsh's real estate buying binge had piled on debt. In only a few short years, Lehman's risk profile had changed dramatically. With a larger debt position and higher leverage ratio, Lehman had nearly destroyed its flexibility to navigate through a financial storm.

During the decade, Lehman was also an active participant in the leverage buyout (LBO) boom, supplying dealmakers with billions in bridge loans. The largest LBO of the decade was the purchase of TXU Corporation, a Dallas-based utility led by buyout firm Kohlberg Kravis Roberts. Lehman along with a handful of other large firms helped to finance this deal. Once the subprime crisis hit by summer 2007, the leverage loan business began to shut down. Lehman was left holding approximately $18 billion in leverage loans. It made efforts to reduce this exposure, but owning junk credit loans in a faltering economy was a hard product to unload.

By 2008 Lehman had $22.5 billion of firm capital. From an equity position, its real estate holdings were three times greater. This meant even a 5 percent to 10 percent decline in real estate prices—now a foregone conclusion—could significantly erode firm capital. Later, Lehman short-seller David Einhorn would point to the McAllister Ranch and Archstone deals, representing 30 percent of firm capital, and question whether these Lehman positions were actually worthless. Even when excluding the leveraged loans, Lehman had more real estate exposure to capital than any other firm on Wall Street. By the second quarter of 2008, Lehman's commercial real estate holdings were 70 percent greater than those of Goldman Sachs and 30 percent greater than Morgan Stanley's. Compared to these much better capitalized competitors, Lehman had to support its risky real estate position with less than one-third to one-fifth the capital. With the help of Walsh, who was under the direction of Fuld and board oversight, Lehman was in effect a speculative real estate hedge fund thinly disguised as an investment bank.

Chapter 12

The Bear Mauling

Bear, Stearns & Company (Bear) had a lot in common with Lehman. It could easily have been mistaken for Lehman's less refined sibling. In 1923, nearly seventy-five years after Lehman's start, Bear was founded by a Jewish businessman. As the nation prospered, Bear did too. It grew into a top-five investment bank dependent on fixed-income revenue, and during the 2000s the firm aggressively built a global mortgage origination platform. Bear was Lehman's mini-me, sharing a similar business strategy and risk profile. Like Lehman, Bear increased its leverage ratio and relied on cheaper, shorter-term, and less stable funding sources. Initially these mortgage and other real estate bets paid off, and billions in profit rolled in. But as Bear's risk accelerated, capital did not keep pace. Like Lehman, Bear had an autocratic leader, who was paid a financial rock-star salary but removed from the day-to-day risks the firm was taking. Bear employees were the company's single largest shareholders.

By early 2007, it became evident that Bear had put too many chips on a single bet—subprime real estate. The firm did not have the revenue diversification, adequate capital, or stable funding to support such risk. Bear's near collapse in March 2008 should have been a clarion call for Lehman's leader Dick Fuld. Lehman had six months to reduce risk positions, get liquid, find a deep-pocketed parent, and gain safe harbor. Instead, Lehman became the largest bankruptcy in U.S. history.

OMINOUS LEADERSHIP PARALLELS

Like Lehman, a key ingredient to Bear's successful track record was strong leadership. Through eighty years, strong personalities shaped Bear and its risk-taking culture. Leaders like Salim "Cy" Lewis (three decades) and Alan "Ace" Greenberg (also three decades) used their own unique styles to nurture and grow the firm. But perhaps no Bear leader would play a more prominent role in the firm's fate than thirty-five-year-old salesman Jimmy Cayne, hired by Bear Stearns CEO Greenberg in 1969.

Cayne was a top-notch bridge player, a card addict. For Cayne, this was not a hobby—it was more like an obsession. While enrolled at Purdue University, he focused on cards instead of books. His academics suffered, and eventually he dropped out one semester shy of graduation. He later jumped around from job to job, selling photocopiers, adding machines, and scrap iron. Jobs changed, but his love for cards remained. In 1961 he won the Midwest Regional Bridge Tournament, and in 1964 he moved to New York City to become a professional bridge player. Between games he drove a taxicab. Growing restless, he interviewed with Greenberg. The interview did not go particularly well, but when Greenberg, who also loved bridge, found out Cayne was a top bridge player, he got the job.[1] Upon joining the firm, Cayne was taken aside by Lewis and given some fatherly advice: either pick Wall Street or bridge because it would be hard to do both well.[2] Cayne chose to ignore this warning.

Cayne joined Bear the same year Fuld joined Lehman. Both men quickly distinguished themselves, Cayne in sales and Fuld in trading. Cayne took to his job, dialing and smiling through wealthy bridge contacts. A born salesman, he showed a knack for getting moneyed people to say yes. Unlike Lewis, Greenberg, or Fuld, Cayne was not a trader. He never traded a bond, stock, or derivative security. His sales success put him on the fast track, and he reached partner in less than four years. By then, Bear had expanded to thirty partners and had more than $500 million in capital.

In 1988, Cayne was promoted to president, but he was not satisfied as second in command. At age sixty, Greenberg showed no sign of stepping down. The friction between these two competitors grew, and, by 1993, it came to a head. Cayne made a persuasive argument and pushed the board to a vote. On July 13, Cayne officially became Bear's CEO. During this same period, Fuld came of age as Lehman's CEO. Two new "Captains of the Universe" were added to Wall Street. In 2001 Cayne assumed the additional role of chairman of the board. Fuld held a similar dual position. In reaching the top, both executives perfected the art of blocking the path of or eliminating potential rivals. Executives who appeared too capable for Cayne's or Fuld's liking seemed to disappear. Both Fuld and Cayne insisted on pulling all the levers. Although pushing out internal competitors was not uncommon in the high-powered, high-salaried realm of banking, it later impacted the quality of both organizations' corporate risk-taking decisions.

CORPORATE ETHOS

Though difficult to quantify with any certainty, Bear's inferiority complex cannot be underestimated when trying to understand its surge in risk taking. Year after year, the corporate ethos at Bear remained the same: one day Bear would rise to eclipse the Big Three—Goldman Sachs, Morgan Stanley, and Merrill Lynch. The Big Three were Porsches; Bear was a Ford Mustang. Bear actually thrived on this categorization. Greenberg used the acronym P.S.D. to describe the ideal Bear hire—poor, smart, and a deep desire to get rich.[3] Colorful adjectives were often used to describe the firm: *freewheeling, scrappy, opportunistic,* and *fiercely independent.* All were considered virtues at Bear. It was a place for guys that liked to eat, drink, work hard, play cards, and, most of all, make lots of money. Bear was built for traders, not prissy investment bankers. It may be fair to assume that Fuld, once known as the Gorilla on the trading floor, had a soft spot for the ethos at Bear Stearns.

THE MAVERICK

As CEO, Cayne was keeper of the flame—the eternal hope of surpassing the Big Three. In the 1980s Bear expanded its corporate mergers and acquisitions business. Up until this time, it was viewed as unsavory for investment banks to support unfriendly takeovers. Always the maverick, Bear did not let this stand in the way of profits, becoming the banker for many hostile takeovers of the decade. As early as 1982, Bear waged a proxy battle against its own client, Global Natural Resources. This was like breaking an unwritten pact in the investment banking world. In spite of the initial stigma, Bear earned the reputation as an incubator for corporate takeovers and raked in handsome profits. By 1985 the firm grew to more than 280 employees, with $1.8 billion in revenue (yet only 6 percent of the revenue came from investment banking). Similar to Lehman, fixed-income trading ran the show.

Deep down, both Bear and Lehman remained envious of their much larger rivals. They were in the club but not really at the top of the investment banking pyramid. For every initial public offering (IPO) or merger and acquisition

Bear completed, the Big Three got two to three times more business. Bear got more than the crumbs that fell off the table, but not the best cuts of meat. Even after being ranked the fifth largest U.S. investment bank, right behind Lehman, Bear could not shake its image as a freewheeling fixed-income shop. The reason was simple: year in and year out, the majority of its income came from capital market activities. What separated the Big Three was revenue diversification—no single business line (investment banking, advisory services, trading, or asset management) contributed more than 40 percent of earnings. Not only did Bear and Lehman rely more heavily on fixed-income trading, they also had greater single product concentration risk. This meant that in a down real estate market, Bear and Lehman would experience greater revenue fluctuation.

MORTGAGE-BACKED SECURITIES

In 1981 Bear officially started its mortgage department, a half decade before Lehman. Initially its product of choice was the lower-risk government agencies—Ginnie Mae, Fannie Mae, and Freddie Mac. Bear then moved into trading the higher-profit, higher-risk pools of mortgages originated by non-bank mortgage lenders. Once Bear started slicing, dicing, packaging, and reselling these private-label securities, it never looked back. Similar to Lehman, Bear viewed mortgages and the growth of securitization as a natural extension of its fixed-income expertise. It quickly developed domestic and international origination platforms, and by 1989 Bear was one of the three top mortgage-backed securities underwriters on Wall Street.

The real push into the risky non-agency mortgage segment occurred with the hiring of trader Howard Rubin—the infamous Merrill Lynch mortgage trader fired for losing $377 million in collateralized mortgage obligation trades that had gone bad. At the time, this was the largest single mortgage securities trading loss ever reported on Wall Street. It was a warning sign that these instruments, in large enough quantities, could be financial dynamite in the wrong hands. In their new hire, Bear saw only upside, and immediately the bet paid off. For the fiscal year ending June 1993, Rubin's mortgage trading desk earned $150 million, just under half of Bear's profits for the year. For his handiwork, Rubin took home $6.5 million in compensation. Bear was also able to ramp up its mortgage-trading platform by hiring traders from defunct Drexel, a mortgage trader fired at Kidder Peabody for alleged sexual harassment, as well as traders from First Boston and Salomon. Bear decided to imitate, buy talent, and gain market advantage.

By 1995 Bear controlled approximately 20 percent of the mortgage-backed securities (MBS) market. Bear was also a larger repo lender to various non-bank originators such as Thornburg Mortgage. Similar to Lehman, Bear took a vertically integrated strategy, buying loan originator EMC Mortgage Corporation (2000) and subprime lender Encore Credit Corporation (2007) in an attempt to capture more profit along the mortgage lending value chain. Real estate–related securities were the ticket to the top. Extending loans and putting more firm capital at risk, Bear also structured the loan approval process to look like a traditional bank, complete with a formalized loan committee. More and more, Bear was acting like a commercial bank in risking firm capital. The difference was that Bear did not have the capital position needed to support this risk taking.

HEDGE FUND HAVOC

In October 2003 Bear established a high-grade mortgage fund. For more than two years this fund had positive returns. In 2006, returns began to fall and investor redemptions increased. To reduce capital flight Bear established two new mortgage-backed hedge funds: the High-Grade Structured Credit Fund and the High-Grade Structured Credit Strategies Enhanced Leverage Fund. Although the names sounded safe, the funds were far from it. Warren Spector, co-president and a twenty-four-year Bear veteran, had broad oversight responsibility for these hedge funds. The firm seeded these funds with $45 million of its own capital. Bear started the High-Grade Structured Credit Strategies Enhanced Leverage Fund with less than $6 million in assets and used leverage to expand the holding size to more than $6 billion. Fees charged by Bear were 2 percent on assets and 20 percent on profits. This provided an incentive for Bear's fund managers to increase the risk to gain higher fees. To increase fund leverage, Bear obtained loans from banks and other lenders who allowed mortgages to be used as collateral.

Many of these lenders were household names, including Merrill Lynch, Lehman, J.P. Morgan, Citigroup, and Deutsche Bank. This borrowed money was then used to purchase more AAA- and AA-rated subprime asset-backed securities (ABS). These funds were a bullish bet that the trend of rising real estate prices and low default rates would continue. To protect against higher than expected default rates, Bear purchased credit default insurance in the form of credit default swaps (CDS). Recall that these instruments were not exchange traded and uniform capital standards were not mandated. Sellers of CDS collected premiums for products sold but were not required to set aside capital reserves to honor these bets. Initially, CDS instruments were created as a way to hedge risk, but they rapidly mutated into a speculative market on the chance of default. At the peak of the market, there were five times more CDS outstanding than the value of the underlying bonds these instruments were insuring. (By 2006 the CDS market reached more than $60 trillion in notional value.) Big commercial banks, investment banks, and insurance companies had formidable balance sheets to offset this growing off-balance-sheet risk. Firms that sold CDS protection—AIG, Lehman, Citigroup, Morgan Stanley, Merrill Lynch, Wachovia, and J.P. Morgan—collected lucrative fees while those that bought it gained insurance against credit default.

As the market value of MBS used as collateral declined, lenders concerned about falling prices began demanding more collateral or seizing it and selling it outright. Bear satisfied these margin calls by offering additional mortgages or providing cash. As the hedge fund community learned that Bear was experiencing significant losses and selling its holdings to meet margin calls, competing funds entered the market to profit or to liquidate trading positions, which drove prices further down. More sellers than buyers caused a price death spiral, forcing Bear to sell securities in a falling market. If Bear had followed a less risky strategy and set aside enough capital, it could have sat on these positions and avoided being forced to unwind them to meet collateral calls. In a last-ditch attempt to save the fund, on June 26, 2007, Bear posted $1.6 billion to bail out the High-Grade Structured Credit Fund.

In a July 17, 2007, letter to investors, Bear reported that this hedge fund had lost more than 90 percent of its value, and the second fund had lost virtually all of its investor capital. The sudden collapse of these two Bear subprime hedge funds set off a crisis. Bear had created radioactive funds, took client money, rolled the dice, and lost big. Bear had been slow to identify its risk, nor did it respond in a timely fashion. Investors were irate, and Bear's reputation was seriously harmed. This was the time for the Bear CEO to lead, but he did not. The very next day Cayne and Spector were busy playing in the ten-day North American Bridge Championship tournament in Nashville, Tennessee. These senior executives made it to the sixteenth round and did not return to work until July 30—thirteen days after the crisis broke. On July 31 the two funds filed for Chapter 15 bankruptcy. Bear wound down the funds and liquidated all holdings. The speed of the collapse of these funds sent tremors through the global financial market. This was an early catalyst that set off what would be known as the Great Credit Crisis of 2008, and it provided Lehman with yet another warning to exit the market.

TOO LITTLE TOO LATE

In good times, Cayne appeared to be the right leader for Bear. In his fourteen years at the helm, stock performance was off the charts. Investors who bought Bear stock in 1993 saw a 600 percent return by 2007. Identical to Lehman, employees owned approximately 30 percent of the firm and represented the largest ownership block. Cayne was the single largest stockholder, and at the market peak his 5.6 million shares were worth approximately $1 billion. In using increased leverage and concentrating on mortgage securitization and real estate lending, Bear was able to push revenue and stock price up.

But risky mortgages were a cancer that had metastasized on the firm's books. As industry-wide losses mounted, Bear's stock dropped like a rock. From its fifty-two-week high in 2007 of $171.51, it dropped to around $88 by year's end. In less than one year, more than $1 billion in firm value was erased. During the biggest crisis of the firm's history, Cayne and his card-playing partner, Spector, had checked into an out-of-state bridge tournament. Cayne was just being himself, doing what he loved best. Lewis's advice three decades earlier was finally catching up to Cayne. To save his own job, Cayne attempted to deflect the blame for the hedge fund losses by firing Spector in August 2007. This management shakeup did little to quell concerns. Short-sellers saw this as further evidence that Bear had more room to fall. Under enormous pressure from institutional investors and his own troops, Cayne relinquished control. On January 4, 2008, the seventy-five-year-old CEO officially retired. As his replacement, the firm turned to Alan Schwartz, a man almost twenty years Cayne's junior. Schwartz was well liked, a leader, and, perhaps most important, not a card player. By the time Schwartz took control, an irrevocable choice had been made. Bear was now hanging on by a thread.

VALENTINE'S DAY MASSACRE

If Bear's losses had been contained to its two private-label hedge funds from the previous summer, it may have been able to survive. But the market was not done claiming victims. At the Zurich headquarters of UBS AG (UBS), February 14, 2008, was a frantic day. Switzerland's largest and most conservative bank, dating back to 1854, was about to drop a financial bombshell with its 2007 fourth-quarter results. Similar to Bear and Lehman, it had jumped into the mortgage securities market with both feet and had even resurrected a Wall Street ghost—investment bank Dillon Reed. Using Dillon Reed as a hedge fund vehicle, UBS set up subprime-focused funds. Similar to Bear, these funds experienced massive losses. Newly appointed UBS CEO Marcel Rohner was the messenger of bad news, reporting a loss of $11.3 billion on subprime mortgage exposure of $27.6 billion. This loss took into account an almost $14 billion write-off of U.S.-related mortgage securities.

Staggering in size, these losses illuminated the speed and seriousness of the deterioration of the U.S. housing market. The losses were not isolated to a small segment of the mortgage market but cut across the real estate spectrum—subprime, Alt-A, credit derivatives, commercial loans, and leveraged buyout loans. Mortgages were now seen as liabilities, not assets. Mortgage products such as residential mortgage–backed securities (RMBS), commercial mortgage–backed securities (CMBS), and ABS quickly acquired the moniker of "toxic sludge." Firms that held mortgage securities on their books were seeing only red ink. Like a giant domino, the write-downs by UBS triggered an industry-wide chain reaction as other firms were forced to re-mark the value of their mortgage securities positions. It was like catching a falling knife. There were not many takers. And while UBS had more than $35 billion in capital to offset these monumental losses, others were not as fortunate. Wall Street quickly assembled a list of the likely walking dead, the soon to be dead, and the deceased. The list included Thornburg Mortgage, IndyMac, Countrywide, Washington Mutual, Wachovia, Fannie Mae, Freddie Mac, Merrill Lynch, and AIG.

Mortgage originators were the first to experience significant trouble. They counted on the willingness of banks, the short-term lenders in the overnight repurchase agreement (repo), to continue to accept mortgages as collateral and lend. Repo markets were used over longer-term debt because it was a cheap way of funding growth. This market was built on the belief that the market would always have confidence enough to make a twenty-four-hour loan. Ironically, the lenders to many of the originators were investment banks such as Bear and Lehman. As the market significantly cut the value of collateral, including AAA-rated mortgages, by as much as 20 percent or more, firms lost confidence and balked at lending. Investor emotion had trumped investor logic, and all mortgage securities were seen as bad bets. The door on a vibrant mortgage-origination market was shut in a matter of weeks.

With their lifeblood shut off, mortgage lenders were thrown into financial turmoil. Thornburg, previously the gold standard of lenders, was a good example. This was one of the nation's largest mortgage lenders and until now a well-respected company. It focused on Alt-A loans, staying away from the more unseemly subprime borrowers. The loans it held on its books were from borrowers with relatively strong credit histories, and default rates remained less than 1 percent. But in this "new" market, even these securities had dropped in value by 10 to 20 percent or more. These price drops were driven by an almost instantaneous drop in market liquidity—there were lots of sellers and few buyers. Margins in the origination end of the business had been strong, but with the value of mortgages plummeting, the lending business had turned into the losing business. Bear and Lehman responded by making significant margin calls on Thornburg and increasing the "haircut" (i.e., discount to face value) used on acceptable collateral. By cutting off their potentially weaker customers, Bear and Lehman were inflicting pain on themselves. While in isolation these cuts were prudent, they also signaled the death of an industry that both of these firms heavily relied on.

MARCH MADNESS

As market prices continued in a downward spiral, Bear's portfolio of assets became less liquid than their competitors'. Lenders had to continue lending if Bear was to stay alive. On March 10, 2008, rumors circulated on Wall Street that Bear was having liquidity problems. For Schwartz and his top executives it made little sense. The firm had taken its lumps the previous summer, reported losses in the fall, and was sitting on $18 billion in cash reserves. But in a crisis cash is king. Bear had only $11.1 billion in tangible equity capital supporting $395 billion in assets and a leverage ratio of 35 to 1.[4] In response to the rumors, Bear fired off a press release including the following statement: "There is absolutely no truth to the rumors of liquidity problems that circulated today in the market." That week, on CNBC's "Mad Money," markets commentator Jim Cramer ranted and raved to viewers that Bear was a survivor and investors should not take their money out. Investors who followed his advice lost big, and Cramer was later immortalized as the poster child of irresponsible financial journalism when television personality Jon Stewart publicly took him to task.

The events of this March day and the weakening stock price worried Bear. Market reputation and perceived financial strength is what kept investment banks in business. Like certain mortgage originators, Bear's funding model relied on the market's willingness to keep the lending spigot flowing. To run the firm's day-to-day activities required borrowing almost $50 billion a day in the repo market, using more than 70 percent of its mortgage securities as collateral. Bear assumed the market would be there for it to keep the lights on. But the overnight lenders—Goldman Sachs, J.P. Morgan, Fidelity, and Federated Investors—were losing confidence and began restricting credit during the second week of March.

On March 11, 2008, in almost laser-like fashion, Goldman Sachs inflicted a debilitating blow to Bear's reputation. Goldman Sachs' Credit Derivatives Group publicly disclosed to its hedge fund clients that Bear's credit was too risky to insure. This added to the growing storm of fear. In response, Bear CFO Sam Molinaro appeared on CNBC to quell rumors, but they had already turned into a growing stampede. Many of Bear's prime brokerage clients were hedge funds that parked billions of dollars in excess cash at Bear. The majority of these unsegregated accounts supplied extra capital to meet Bear's daily operational demands.

By March 12, in accelerating numbers, hedge funds with deposits totaling more than $25 billion left Bear. On this day, in an attempt to stop the mass exodus, CEO Schwartz appeared on CNBC stating that trading partners were still accepting Bear's credit. Yet, by March 13, other clients and trading partners headed for the door. Even with billions in cash, Bear did not have enough money to make it to the next week. In an attempt to provide needed liquidity, working through J.P. Morgan as a surrogate, the Federal Reserve (Fed) set up a temporary lending facility for up to $30 billion. On Friday morning, March 14, at 9 A.M., Bear announced this sizable lending agreement, but its stock still dropped by almost 40 percent. By then, the damage was done. In a second attempt to rescue Bear on the same day, the Fed put together a meeting at its New York headquarters with New York Fed President Tim Geithner in charge. The Fed was concerned about systemic risk and the impact that a collapse of the fifth largest investment bank might have on the already fragile U.S. economy. To all in attendance it was clear by the following business day that Bear was going to be quickly sold off or forced into bankruptcy. On the Friday market close, Bear's stock was trading in excess of $30 per share. During a closed-door emergency meeting on Sunday, March 16, the Fed approved a $30 billion credit line to facilitate the rescue of Bear.

Having a commitment in hand from the Fed to backstop losses on toxic assets, J.P. Morgan made an offer to buy Bear at $2 per share. The total purchase price was about $240 million—less than the contract of Yankees third baseman Alex Rodriguez. Bear's headquarters at 383 Madison Avenue was worth $1 billion alone. That Sunday evening, Bear's board approved the low offer. When the market opened on Monday, March 17, Bear became a subsidiary of J.P. Morgan. One week later, in an attempt to appease irate shareholders and make sure Bear would not go into liquidation, J.P. Morgan upped its offer to $10 a share, after gaining approval from the government. The next day, March 25, 2008, Cayne and his wife sold 5.66 million shares, their entire holdings, pocketing $61.3 million. In a last jab at the fallen CEO, Greenberg charged Cayne $77,000 in commission fees to execute this trade instead of the much smaller employee discount rate of $2,500.[5] Greenberg later told the *New York Times*, "If he doesn't like it, he should do his future business elsewhere."[6]

In the end, J.P. Morgan got a steal with the Fed's help. Worried about both systemic risk and moral hazard, it seems the Fed attempted to thread the needle. Ostensibly, the lowball bid was supposed to send a clear message to the market: the government will not reward firms that take excessive risk. Treasury Secretary Hank Paulson was instrumental in engineering the original rescue and recommending the $2-per-share offer. Even that price he felt was too high. Upon first hearing that the offer was being raised to $10 a share, Paulson reportedly said that the news made him want to puke. He realized that the public wouldn't perceive this better offer as punishment—and former employees like Cayne who were cashing in their holdings did nothing to improve the public's perception. J.P. Morgan was able to play the role of white knight only because the government's financial guarantees made the deal a steal.

THE DUST SETTLES

Paulson officially claimed that a liquidity event caused Bear's fall. On this point he was correct. In only a few days, market rumors had put in question firm viability and eroded support from other trading partners. It was a crisis of confidence and an investment bank's worst nightmare. Goldman Sachs, for example, did little to help Bear. Could this have had anything to do with Cayne's actions a decade earlier when Long-Term Capital Management (LTCM) was on the Fed's operating table? Recall that when LTCM was on the brink of collapse, Bear left the negotiation table and did not participate in the rescue. Of the sixteen powerful Wall Street firms then assembled, only Bear said no to the Fed's attempt to arm-twist help for LTCM. That original plan was for each bank to ante up $250 million. When it came time to vote on the plan, the Fed did an alphabetical role call, starting with Bankers Trust, then Barclays, and then Bear. After Bear bucked the crowd, a period of shocked silence was followed by chaos. The meeting was abruptly stopped, and Cayne was taken to a side room to reconsider. But the Fed's cry of systemic risk—and the importance of rescuing LTCM for the market's sake—continued to fall on deaf ears. Fifteen firms would not forget what Bear had done.

Though the global markets were visibly shaken by the sale of Bear to J.P. Morgan, the efforts of Geithner and Paulson appeared to have bypassed the sort of financial catastrophe that was feared possible if Bear had completely collapsed. The government actions taken were not necessarily following any precedent, nor were they creating one. The sale of Bear seemed to produce more questions than it answered. How exactly were the threats of systemic risk and moral hazard balanced? Was any rationale used as a guiding principle, or was Bear's sale a convergence of last-second conjecture and deal making between public and private entities? Most on Wall Street saw the Fed and Treasury intervention through J.P. Morgan as proof that Bear was considered "too big to fail," which explained the reluctance to force Bear into bankruptcy. But then why wasn't this model followed six months later when attempting to rescue Lehman?

Lehman received several clear warnings through the years about the dangers of excessive risk taking, derivatives, mortgage-related securities, and high leverage—Shearson's ability to purchase rival E. F. Hutton at a fire-sale price (1987), Merrill Lynch's $377 million in trading losses (1987), Kidder Peabody's sale to Paine Webber (1994), and LTCM's meltdown (1998). Yet perhaps no warning was louder than the unraveling of Bear, Lehman's mini-me. How would Lehman respond to this?

Chapter 13

Time Runs Out

The "Bear mauling" provided Lehman with valuable lessons. First, in times of trouble, raise excess capital and dump bad assets. Second, get out in front of market rumors, stomp them out, and protect the stock price. Third, last-minute deals should be avoided because they are difficult to execute and struck at deep discounts. And, last, when all else fails, the federal government will be there to help bail you out. Did CEO Dick Fuld apply these lessons and move to save the Mother Ship before government intervention was necessary?

The skittish market was looking for the next Bear, and Lehman stood out as a likely candidate. Several skeptics took large short positions on Lehman stock. A confluence of dismal events—a flood of mortgage lender bankruptcies, increased loan delinquencies, plummeting real estate values, a drop in investor sentiment, and billions in losses reported by rival banking firms—continued to turn the global markets downward. During the first quarter of 2008, many larger banks with similar mortgage-related exposure, including Deutsche Bank, Morgan Stanley, UBS AG, and Merrill Lynch, reported multibillion-dollar real estate write-downs. Lehman remained an oddity. For the first quarter of 2008, it reported positive earnings. Earnings fell 59 percent but easily beat forecasts. The market was puzzled. Lehman was by far the largest mortgage originator on Wall Street, active in risky subprime, Alt-A, residential mortgage–backed securities (RMBS), commercial mortgage–backed securities (CMBS), and commercial lending. With more than $89 billion in residential and commercial securities and related loans on its books, even if Lehman assumed a modest decline in value of 5 percent, this would represent at least a $4 billion pre-tax hit to earnings. The skeptics believed Lehman was the next firm to fall.

DEATH OF LEHMAN?

The global financial markets are driven by a combination of logic and emotion. Sometimes numbers rule; other times fear takes control. On Sunday, March 16, 2008, it was a combination of both. If Bear in a forced rescue was worth only $2 per share (a week later adjusted to $10), how much was Lehman worth? On Monday morning, March 17, the next day of trading, the market responded by knocking Lehman's stock down 38 percent to $24.20. In a single day, Lehman shares lost $3 billion in market value. The markets were painfully efficient. The trading of options, including calls and puts, began to show higher-risk premiums. Implied volatilities on Lehman stock, the risk meter used by option investors, increased to 132 percent, twice that of Goldman Sachs or Merrill Lynch. Only Bear's stock options, the company just sold at a fire-sale price, traded at a higher implied volatility (248 percent).

The market was not done showing its skepticism of Lehman's survival. That same day, credit default swaps purchased by speculators and hedgers as a way to bet on credit default also began to spike. These swaps that traded one week earlier at 365 basis points above U.S. Treasury rates were now trading at 443 basis points. The perceived risk of a Lehman default had dramatically increased. The broader stock market was also showing signs of fear. The most widely watched market sentiment gauge, the Chicago Board Option Exchange Volatility Index (VIX), began to spike, hitting 32.24. The higher the VIX, the higher the perceived near-term risk associated with the Standard & Poor's 500. By March 17, 2008, the VIX was at levels not seen since 2002.

After Bear was taken over by J.P. Morgan, the market made it clear that the highly leveraged investment banks that depended on the overnight repo market to fund day-to-day operations were under attack. Lehman was not singled out. Goldman Sachs, Morgan Stanley, and Merrill Lynch were also put on notice. But Lehman had two more marks against it: it had only half the capital of Merrill Lynch, its next largest competitor, and it had about two times the amount of risky real estate. Compared to its much larger rivals, Lehman stood out like a sore thumb. While the market had determined that Lehman was teetering, Fuld and other top Lehman executives refused to believe it. Unfortunately for Lehman's shareholders, bondholders, and employees, not to mention the investors who later suffered from the effects of its collapse, Lehman's leaders refused to fully acknowledge the severity of the situation. To an outside observer, it appeared as if Lehman's top brass were going through the same stages of grief experienced after the loss of a loved one: denial, anger, bargaining, depression, and, only *after* the fall, acceptance.

MARCH 2008: DENIAL

When Lehman's 2007 annual report was mailed to shareholders, it showed another record-breaking year that merited record-breaking bonuses. Addressing shareholders, Fuld boasted it had been the most profitable year in firm history yet also one of the most challenging. Lehman had navigated the market turbulence and earned more than $1 billion of profit per quarter and had in excess of $22 billion in equity capital to cushion against a weakening real estate market. For first quarter 2008, when other firms showed crippling mortgage-related losses, Lehman showed profit.

For Fuld, the March run on Bear and the rumors that were battering his stock were malicious, concocted by those out to profit at Lehman's expense. What was happening in 2008 was not different than a decade earlier with Long-Term Capital Management (LTCM). Lehman would live to trade another day. Fuld was convinced that Lehman was financially stronger, safer, and more vital to the financial markets than Bear. Lehman ranked just one notch above Bear in the investment banking league tables, but it lived and operated in a different universe. It had twice the capital, twice the revenue, twice the history, and more than twice the smarts. Lehman had a much greater international footprint. More than 60 percent of Lehman's profit came from outside the United States. Both firms were fixed-income centric, but Lehman still could count on about half of earnings flowing from investment banking and asset management activities.

The Federal Reserve (Fed) was also improving market liquidity and, taking unprecedented steps, providing support that had not been available to Bear. After the Bear rescue, the Fed established a twenty-eight-day lending facility providing a backstop to the twenty top primary dealers. Starting on March 27, 2008, the Fed agreed to step in for the market and accept collateral, including mortgage-backed and asset-backed securities (the toxic and increasingly illiquid assets that Lehman had too much of). Even if the repo market closed its door, Lehman could always count on the Fed as its lender of last resort. Unlike Bear, Lehman performed a statesman role in the global financial markets and served as an advisor to numerous central bankers. Since 2005 Fuld had served on the Federal Reserve Bank of New York's board of directors. Lehman was an approved prime dealer in U.S. Treasuries. When the government wanted to raise capital, Bear may have helped but Lehman did the heavy lifting. The most widely followed bond index was created and managed by the company. If the government helped the less vital Bear avoid bankruptcy, then it would certainly do the same for Lehman, right? What's more, when the real estate bubble began deflating, Lehman did not sit still. In August 2007 Lehman closed down BNC Mortgage, its California-based subprime lending factory. Lehman was the first Wall Street firm to do so, and the market applauded this decision. Other Wall Street firms even followed Lehman's lead.

Denial of Lehman's poor financial health led to serious errors in judgment. First, the firm did not go far enough when exiting the mortgage-related market. Lehman may have begun to exit the subprime lending business, stopping new loans flowing on its books, but it failed to take more than $20 billion in existing mortgages and related securities off its books. It forgot a fundamental lesson: inventory sold today is worth more than inventory that sits on the shelf tomorrow. Lehman needed to dump these securities and cut its losses.

Lehman's second error in judgment was the mixed message it was sending: sell subprime and keep doing commercial real estate deals. The real estate boom was obviously coming to an end, but for Mark Walsh's Global Real Estate Group it was business as usual. He would continue to swing for the fence. As far back as 2006, Michael Gelband, former head of Global Fixed Income, had warned Fuld about the overheated real estate market and the need to change the firm's real estate dependent business model. As discussed in Chapter 11, the $22.2 billion Archstone-Smith deal that closed at the top of the market symbolized Lehman's excessive risk-taking culture. This single deal put at risk 20 percent of Lehman's capital. It was also a risky concentrated bet on the bubble states. This deal involved more than 360 high-end apartment complexes, almost half in Florida, California, and Arizona.

Lehman had broken two basic investment rules: it bought at the top of the market and it failed to diversify its bets. As the largest mortgage underwriter on the Street, Lehman's balance sheet of global real estate bets ballooned to more than $89 billion, with commercial loans representing two-thirds of this exposure. By 2007 real estate positions were almost four times greater than the firm's capital. The firm's massive bets had grown out of proportion to the company's sliver of a capital position. Commercial real estate became a millstone around Lehman's neck.

While still in denial, Lehman's survival plan was shaped by lessons from a decade earlier. Once again Fuld was at war with the market, even handing out plastic swords to convey this message. The battle was market perception versus reality. The market attack on Bear Stearns had reinforced the importance of getting out in front of market rumors. Like a firefighter, it was paramount for Lehman to stomp out the embers before they turned into a raging fire. For Fuld and Lehman to win, this battle needed to be fought on two fronts: *internally*, by winning the hearts and minds of employees; and, *externally*, in the marketplace, where short-sellers and doubters roamed.

Internal Campaign

Fuld knew he needed his employees' help to beat the market rumors into submission. In 1998 he had rallied the troops, and their commitment and hard work helped win the battle. He also knew the fastest way to gain employee loyalty was through stock grants. Since Fuld had taken the corner office, employee stock ownership had increased from 5 percent to 30 percent. Employees were the single largest owner of firm stock. Many employees had the bulk of their net worth tied up in Lehman stock. At the peak of the market, Fuld's holdings were worth in excess of $1 billion. Fuld knew falling stock prices could quickly undermine team unity and morale. When the firm's stock plummeted during the LTCM crisis, he responded by re-striking employee stock grants to the September 1998 market close price. By happenstance, his timing was impeccable. Thousands of employees received stock at the market low price of approximately $25. As Lehman came out of the crisis and the stock rebounded, employees were rewarded handsomely.

Falling back on this previous success, Fuld decided to re-strike stock options again. For employees with the firm since the LTCM days, the new stock grants for 2008, struck at a low market price, reinforced the strongly held internal view that the firm would survive and employees would profit again. The only catch to this strategy was that the stock price needed to rebound, but market forces and the aggressive short-sellers were continually pushing the stock price lower and lower. There was not even a dead-cat bounce.

External Campaign

For investment banks, the chief financial officer (CFO) is the financial face to the market. This officer interacts with the investor community and sets the tone. CFOs discuss firm earnings and capital structure and do the cheerleading when new capital is being raised. Some CFOs are formal, others informal. Some provide more financial information than required by Securities and Exchange Commission (SEC) rules, and others provide only the bare-bones minimum. Since the Sarbanes-Oxley Act in 2002, CFOs must sign off on all financials. The logic is that a signature increases officer accountability. Since 1994, with the exception of David Goldfarb's multi-year tenure, Lehman's CFO slot had been a virtual revolving door. In fourteen years there had been six different CFOs.

In December 2007 Fuld had hired Erin Callan as Lehman's newest CFO. Callan did not fit the typical mold—she was not a trained accountant, nor did she have experience in Lehman's finance or treasury department. She had spent her entire thirteen-year career at Lehman on the investment banking side of the business. Joe Gregory, Lehman's president and COO, had taken Callan under his wing, and when the critical CFO seat became vacant she got the nod. Callan was an overnight sensation. The rapid accession of the daughter of a New York police officer to CFO of the fourth largest investment bank in the country catapulted her to the most powerful spot of any woman on Wall Street. She had smarts, drive, and now power. Unlike David Viniar of Goldman Sachs, the longest standing CFO on Wall Street, Callan was not wary of public appearances. Her detractors said she was unseasoned for her new role. But in Fuld's and Gregory's minds, Callan was a Tomahawk missile programmed on a seek-and-destroy mission. Her primary goal was to eliminate the growing threat of rumors and get Lehman stock moving back in the right direction.

As Bear collapsed on March 18, 2008, Lehman's external campaign began when CFO Callan orchestrated a blitzkrieg on short-sellers. During Lehman's first-quarter conference call, which had been moved up by a week to reassure investors, Callan stayed on script and was charismatic and to the point. She methodically answered more than twenty questions and provided the market with more financial transparency than was (perceived) necessary. She provided the jittery market with a $489 million earnings surprise. Although substantially down from the previous quarter, these earnings easily beat Street estimates. The firm had successfully delivered its fifty-fifth consecutive profitable quarter. The market responded favorably. By end of day, Lehman's stock price had surged by 46 percent. The *Wall Street Journal* reported that after this call, Callan walked the trade floor and was greeted with high fives, applause, and a standing ovation, usually reserved only for Fuld. It appeared the radioactive fallout from Bear had been averted and the rumors blasted to smithereens.

But the March 18 earnings call did not pacify all investors. Some remained skeptical and for good reason. Many were hedge fund managers who made their money by shorting stocks. To some on Wall Street and Main Street, betting against a company almost seemed anti-American, and frustration with short-sellers appeared to peak when stocks were falling. To these hedge funds, utilizing short-selling techniques was purely business. For Fuld, the single largest Lehman shareholder, it was personal. He was convinced that hedge funds were planting bogus rumors—an illegal practice—and talking up their positions in an attempt to push his firm's stock down. The real estate bubble had popped, which provided a multitude of opportunities to bet against the mortgage origination sector. Lehman was a logical choice. How could a firm that made billions on the way up not lose on the way down? Short-selling was based on a reasonable premise: Lehman stock was overvalued.

David Einhorn was one prominent short-seller who hoped to profit from this investment hunch. He made a good living by being skeptical. When others were buying stock, he was shorting stock.[1] At the top of his list was Lehman. Einhorn was convinced that Lehman was a tower of sludge. Fuld had built a franchise, setting the pins in place. Einhorn was now attempting to take one ball and roll a perfect strike. In the process he earned a special brand of disdain from the very top of Lehman. In an April 2008 e-mail to Fuld, former Lehman CFO Goldfarb suggested that if Lehman was successful in getting capital from a joint venture partner, it should use half of the money to buy back Lehman stock, "hurting Einhorn bad." Fuld responded, "I agree with all of it." This exchange demonstrated the priority Lehman management placed on defending the stock price. But whether or not one liked Einhorn's style or his media-seeking persona, the question he asked was valid: Was Lehman actually a weaker company than what it was reporting?

For Lehman, the Great Credit Crisis of 2008 was not the same as the LTCM near-death experience. In spite of all the public relations spinning by Lehman and CFO Callan, something was fundamentally different this time. Now the rumors were built on fact—Lehman had significant skeletons in its closet. Lehman had bet big that prices would continue to rise across residential and global commercial real estate markets as well as that any fallout from the subprime market would be self-contained and not spill over to the Alt-A or commercial real estate market. This time Lehman's exposure was not linked to the $13 billion Russian debt market but cemented to the $14 trillion real estate market. In 1998 less than 2 percent of the firm's equity was exposed to LTCM or Russian-related bonds. By 2008 four times Lehman's equity was exposed to a plummeting real estate market. In 1998 rumors grew because people did not know what Lehman's books looked like. In 2008 the market knew and did not like what it saw.

APRIL 2008: ANGER SETS IN

Fuld was hopping mad. He believed short-seller hedge funds had colluded in targeting and causing Bear's demise, and now they were coming after Lehman. Data from the SEC showed that on March 17, 2008, the first trading day after Bear's sale to J.P. Morgan, naked short-selling (selling shares short without actually borrowing them first) rose on Bear to 1.2 million shares and three times greater than the previous year's peak. Technically, naked short-selling is illegal because it can cause market imbalance by allowing an infinite amount of shares to be sold, putting immense downward pressure on stock price. Was the SEC not enforcing this rule? Another market safeguard, the "uptick rule," which prevents short-selling of securities except on a price uptick, was eliminated by the SEC in July 2007.[2]

The willingness of the SEC to relax market rules and enforcement increased firms' vulnerability to speculative stock attacks. To Fuld these brash underregulated hedge funds were the enemy. They were creating fear and destroying the market's confidence in the Lehman brand. Lehman stock was not getting breathing room to stabilize price, which would allow the firm critical time to find a buyer. The SEC's complacency had helped Einhorn and other hedge funds gain the upper hand. Fuld was agitated enough that by late March 2008 he instructed his legal staff to contact the SEC. It was suspected that the Goldman Sachs London office was the source of damaging rumors that helped to precipitate the run on Bear.[3] The SEC looked into these allegations and, by July, sent subpoenas to fifty hedge funds and other broker-dealers, including Goldman Sachs, seeking trading records and e-mails. On July 21, 2008, the SEC instituted an emergency order prohibiting the short-selling of nineteen financial companies, including Lehman. Fuld's insistence appeared to bear fruit, even though this restriction was temporary, extended in August and finally lifted on August 12, 2008. In this protective bubble, ten stocks gained in value, but Lehman's did not. The wolves were at the door. Once the restriction was lifted, short-sellers resumed their feast.

In the month after the Bear sale, Lehman increased its correspondence with Treasury Secretary Hank Paulson. Fuld was keeping an open pipeline to Beltway decision makers, and Paulson was gaining hard market data he needed in formulating his opinions. On April 12, 2008, Fuld had dinner with Paulson, where Paulson discussed his concerns about Merrill Lynch, also heavily involved in mortgage-backed securitization. He further intimated that he might be working the levers to find a buyer for Lehman. Reports suggest this meeting was tense. Apparently Fuld did not appreciate the advice given by this former Goldman Sachs counterpart. Fuld shot back, "I have been in my seat a lot longer than you were at yours at Goldman. Don't tell me how to run my company. I'll play ball, but at my speed."[4] After this meeting, Fuld sent out an e-mail to the firm's general counsel saying the meeting went well and "we have huge brand at Treasury," meaning that the Treasury understood the importance of Lehman to the marketplace.[5]

MAY 2008: ANGER GROWS

Things got pretty ugly for Lehman in May. By May 19, Lehman's stock closed at $36.81. The stock was at levels not experienced since the height of the run on Bear. Clearly, the market was no longer buying the "we are not Bear" message. Lehman management had good reason to be concerned. The stock price was the most important barometer of the firm's health and, in some ways, was also a scorecard to measure Callan's success in fighting the rumor mill. With the stock in steady retreat, the star appeal that Callan had initially enjoyed was fading. Callan's troubles can be traced to a single day—May 21, 2008. On this day, in a speech before a large group of well-connected investors at the annual Ira W. Sohn Investment Conference, Einhorn came out swinging. He wasted no time in challenging Callan's credibility in Lehman's accounting for real estate investments, pointing out a perceived $1.1 billion discrepancy and questioning why Lehman had not written down the top-of-the-market purchase price of Archstone-Smith.[6] In a public setting, he basically claimed Lehman was full of shit and he was shorting the stock—betting that Lehman stock would fall. At the end of this thirty-minute speech, the doomsayer of Lehman sent another equally important message, this time to Lehman's government overseers. In an eerie foreshadowing he concluded his remarks by stating, "My hope is that Mr. Cox and Mr. Bernanke and Mr. Paulson will pay heed to the risk to the financial system that Lehman is creating, and that they will guide Lehman toward a recapitalization and recognition of its losses—hopefully before federal taxpayer assistance is required."[7] Unfortunately on this day in late May 2008, niether Cox, Bernanke, nor Paulson bothered to attend the conference. Less than two weeks later, Einhorn made other media appearances, including one on CNBC, reiterating his bearish view on Lehman. Albeit Einhorn had self-serving views, now many in the investment world were finally listening—Lehman was at risk of failure.

Lehman responded to these attacks, but the damage had been inflicted. In a matter of weeks, the stock dropped to less than $30 and then less than $20 per share, never to recover. Einhorn and other short-sellers were making money at Lehman's expense. Increasingly, Lehman was looking and feeling like Bear. The only difference was that Lehman was imploding over several months instead of several days. In less than three weeks, the stock dropped another 20 percent, wiping out more than $1 billion in shareholder value. In a lengthy *New York Times* article written by Louise Story on June 4, 2008, Einhorn stated, "Lehman has been one of the deniers," referring to financial firms with real estate exposure.[8] The press painted this story as a boxing match: Einhorn vs. Callan, complete with a half-page full-color picture. Hedge funds might have been hitting below the belt, but Lehman's CFO was losing rounds quickly.

JUNE 2008: TIME TO BARGAIN

In June, Standard & Poor's (S&P) downgraded Lehman's credit rating from A+ to A. This one-notch downgrade increased Lehman's incremental cost in funding daily operations. It also sent a message that market experts were seeing a pronounced weakness not just at Lehman but across the investment banking sector. In this environment, the firm's stock became hypersensitive to any mortgage-related news. The preannouncement of first-quarter earnings in March had briefly put a floor on the stock price. So on June 9, 2008, in another attempt to create a firebreak, Callan preannounced second-quarter earnings, but this time the market turned hostile. Lehman had lost a total of $2.8 billion, much of which came from the sale of 20 percent of the firm's mortgage-related securities. This quarterly loss rocked the market because it was the first in Lehman's fourteen years as a public company. To soften the earnings blow, Lehman announced it was raising $6 billion in fresh capital. On its own, that announcement would have been great news. But the market decided that the significant earnings loss, four times greater than estimates, trumped the benefit of new capital. It also viewed this rushed capital raise as further proof of Lehman's liquidity problems.

That day the market put a sledgehammer to the stock. From the fifty-two-week high, the stock was now down 86 percent. Lehman was on the operating table. It was a race against time if the firm was to be saved. As the stock hit new lows and more wealth evaporated, tension at senior levels reached a boiling point.

On June 12, 2008, Callan was fired, replaced by Ian Lowitt, most recently co–chief administration officer. Lowitt would become the third CFO in less than one year. On the same day, Skip McGee forwarded an e-mail to Fuld from an employee who had just left the firm saying, "Senior managers have to be much less arrogant and internally admit that some major mistakes have been made." The e-mail further stated: "[They] can't continue to say we are great and the market doesn't understand."[9] This was a telling e-mail, revealing that denial and anger were still a part of the Lehman culture.

Other heads rolled on this day as well. With Lehman's balance sheet oozing losses, the stock at new lows, and rumors intensifying, it was time for Joe Gregory, president and COO, a thirty-four-year Lehman employee and close friend of Fuld, to go. During Gregory's tenure it became apparent that he spent too much time focusing on the firm's culture issues and not enough time on risk management. By all measures, Lehman was a riskier shop than before Gregory had filled the number-two spot. Debt had increased by more than $150 billion; Value-at-Risk (VaR), the measure of daily potential market loss, had increased from $25 million to more than $120 million; and leverage had skyrocketed to more than 30 to 1. Later it was reported that Fuld saved his own job by sacrificing Gregory. There is an indication that Fuld was given an ultimatum from his alarmed executive management committee—either Fuld or Gregory, but one scalp had to be taken.

The doomsday real estate bust predicted by Michael Gelband, former head of Global Fixed Income, had come true. The fact that Gregory had fired Gelband in March 2007, the bearer of bad but accurate news, further diminished Gregory's credibility. The decision by Gregory to promote the bright but inexperienced Callan to CFO and her inability to keep the stock price from collapsing was proof enough that senior-level change had to be made. Herbert "Bart" McDade, the former fixed-income and equity head, was Gregory's replacement. McDade had developed a reputation as a hands-on and well-liked manager. He was also known as a prudent risk taker. While Fuld remained CEO and chairman, his power was diminishing. Increasingly, McDade and his handpicked team of executives were making day-to-day decisions. As one of his first acts, McDade rehired Gelband. While rehiring Gelband may have been vindication, it was too little too late. Once McDade and his team began digging into the books, they were shocked at what they saw.

JUNE–JULY 2008: SERIOUS BARGAINING

The market assault on Lehman stock continued. The fire-sale price of Bear had demonstrated the consequences of waiting too long to strike a deal. In a forced sale, the buyer has the upper hand. Though Fuld had reservations about selling, the market looked favorably at a deep-pocketed partner willing to make a sizable investment. A strategic partner could help stabilize a plummeting stock price. This was part of Lehman's strategy since Bear's collapse, but it became increasingly important (and desperate) during the summer.

As early as March, Fuld had instructed Hugh "Skip" McGee, head of investment banking, to see if famed investor Warren Buffett was interested in investing in Lehman. In times of crisis, financial companies often called Buffett for a bailout. Buffett's terms were always stiff, but his willingness to invest could lift market confidence and protect a firm against bankruptcy. Contacted in his Omaha office, Buffett indicated to Fuld a willingness to invest. His terms were straightforward. Lehman would get $5 billion in needed capital, and Buffett would get the equivalent value in preferred shares yielding 9 percent, able to be converted at a stock price of $40.[10] Fuld hung up the phone and did some research. Buffett's terms were discussed internally and determined to be above market rate. Fuld respectfully declined the offer. Within the week, Lehman went directly to the market and successfully issued preferred stock at the lower 7.25 percent, and with a more favorable stock conversion rate. But in declining Buffett's offer, Fuld had said no to one of the smartest and most well-respected investors in the world, a refusal that reeked of hubris and short-sightedness.

Other partnerships explored that spring included the Korea Development Bank (KDB), with which Lehman negotiated for a $5 billion capital infusion. This government-backed bank had plenty of capital, and an inked deal would have let the market know that Lehman's franchise had secured a safe harbor. Discussions with KDB took various twists and turns, but consensus remained elusive. By June 2008, once Lehman's second-quarter multibillion-dollar losses were announced, alarm bells were set off at the Treasury and the pressure—let's get Lehman sold—began in earnest.

Paulson continued to be in frequent contact with Fuld, now taking his calls on a daily basis. From this period on, Paulson began *urging* Fuld to find a partner. Back in April, Paulson had planted a seed by encouraging Barclays Plc (Barclays), a large London-based commercial bank, to start talks with Lehman. Paulson approached General Electric CEO Jeffrey Immelt, but he declined. HSBC Holdings Plc was also approached, but talks did not advance. By July Paulson indentified Bank of America as another potential buyer. On July 21, 2008, Fuld met with Ken Lewis, Bank of America CEO, and indicated that he wanted at least $25 per share. At the time, Lehman stock was trading around $18. Though the size of Lehman's mortgage-backed securities portfolio was known in the market, discussions with Bank of America broke down when it saw that the sheer size of the illiquid commercial portfolio exceeded $37 billion. Bank of America only wanted Lehman's good assets; Lehman needed to sell its bad assets.

By August discussions with KDB intensified. Talks with Barclays also picked up. Barclays had a small presence in investment banking, and Lehman seemed like a good fit. But neither deal moved forward. Paulson later admitted he was frustrated with the overinflated value Fuld had placed on Lehman. Viewing the value of his firm through a 2006 prism, Fuld did not readjust the price for the new market dynamic. This higher-than-market price tag most likely hindered finding a buyer.

JULY–AUGUST 2008: DEPRESSION

Fuld was losing the internal battle to keep his employees' hearts and minds. As the largest ownership block of Lehman stock, employees had a vested interest in Lehman's survival. Many had the bulk of their net worths tied up in Lehman, and much of their stock was restricted by a three- to five-year period before it could be sold. Employees began to feel helpless as their life savings evaporated. On TV, Internet, radio, and print the news was all about Lehman. The dramatic fall in stock value became a justifiable preoccupation across the firm. From London to New York to Tokyo, employees kept the stock ticker symbol LEH on their computer monitors to measure the health of their company. Trust in the internal communication coming from the top floor of the Lehman headquarters, known as "Club 31," was breaking down.

To fill this void, employees looked to other sources. At first, employees discreetly used headsets to follow market pundits predicting the fate of Lehman, but by midsummer the headsets were off and the volume turned up as employees were transfixed by TVs tuned to CNBC, Bloomberg, and others. Many employees scanned the Wall Street tabloid Dealbreaker.com, which had been one of the more accurate to date, to read the latest gossip on Lehman and its battle to survive. Lehman employees found humor in the tabloid's unofficial slogan, "if your firm is on Dealbreaker it might be time to find a new job." On July 3, 2008, CNN Money published a damaging online article outlining how Lehman had lost its way, emphasizing the likelihood of a Bear Stearns–type collapse or a sale. The word was out: Lehman was in trouble and had to move quickly.

The market remained skittish. On July 11, 2008, in response to general market rumors that Freddie Mac and Fannie Mae might have to be bailed out, Lehman stock dropped another 17 percent. The firm was thrown into a state of turmoil. In response, Fuld joined many other broker-dealers pleading to the SEC for help against the growing army of short-sellers. In a further attempt to save the body, Lehman started cutting off appendages, including 6 percent of its workforce. Lehman's turmoil was visible to the outside world, giving more credence to Einhorn's hunch. If he was correct, for the next quarter, Lehman would have to write down billions more in bad real estate bets. Lehman had two times as much capital as Bear, but the size of its bets was about three times greater than Bear. Lehman was also losing its external battle (measured by stock price and the inability to attract a joint partner).

Recall that back in March 2008, the repo desks at Lehman were busy calling clients, discounting collateral, and making margin calls. They were the aggressor, exercising prudent risk management. By June the tide had turned, and Lehman was on the other end of these calls. Its largest clients were nervous. During the past five years, the growth of the firm's prime brokerage operation mirrored the rapid growth of the hedge fund industry. In almost lockstep, hedge funds began withdrawing billions of dollars and putting a squeeze on Lehman's cash flow. Lehman also received a flood of hedge fund requests that the firm rewrite business contracts so that cash retained was legally segregated from Lehman's general account. This reduced the chance that Lehman would use these funds to meet day-to-day operating expenses. It was another sign that hedge funds, some of Lehman's largest customers, were preparing for a possible bankruptcy.[11] The troops in the trenches, like those on the repo desk, knew all was not fine, but the generals in Club 31 kept spinning positive nonsense. In one attempt to ease employees' minds, Alastair Blackwell, head of Lehman global operations, addressed his team in late July. He started the meeting by urging employees not to believe the rumors floating around. All is well, and Fuld personally had told him that he expected next quarter return on equity to top double digits. Based on Fuld's actions, it appears that he might have truly believed his own press releases.

But Lehman was a very sick company, and denial or lack of comprehension of its true state was not an acceptable defense. Blackwell's monotone message fell on deaf ears. The market had changed, but all in the room knew Lehman had moved too slowly to keep up. As Blackwell finished his speech, he could not help but look more at his shoes than at the group he was trying to comfort. He would have been more credible if he had borrowed a line from an 1862 letter by Emanuel Lehman, one of the firm's original founders. Responding to economic hardship caused by the blockades of the Civil War, Emanuel Lehman had simply stated: "Everything is over."[12] Nearly 146 years later, his premonition was coming true.

During the third week of August, Lehman stock staged a mini rally, up 16 percent for the week on news that KDB was still in discussions to buy Lehman. Shareholders were pinning the future of Lehman on this single deal. Just as J.P. Morgan had rescued Bear, KDB could do the same for Lehman. Then news began to leak that KDB was having difficulty attracting partners in the deal and experiencing regulatory hurdles. Realistically, Lehman had no remaining options without some kind of government intervention. With the significant second-quarter losses, sizable mortgage portfolio, and real estate prices that continued to decline, it was too difficult for Lehman to find a partner or an outright buyer. Employees sensed this and depression fully set in. Without warning, management sent out an e-mail immediately prohibiting all employees from selling Lehman stock. Now even if employees wanted to, they had no way to cut their losses. They were strapped to a ship that was sinking fast.

Chapter 14

The Death of Lehman, Regulation, and Investment Banking

After 158 years, Lehman's fate hinged on the events of fourteen days in September 2008. Lehman's stock, the most important barometer of market confidence, was in free fall. Trading partners and clients ran for the door, and essential funding was cut off. Chairman Dick Fuld and his lieutenants were in crisis mode. Numerous strategic partners were contacted but none materialized. The federal government attempted to help, but then, at the last minute, lost its resolve. In the span of one week, the same government that applied the "too big to fail" doctrine to save two of the nation's largest mortgage financing firms was unwilling to do the same for Lehman. Was the House of Lehman sacrificed to show that free market discipline still worked and excessive risk taking would be punished? Once the government's decision was made, there was no crisis planning to allow for an orderly bankruptcy, and the market responded with great displeasure. Lehman trading partners ducked for cover, systemic risk was unleashed, and a global financial panic ensued. Trillions of dollars were lost as investors stampeded out of the market.

The desperate situation was proof that both government regulation and "self-regulation" had failed. Those appointed to police Wall Street had fallen asleep, and excessive risk taking had permeated the market so thoroughly that auto-correction was out of the question. Attempting to calm the growing meltdown, Congress begrudgingly approved the Troubled Asset Relief Program (TARP), a $700 billion bailout and a series of other targeted programs to help prop up the financial market. The nominal value of government-backed guarantees would register in the trillions. By the end, a large English commercial bank and a Japanese securities firm went bargain hunting, the Fed rushed to grant special banking powers, and the death of investment banking became complete.

SEPTEMBER 2008

For Lehman, September provided no respite from the August swelter. In mid-August, the Securities and Exchange Commission (SEC) had lifted the temporary short-seller ban, and the pent-up imbalance of sellers immediately pushed Lehman stock to less than $14 a share. The market had turned into a giant wrecking ball looking for companies that were built on risky mortgage-backed securities. Among these fragile companies were the nation's two largest mortgage finance companies, Freddie Mac and Fannie Mae, both of which became the next scheduled for demolition. Dick Syron, the embattled CEO of Freddie Mac and a former president of the Federal Reserve Bank of Boston, had spent the summer with hat in hand attempting to raise needed capital. Wall Street was not willing to save this damaged company. As government-sponsored lending factories, Freddie Mac and Fannie Mae generated $6 trillion in mortgages in 2007, keeping billions of dollars in works in progress on their balance sheets. Their government-imposed mandate to lend to median- and lower-income borrowers coupled with their drive for high profit caused them to relax credit standards. Through the Department of Housing and Urban Development (HUD) social policy for affordable housing, Congress had inadvertently exposed the U.S. mortgage market to greater credit risk.[1] Loan delinquency data were disturbing. Rates for mortgages made in 2007 were now higher than the 2006 vintage, indicating that the U.S. housing woes were much greater than initially expected.

At the epicenter of the crisis when the housing and credit bubble popped, highly leveraged Freddie Mac (60 to 1) and Fannie Mae (20 to 1) were left holding billions in risky subprime mortgages. Even though subprime mortgages represented only a portion of holdings, increasingly, market rumors pointed to insolvency. Stocks in both companies dropped to less than $5 per share from fifty-two-week highs of more than $50. With no private buyers, the market backed the government in a corner. These mortgage giants controlled half of the mortgages issued in the United States. Bond investors in these companies included foreign governments such as China and India. If Freddie Mac and

Fannie Mae failed—in the middle of a hard-fought presidential campaign no less—a crisis of confidence could spread through an already weak U.S. housing market.

These unfolding crises conflicted with the free market ideology that had pervaded at the Federal Reserve (Fed) since President Ronald Reagan had appointed Alan Greenspan chairman in 1987. According to Greenspan, free markets self-regulate, fix themselves, and should not break down. Yet the housing and credit bubbles were proof that when free markets stray off course, government intervention may be necessary.[2] Over Labor Day weekend 2008, on the heels of the Bear rescue, Treasury Secretary Hank Paulson and Fed Chairman Ben Bernanke met and agreed that government takeovers of Freddie Mac and Fannie Mae were the best options.[3] Initially, $200 billion was committed, which later doubled in size.[4] In a snap of a finger, both firms were deemed "too big to fail," and the free market ideology of the Greenspan-era was again cast aside.

Paulson made the news official on September 7: Fannie Mae and Freddie Mac were put in conservatorship and nationalized—the largest government-engineered takeover in U.S. history. This action validated the market's long-held belief that the government would honor its implicit guarantee backing the two lenders. Equity shareholders in both companies were wiped out, but bondholders were protected. As part of the nationalization, the government acquired an 80 percent ownership stake in each, replaced the CEOs, and provided both companies with a capital lifeline of up to $200 billion. This takeover, combined with the Bear rescue, confirmed to the market that the government was willing to put money on the table for companies deemed vital to the economy. Investor Warren Buffett publicly endorsed the government's bold move as exactly what was needed. In response to the takeover news, on Monday, September 8, the stock market rallied with the Dow Jones Industrial Average (Dow) closing up almost 300 points. The government's aggressive actions appeared to have worked.

TUESDAY, SEPTEMBER 9

If the time was right for celebration, Lehman spoiled the party. On Tuesday, September 9, rumors circulated that the merger negotiations with Korea Development Bank (KDB) to buy a stake in Lehman had fallen through. Even as Lehman stock tumbled, Fuld was unwilling to accept a price less than $17 a share. Now, even at $8 per share, KDB was no longer interested. The single thread of hope supporting the stock had been cut. The stock price dropped

45 percent, the largest one-day decline in Lehman's history. The firm had a market value of about $5 billion, six times less than it had one year earlier. At less than $8 per share, the stock was trading at pizza prices. The market was placing its bets on a Lehman bankruptcy. Credit default swap (CDS) insurance on Lehman now cost more than 500 basis points, an increase of 100 basis points.

Lehman's heavy reliance on the overnight repo market to support daily operations had become its Achilles' heel. The firm was borrowing short term to fund long-term assets. In good times, lenders were willing to accept asset-backed securities (ABS), residential mortgage–backed securities (RMBS), and commercial mortgage–backed securities (CMBS) as collateral and provide Lehman with $180 billion in daily loans. Now, with a crippled stock price and doubts about Lehman's survival, many trading partners stopped doing business with the firm or extracted more onerous terms. On September 9, Steven Black, the co-head of J.P. Morgan investment banking, called Fuld demanding that Lehman post additional securities and cash of $5 billion. J.P. Morgan was acting in its own best interests, but at Lehman's expense. In a matter of days, Lehman's liquidity, access to cash, and market brand were evaporating.

Lehman's third-quarter earnings were not scheduled to be released until September 18, but rumormongers forced the firm's hand. As in the previous two quarters, Fuld knew the earnings news needed to get out fast. On Wednesday, September 10, newly appointed CFO Ian Lowitt preannounced third-quarter losses of $3.9 billion, after $5.6 billion in real estate–related write-downs. Residential and commercial real estate exposures were reduced by 31 percent to $17.2 billion and by 18 percent to $32.6 billion, respectively.

On this early morning earnings call, Lehman also outlined a three-pronged survival plan: raise capital by selling Neuberger Berman, its profitable asset management business; spin off its troubled commercial real estate assets; and slash its dividend from 68 cents to 5 cents.[5] These actions would also reduce Lehman's skyrocketing leverage ratio. On this call Fuld chimed in, "We have a long track record of pulling together when times are tough." But the billions in fresh quarterly losses only confirmed what the market already knew—Lehman was a tower of sludge. The market responded by further punishing the stock. That same day Lehman received even more bad news—Moody's was preparing to downgrade the firm unless it found a strategic partner. The horror film was rolling, and Fuld and his lieutenants could only sit and watch in disbelief. Reminiscent of the 1950s science-fiction thriller *The Blob*, mortgages had morphed into a toxic substance, engulfing the firm and surrounding financial community and then spreading globally. By Thursday Lehman stock traded for less than $5 per share. Somewhere, David Einhorn and other short-sellers were smiling.

NO FRIENDS TO BE FOUND

The run on Lehman was a highly visible event, reflected in the single-digit stock price, rising media attention, increase in CDS rates, volume of short sales, panic on the faces of Lehman executives, and mass exodus of large trading partners and customers. In the last six months, Fuld and his investment banking team had reached out to numerous prospects—Bank of America, Barclays, GE, HSBC, Morgan Stanley, and KDB—but had no takers. Lehman was in imminent danger of collapse. The market knew it. Hank Paulson and the Fed knew it. And Fuld knew it. The Fed also believed—incorrectly—that this well-telegraphed risk had given investors ample time to prepare for a possible Lehman bankruptcy.

For Bear, the definitive shove came from Goldman Sachs; for Lehman, J.P. Morgan had the honor. On Thursday, September 11, J.P. Morgan cut off Lehman credit. Through the years, J.P. Morgan had been the firm's clearing bank, which meant once a Lehman trade was made, J.P. Morgan was responsible for transferring the cash and securities. J.P. Morgan also supplied Lehman with working capital loans that kept the lights on. During the first week of September, J.P. Morgan had stepped up and lent Lehman in excess of $100 billion in overnight loans. If Lehman went bankrupt, being its banker meant a significant loss. J.P. Morgan had reached the same conclusion as others—the risk of lending to Lehman was too great. At day's end, J.P. Morgan froze $17 billion in cash and securities. Lehman's liquid cash position was now dangerously low.

Lehman was in a vulnerable state and needed a friend. Abandoned by its clearing bank and with only $1 billion in cash remaining, Lehman turned to the Fed's newly created broker-dealer facility to stay afloat. Surely Lehman could rely on Mother Fed to help. But that Thursday the Fed refused. Instead, responding to the growing market turmoil, the Fed increased its collateral requirements—and much of Lehman's collateral was deemed nonconforming. Lehman's collateral was no different than that posted days before by rival firms, but now the Fed was shutting the window. In essence, by September 11, Lehman was deemed "small enough to fail." It would have to live by and die by the free market sword.

Even if the Fed wouldn't help, Lehman still thought it had a friend in Washington. There was no one better equipped to understand and fix Lehman's plight than Paulson, backed by the government's balance sheet. The Treasury secretary reported directly to President George Bush, the first sitting U.S. President with a Harvard M.B.A. They were businessmen at heart and understood financial markets can quickly bury a firm.

Another reason Fuld thought he had a friend in Washington was as simple as "family comes first." The Treasury secretary might have worked at Goldman Sachs, but his younger brother Richard had chosen Lehman. For more than a decade, Richard had worked as a fixed-income salesman in Lehman's Chicago office. Could Paulson let his own brother down? Lehman also had several other family connections to the White House. Since 2007, Jeb Bush, the president's brother, was a paid advisor to Lehman's private equity business. In addition, the president's second cousin, George H. Walker IV, was global head of Lehman's profitable investment management division. With these close family connections surely Lehman would get Washington's utmost attention. But it appears the family ties only heightened Paulson's sensitivity to the appearance of favoritism. A principled businessman turned politician, Paulson had to walk a tight line. He would help Lehman but only at arm's length.

On the previous day, Wednesday, Paulson received unsettling news from New York Fed President Tim Geithner that Lehman's cash position made it unlikely it could open for business on the following Monday.[6] Jumping to action, Paulson took the reins. He intended to get Lehman sold, doing what Fuld could not. On September 11, Paulson called Bob Diamond, CEO of Barclays. Barclays had already had discussions with Lehman, but the phone call rekindled interest. Diamond had great aspirations for his bank, seeing it as a universal bank modeled after such powerful European banks as Deutsche Bank, UBS AG, and HSBC. Owning a global broker-dealer franchise would bring him closer to this dream. In this conversation, Paulson towed a hard line, indicating there would be no government money to help with the deal. Diamond appeared to understand this condition. Even without government assistance, the idea was intriguing to Diamond. Seeing a unique opportunity, Diamond and a few other senior executives boarded a late-night commercial flight to New York. Shortly after arriving on Friday, September 12, Diamond was picked up by Fuld's chauffeur and driven to Lehman headquarters, where he was whisked up to Club 31 to meet with Fuld. In this meeting, Fuld offered his resignation if it would cement the deal. Afterward, Diamond and his team proceeded to the law firm of Simpson Thatcher & Bartlett LLP, where they pored over Lehman's books. From the start, they were struck by the size and concentration of commercial real estate positions. Quickly, Diamond concluded that without government assistance, a deal could only be made if the bad real estate assets were stripped out.

Back in July, Fuld's inflated asking price had turned off a lukewarm Bank of America. But now the potential to pick up a brand-name franchise on the cheap intrigued Bank of America CEO Ken Lewis. Unlike Diamond, Lewis had never had a strong desire to own an investment banking franchise. But he, too, had dreams of turning his bank into a universal bank that could compete with J.P. Morgan or those abroad. Though owning Lehman was not a core part of his corporate strategy, at the right price a deal might make sense. Earlier in the week, Bank of America had contacted J. C. Flowers & Company, a New York private-equity firm, which agreed to team up. By Friday, September 12, Lewis and others assembled at the law firm of Sullivan & Cromwell LLP to look at Lehman's books. They completed due diligence. In a distressed situation, Fuld understood the benefits of multiple suitors. Bear proved what can happen to stock price when there is only one willing buyer. A call was also placed to Nomura Holdings Inc., Japan's largest brokerage shop. Nomura declined, indicating it could not move fast enough. Still on Friday, September 12, Lehman had two interested buyers. Its survival hinged on sealing a deal.

EMERGENCY MEETING AT THE FED

On September 12, while teams from Barclays and Bank of America were busy assessing the risk of buying Lehman, the government was busy setting up an emergency rescue meeting. Paulson, Geithner, and SEC Chairman Christopher Cox—the Three Musketeers—made calls to top banking executives. Though the goal was simple—hold a weekend powwow, sell Lehman, and extinguish the flames of a global financial crisis—the means to achieve this goal were not clear. Worse still, the Three Musketeers had no reliable way of measuring what the fallout would be if they failed. It was uncharted territory, and they were flying by the seat of their pants. The series of meetings was set to start Friday evening and last until mission accomplished. A deal had to be done by Sunday. The Federal Reserve Bank of New York, a seventeen-story fortress at 33 Liberty Street, served as the war room. The fate of Lehman was in the hands of this very tight fraternity.

Although Lehman was billed as the weekend's top attraction, the Fed had other problem children. Merrill Lynch, the nation's third largest investment bank, had also aggressively pursued a mortgage-backed securities strategy. In contrast to Lehman, Merrill had acknowledged its billions in losses and replaced senior management, but its stock was still decimated. Clients and trading partners were departing, and liquidity was being squeezed. Confidence in Merrill as a stand-alone firm was in question, and CEO John Thain knew the fate of Merrill was inextricably tied to Lehman's. He, too, needed to find a partner fast.

The Fed's third problem child was AIG. Actually, it was the adopted problem child. The Fed did not have regulatory oversight responsibility for the insurance giant but felt forced to act. For Paulson, Geithner, and Cox, AIG symbolized all that was wrong with the shadow banking system. These lightly regulated non-banks controlled a growing percentage of global capital, and their proclivity for exploiting regulatory gaps and placing risky bets increased the chance of inflicting economic harm.

While AIG's core franchise of insurance underwriting was financially sound and regulated by a web of state regulators, other more dubious activities were not as safe. The Financial Products division, located in London, proved to be a small but deadly tumor. Operating outside of regulation, this group churned out $500 billion in credit default insurance (e.g., CDS). In less than a decade, the highly rated AIG became the world's largest CDS bookie, initially reaping enormous profits. The main buyers were major banks, hedge funds, and others wanting to speculate, hedge, or meet regulatory capital requirements. Despite a mountainous portfolio of CDS, AIG did not hedge this risk, considering the chance of default low. By 2008, the improbable events AIG had insured against—but not hedged against—were beginning to happen. Real estate price declines, mortgage delinquencies, defaults, and company bankruptcies spiked well above historical norms. During the summer of 2008, the rating agencies began to downgrade mortgage-backed securities en masse. These rating actions triggered billions of dollars in collateral calls and exposed the riskiness of AIG's CDS-driven strategy.

In a matter of weeks, AIG ran into liquidity problems. By the summer of 2008, one Lehman employee who worked in the operations area remembers having to call AIG on a daily basis in an attempt to gain additional collateral. By the first week of September, market-driven cash demands intensified. In another week, AIG estimated its cash shortfall would be $6 billion, increasing to $25 billion the following week. In a virtual avalanche, holders of CDS insurance were calling in their bets. The previously highly rated AIG also had credit exposure. Rating agencies were threatening to downgrade the firm (and subsequently did) by the following Monday (September 15), an event that could trigger additional margin calls of up to $18 billion. In the unregulated $60 trillion CDS market, trading was done over the counter and there were not standardized credit requirements to minimize credit risk. Having taken on significant exposure, AIG did not have enough cash or credit to cover its bets.

If AIG failed, firms across the globe that thought they were hedged would be exposed. The Wall Street elite—Goldman Sachs, J.P. Morgan, Morgan Stanley, Merrill Lynch, and Lehman—all had AIG exposure. Goldman Sachs alone had $13 billion in AIG exposure. Only a year earlier AIG stock was trading above $80; now it was selling for $12 per share. Similar to Lehman, AIG was running out of cash. As Lehman and LTCM had in a time of need, AIG's CEO Robert Willumstad now made a desperate call to Buffett. This time Buffett wisely passed. The market deathwatch was on. Rumors swirled that Washington Mutual, Wachovia, and Citigroup were mortally wounded. Even Goldman Sachs and Morgan Stanley appeared to be teetering.

Getting the Wall Street elite together in one room, locking the doors, and twisting arms to solve a crisis was not a new idea. Such tactics had assisted in averting financial meltdowns with the rescue of Bear and the orderly wind-down of Long-Term Capital Management (LTCM) a decade earlier. This time around Lehman was on the operating table, with Merrill Lynch and AIG in the waiting room. In attendance at the emergency rescue meeting were CEOs and senior executives from major firms such as Goldman Sachs, Morgan Stanley, J.P. Morgan, Merrill Lynch, Credit Suisse Group, and Citigroup. On the previous day, to avoid appearance of conflict of interest, the Fed requested that Fuld resign from the Federal Bank of New York's board of directors. He quickly complied. He was also not in attendance at the rescue meeting. Representing Lehman were recently minted president Bart McDade and newly rehired executive Alex Kirk, former head of global credit. Since replacing Joe Gregory in June, McDade was calling the day-to-day shots. Fuld's physical absence at this critical meeting was further proof of McDade's growing power.

That Friday evening, Geithner wasted no time challenging the assembled to find a "private" solution in rescuing Lehman. The meeting was then turned over to Paulson. At a table surrounded by a virtual Who's Who of banking, he made it clear the government was not willing to foot the bill for a Lehman takeover, nor would it provide a backstop guarantee. The rescue of Freddie Mac and Fannie Mae only a week earlier had provided enough political consternation for the Bush administration. This time around moral hazard would not be exacerbated. Without providing details, Paulson indicated to the group of bankers that there were two potential bidders. Geithner then suggested that a Lehman bankruptcy could be "catastrophic" and the damage hard to contain. In addition, SEC Chairman Cox emphasized the importance of putting aside competitive differences and working together to restore the health of the market.[7] The bankers were being asked to help Lehman, but they had their own self-interests to protect. Many in the room had benefited as Bear's and Lehman's larger customers looked for a safer home. Now they were being asked to help a wounded competitor. Some in the room, including Goldman Sachs CEO Lloyd Blankfein, questioned why. They were responsible for saving their own backsides, not that of rivals or the American people. In setting the time clock, Paulson indicated that Lehman was unlikely to open on Monday. They had forty-eight hours to solve the problem. The government would serve as moderator.

With the ground rules laid out, the bankers were divided into three working groups: Goldman Sachs and Credit Suisse were assigned valuation of Lehman's bad assets; Morgan Stanley, Merrill Lynch, and Citigroup were asked to determine the various structures that could be used to sell Lehman; and the remaining bankers, led by Bank of New York–Mellon, prepared for a Lehman bankruptcy. The first series of meetings lasted well into the late evening, with the group agreeing to meet again early the following morning.

SATURDAY, SEPTEMBER 13

Dressed in more casual attire, the bankers began to stream into 33 Liberty Street by 8:00 A.M., and the Lehman rescue meeting reconvened. Geithner and Paulson updated the group that Barclays was now the only potential buyer. After a closer look at Lehman's books and without government financial support, Bank of America had gotten cold feet. By Saturday, Ken Lewis was not returning Fuld's calls. That morning, Merrill Lynch's Thain stepped out of the group meetings to call Lewis at his home in North Carolina. Realizing the increasing fragility of his own firm and the likelihood of a Lehman bankruptcy, Thain suggested they talk. He wanted to save his own skin and was not responsible for Fuld or the broader market—that was the role of government.

Lewis was interested in Thain's overtures and quickly turned his attention to acquiring the hobbled Merrill Lynch. Secretly, they met in Bank of America's corporate apartment in the Time Warner Center. That afternoon, Thain notified Paulson of the deal between Merrill Lynch and Bank of America, which Paulson quickly approved. Bank of America had abandoned Lehman on the way to the altar for what it perceived to be a healthier, more beautiful bride. After less than forty-eight hours of due diligence, Bank of America announced publicly it had made the deal. Merrill Lynch, the third largest investment bank, was saved. One problem child was taken care of.

That same Saturday, as Merrill Lynch was heading toward safe harbor, AIG was on a collision course with an iceberg. At the behest of Fed officials,

AIG CEO Willumstad was summoned to the New York Fed. At this meeting, Willumstad quickly confirmed AIG's liquidity crisis. Markets continued to move against AIG's enormous CDS positions and collateral calls had drained it of available cash. That evening, Willumstad also indicated that a Lehman bankruptcy would substantially increase the cash calls on his firm. To withstand such a storm, AIG indicated it would need to raise $20 billion. Paulson, Geithner, and Cox had a problem. Saving an investment bank such as Bear may have stretched Fed doctrine, but bailing out a giant insurance company over which the Fed had no direct regulatory authority was really pushing the envelope.

SUNDAY MORNING: DEAL DONE . . . THEN UNDONE

As Lehman's sole bidder, Barclays had increased leverage to dictate terms. The working group of bankers determined that the commercial real estate assets on Lehman's books were at unrealistically high prices. The bad assets were burning a multibillion-dollar hole in Lehman's balance sheet. To get a deal done, these bad assets would need to be carved out. By that evening, the syndicate of bankers hammered out their private solution. It was agreed that $50 billion in risky commercial real estate would be transferred to a separate private entity and backstopped by the participating banks. The bankers were agreeing to take on the role the government was no longer willing to assume. With this private backstop in place, Barclays agreed to buy Lehman. Bob Diamond would run Lehman, and Fuld would be out. Around 10 A.M. Sunday morning, Bart McDade e-mailed Michael Gelband, who had his sleeves rolled up at Simpson, Thatcher & Bartlett LLP assisting Barclays in its due diligence.[8] Cloistered in Club 31, the increasingly detached Fuld was notified. After a harrowing ride, a plummeting stock price, and a near-death experience, Lehman would live to trade another day. The price was considerably less than the Friday closing price of $8 per share, but it was a price. Paulson, Geithner, and Cox were pleased.

The only remaining hurdle was obtaining regulatory approval from the Financial Services Authority (FSA), the UK equivalent of the Fed. Approval was assured, as long as the FSA stuck to its script. Yet, as Sunday progressed the FSA refused to waive the shareholder-approval requirement or allow Barclays to back Lehman's debt until a vote occurred. If Lehman wanted a deal, it would have to go through a lengthy shareholder approval process—time the firm didn't have. The interim gap could be bridged if a temporary U.S. government guarantee was obtained. This was similar to the terms used to entice J.P. Morgan to buy Bear. But Paulson remained unwavering. True to the nickname he earned playing college football, "the Hammer" came down. No government assistance would be given. With no government guarantee, no other takers, and not enough cash to open for business the next day, Lehman had exhausted its options. In an instant, Lehman had gone from being rescued to being out of luck. After going to such great lengths over the weekend, the government men in the room were willing to throw in the towel.

FINALLY, ACCEPTANCE

The bankers assembled at the Fed for another day of meetings were surprised to learn FSA approval was not forthcoming, and the tone that morning was somber. A Treasury official summarized it well in a noon e-mail to colleagues: "We lost the patient." News of pending doom swept through Lehman, and many employees, worried about being locked out of the building post-bankruptcy, arrived at the office to fill up boxes with their personal belongings. By Sunday afternoon the government summoned the undertaker, Harvey Miller of the law firm Weil, Gotshal & Manges. The message communicated to Miller was loud and clear—he needed to file before the markets opened on Monday. A Lehman filing required a full board of directors vote.

The political winds had shifted. The pitchforks were out and taxpayers were mad, and their congressmen were too. Paulson had expended too much political capital on Bear, Freddie Mac, and Fannie Mae. The government had no reliable way to measure how a Lehman bankruptcy would systemically affect the market. It was as if there were a scale with further populist outrage on one side, and on the other, the ripple effects of a major bank crashing. For reasons impossible to explain clearly, Paulson, Geithner, and Cox rolled the dice on Lehman crashing.

This fateful decision was first communicated to McDade, who was left to tell Fuld the devastating news. What Fuld heard made him want to throw up.[9] He was shocked by Paulson's unwillingness to provide a lifeboat. Perhaps unfairly, the Lehman brass accused the former investment banker of turning his back on one of his kind. In terms of time spent, Paulson had clocked in more hours in discussions with Lehman than with Bear, Freddie Mac, or Fannie Mae.

A more valid criticism of Paulson and his colleagues was the utter lack of preparedness for such an event. Lehman had operations in twenty-eight countries with clients spanning the globe. Bankruptcy would trigger defaults on billions of dollars of debt and assets held to the vagaries of bankruptcy courts.

Many clients would lose the ability to access their accounts. Credit default swap contracts written on or by Lehman in the billions would be redeemed. At the time, the government did not have "resolution authority" to put Lehman in conservatorship, reorganization, or a wind-down.[10] Going into the weekend rescue meeting, knowing this should have motivated Paulson and others to formulate an anything-else-but-bankruptcy strategy. The Fed, Treasury, and SEC had a duty to understand more fully how their decision would impact the broader market and plan accordingly. As part of this decision process, it was surprising that a comprehensive crisis management plan to shore up market confidence was not developed and executed. Instead, the government washed its hands of Lehman and walked away. Later, Paulson would use the lack of "resolution authority" as the reason why he could not rescue Lehman. This does not negate the fact that a crisis management plan would have softened the blow to the market. It remains unclear why more government resources were not dedicated to the real chance that a bankruptcy would occur and how best to manage it.

By Sunday afternoon, SEC Chairman Cox addressed Lehman's board members via conference call and in a stern voice stated they had a fiduciary duty to shareholders. He indicated he did not want to interfere with corporate governance of the company but made it clear his preference was for Lehman to file bankruptcy. This was an unprecedented action. With that said, Lehman's board had run out of options and voted unanimously (Fuld included) to file. Racing against time, Lehman's lawyers worked through the night to prepare the filing. Around 2:00 a.m. Monday, September 15, 2008, the Chapter 11 documents signed by CFO Ian Lowitt were filed in the U.S. Bankruptcy Court in the southern district of New York. The largest bankruptcy in U.S. history was official.

That Monday the market woke to news that Merrill Lynch had been rushed to safety and Lehman pushed into bankruptcy. The bankruptcy announcement was made before the market opened, and LEH was delisted from the NYSE. A 158-year-old company that had weathered many a storm was no more. The nation's third and fourth largest investment banks were gone. Bear, the fifth largest, had been disposed of in March. Three pillars of Wall Street had vaporized. In response that day, the Dow lost more than 500 points, or 4.4 percent. It was the largest single-day drop since the market opened after the 9/11 terrorists attacks. The Lehman bankruptcy eventually helped push the Dow down by more than 4,000 points to below 6,700 in March 2009. A deep recession that had been only a possibility was now a market reality. A financial Armageddon had occurred.

SYSTEMIC RISK UNCORKED

The willingness of the Fed and the Treasury to allow Lehman to fall triggered a cascade of market events that shook the global financial market to its core. The market had received mixed messages. Only months earlier, testifying before the Senate Banking Committee on April 3, 2008, Geithner demonstrated that he understood the potential systemic risk associated with Bear, using it to justify Fed financial assistance. At this hearing he stated:

> . . . [I]t became clear that Bear's involvement in the complex and intricate web of relationships that characterize our financial system, at a point in time when markets were especially vulnerable, was such that a sudden failure would likely lead to a chaotic unwinding of positions in [an] already damaged market.[11]

Geithner's statement reinforced the market consensus that Lehman would be rescued. The government had many months to correct this public view, if it was not accurate. The rescue of Freddie Mac and Fannie Mae on September 9 also reinforced the belief that Lehman was too important to let fail. In one fateful weekend, Geithner, Paulson, and other government officials had changed their tune. They decided to let systemic risk out of the bottle. Government inaction actually *increased* the chaos it was supposed to protect the market against. Once Lehman announced its bankruptcy, the market was left completely on its own. Naturally, panic set in as the market readjusted to the fact that the government would not behave as expected. Running for cover, investors acted in ways the Fed did not think possible. Though government officials may have determined that Lehman was not "too big to fail," they had overlooked the fact that it was "too interconnected to fail."

No sooner had Lehman filed than the Reserve Management Company, the oldest money-market fund in the United States, received a flood of redemption calls. Since 1971, the company's flagship fund, the Reserve Primary Fund, was a popular place for corporations (and wealthy investors) to park excess cash. Money markets were liquid, higher yielding than banks, and safe as cash. Investors bought and sold ownership shares on a net asset value (NAV) basis of $1 per unit. Through the years to increase yield, the Reserve Primary Fund substituted lower-rated corporate commercial paper for higher-rated U.S. Treasuries. Of this fund, approximately 1.2 percent ($785 million) was made up of Lehman commercial paper. Rating agencies, including Moody's and Standard & Poor's, rated the fund AAA.

By September 2008, the money-market industry had grown to more than $3.5 trillion, and the Reserve Primary Fund held in excess of $60 billion of this market. The Reserve Primary Fund was a rock-solid fund for rock-solid investors. Yet the Lehman bankruptcy made investors behave strangely. On Monday, September 15, 2008, redemption requests from the Reserve Primary Fund swelled to $5.2 billion. By the end of the day, this total exceeded $20 billion. By Tuesday, redemptions doubled from the previous day. There was now a run on the Reserve Primary Fund. It made no logical sense. In times of uncertainty, cash is where investors put their money. This was an AAA-rated fund, as good as cash, and almost 99 percent Lehman-risk free, yet investors wanted to grab their money and run. The requests overwhelmed the Reserve Primary Fund and it limited redemptions, but not before over-drawing its account at clearing agent State Street Bank in Boston. Starting on September 15, 2008, the Reserve Primary Fund was no longer able to find a buyer for Lehman commercial paper. It decided to hold on to this paper and arbitrarily priced it at a 20 percent discount. Even at this liberal valuation, the NAV dropped to 99.75 cents.

Externally, management continued to indicate to the market that the fund did not drop below a $1 net asset value.[12] While not yet public knowledge, the Lehman bankruptcy had actually triggered the Reserve Primary Fund to "break the buck." The sacred $1 market was breached.[13] In Fed speak, this was a Code Orange—a sign of how swiftly the market was becoming unhinged. The credit markets were beginning to freeze.

On that same Monday, September 15, the market also staged a run on AIG. Shares dropped an astonishing 61 percent. Shareholders also fled from Goldman Sachs and Morgan Stanley, the last two independent investment banks still standing. By market close, it was clear that letting Lehman fail had unleashed an entirely new set of dangerous circumstances. Paulson, Geithner, and Cox had their work cut out for them. Following the Lehman bankruptcy, Bernanke become instrumental in the government's crisis management strategy. By lunchtime, the exhausted group of bankers was back at 33 Liberty Street, this time to help save AIG. Geithner started the meeting with a well-worn (and failed) script, preaching that no financial support from the government was forthcoming and pushing the bankers to find a private solution. J.P. Morgan and Goldman Sachs were chosen as the lead banks to find a solution. That afternoon, the public rating agencies also downgraded AIG debt, triggering even more calls for posting collateral. At this late stage of the game, the working group was not able to find a private solution. The shock waves of Lehman's failure put much more urgency on saving AIG. The government could not afford to make the same mistake they had made with Lehman. By early the next morning an internal consensus was reached that AIG could not fail.

TUESDAY, SEPTEMBER 16

On Tuesday morning, AIG was out of cash and preparing to draw down its remaining credit line, a final sign of desperation. Geithner relayed this distressing news to Paulson, who then worked with Bernanke to put together a bailout.[14] This process included an emergency meeting held at the Board of Governors in Washington, D.C., the policy arm and overseer of the entire Federal Reserve System. The Fed specifically made the case that AIG was "too big to fail." Bernanke even pointed out that AIG was on the top-ten list of the most widely held stocks in 401(k) retirement accounts.[15] Paulson notified Congress. An agreement was reached that AIG would be provided with an $85 billion loan at an interest rate of 11.5 percent. In return, the government (that is, U.S. taxpayers) received an equity ownership stake of approximately 80 percent. This loan represented 1 percent of the Fed's balance sheet. The rescue eventually cost taxpayers $180 billion. Similar to Freddie Mac and Fannie Mae a week earlier, AIG was nationalized. Without voting, the American people became majority owners of the world's largest risk-taking insurance company. The announcement was made after market close.

One day after Lehman's bankruptcy, the vultures also arrived. A giddy Diamond announced that Barclays had reached an agreement, subject to regulatory and court approval, for buying the trading and investment banking operations of Lehman. This included nine thousand employees. In a $1.75 billion deal, it also acquired Lehman's valuable headquarters building and its New Jersey data center. Barclays would have paid several times that figure if it had agreed to purchase Lehman before the bankruptcy. By waiting just two days, netting out the value of office buildings, Barclays was able to pick up the best parts of Lehman for less than $300 million.

It was a given that Fuld was not a part of Barclays' purchase. The first order of business was to dismiss Lehman's real estate cowboy, Mark Walsh, and most of his risk-taking team.[16] The second order of business was pulling down, floor by floor, the green Lehman signs, replacing them with the more conservative blue Barclays signs. Shortly afterward, Nomura Holdings snatched up Lehman's Asia-Pacific operation for $225 million and the European and Middle Eastern operations for a token $2 dollars. With this move, Nomura gained 5,500 employees. Nomura played its cards well. In declining

Fuld's last-minute solicitation and sitting on the sidelines as the U.S. government let Lehman fall, it profited.[17] Similar to J.P. Morgan's purchase of Bear, Barclays and Nomura got steals. This time the bargain basement price was set by government inaction instead of government action.

Though AIG had been saved, the fallout from systemic risk continued to grow. On Tuesday, September 16, the Reserve Primary Fund officially disclosed to the market it had broken the buck. The NAV had dropped to 97 cents a share. The most secure of investments was no longer safe. The market's response to this news was similar to one stick of dynamite igniting an entire string. Money-market redemption activity spread to other brand-name firms, including Vanguard, Fidelity, Federated, and Dreyfus. Redemptions were heavy even on funds that had no Lehman exposure. Boston's Putnam Funds announced it would close its flagship $12 billion fund. The buck had not been broken in this fund, but investors wanted out. In a counterattack, the Fed pumped $70 billion of extra liquidity into the market, but banks continued lending less, not more.

With money-market redemptions at historic highs and funds shutting down, it became difficult to find buyers for commercial paper. This set off yet another powerful market explosion. Companies with strong credits began to find it virtually impossible to issue lower-risk paper in a market with no buyers. Lehman, the original detonator, had set off a market avalanche.

WEDNESDAY–FRIDAY, SEPTEMBER 17–19

On September 17, Paulson received an alarming call from Jeffrey Immelt, head of GE, indicating that GE was having problems issuing commercial paper at reasonable or predictable rates.[18] If GE, one of America's most successful brand names, was having difficulty using short-term paper to raise funds, the credit markets must be in serious turmoil. The Fed now had a real-life example of the consequences of systemic risk. The market—not Paulson, Geithner, or Cox—was firmly in control. In three days, the Dow dropped more than 1,000 points. The market was producing other disturbing news.

With two shaky independent investment banks remaining, short-sellers began aggressively targeting Goldman Sachs and Morgan Stanley. Of the two, Morgan Stanley appeared the most vulnerable. CEO John Mack tried to stomp out the market rumors as had Fuld, but the market was winning. It appeared that what happened at Bear, Lehman, and Merrill Lynch was going to happen again. Paulson and Geithner told Mack that he needed to follow Merrill Lynch's example and find a partner fast. At the time, Mack spoke to

Citigroup CEO Vikram Pandit, but a merger between two sick firms did not make sense. By day's end, the market had dropped another 400 points. For the day, Morgan Stanley stock was down 24 percent and Goldman Sachs stock was down 14 percent. Combined, these firms had lost $15 billion of shareholder wealth.

By Thursday, the credit markets were seizing up globally. Banks were not lending to each other or to customers. In synchronized destruction, markets from Europe to Asia were in disarray and plunging. The sudden death of Lehman had triggered a run on banks around the world. Confidence had left the system, and banks that had trusted one another were now hoarding valuable cash. Short-sellers were out—Britain enacted a monthlong ban on short-selling. In Russia trading had been suspended for two days. Together, these actions qualified as a global financial meltdown. The consequences of allowing Lehman to fail had been far greater than anticipated. One thing was clear: systemic risk, though difficult to define, was authentic.

The financial firefighters who helped fuel systemic risk were now attempting to put out the flames. Paulson, Geithner, and Bernanke were forced to take drastic measures, crafting TARP. This multibillion-dollar financial-market rescue package was made on the fly, in the heat of a crisis. On Monday, September 15, 2008, there wasn't TARP. By that Friday, it had been invented. Bernanke, falling back on his academic studies of Depression-era economic policies, took an active role in devising TARP. This plan called for removing bad assets from bank balance sheets and replacing them with cash, which would strengthen bank financials and thaw out frozen credit markets. The government would buy toxic securities (CMBS, RMBS, and ABS) that the market no longer wanted. Similar to the Resolution Trust Company model used two decades earlier, the government planned on holding these assets and selling them back when the market stabilized. Paulson was the face of the bailout plan, appearing in front of Congress asking for $700 billion. If approved, it would be the largest one-time expenditure in U.S. government history. The Treasury, not the Fed, would be responsible for disbursing the funds.

On Thursday, once word leaked out to the market that a more comprehensive plan was being formulated, the Dow moved up more than 400 points, the largest single-day climb in six years. Paulson, Bernanke, and Cox met with various congressional leaders to discuss their master plan. Representative Barney Frank, Democrat from Massachusetts, and chairman of the House Financial Services Committee, indicated that it could not be only a Wall Street bailout; Paulson emphasized that a collapsed banking system would certainly hurt Main Street.[19] After much discussion, a plan was hammered out. Before the markets opened on Friday, September 19, Paulson also announced a temporary guarantee program for money-market funds. These guarantees would have a nominal value of $4 trillion. The Lehman collapse had started the Reserve Primary Fund stampede that infected the broader market; now the government was stepping in with massive government guarantees to restore market confidence. At this meeting, the Treasury also provided additional details on TARP as well as a proposal to temporarily raise the FDIC insurance limit to $250,000 per account holder.[20] TARP ensured that a list of critical banks would receive exceptional government assistance and that greater FDIC insurance would lessen depositors' fears. The market responded favorably to the news, and the Dow experienced another triple-digit move up. For the first time, it appeared that the government had a more comprehensive plan and was not just reacting to market events in ad hoc fashion.

DEATH OF INVESTMENT BANKING

Morgan Stanley's and Goldman Sachs' stock ticked up but remained under pressure. Both firms appeared to be sitting ducks. Moving quickly, these firms contacted the Fed and requested bank-holding company powers. In the past, the Fed used this power sparingly. If approved, it would allow the firms to expand their funding bases to raise capital through customer deposits and the Fed discount window instead of through the volatile shorter-term funding (e.g., repo) or broker-dealer lending markets. As bank-holding companies, these risk-taking investment banks would be under tighter regulation, held to higher capital standards, and required to reduce firm leverage.

Two months previously, in July 2008, Lehman had approached Geithner with a similar request. At the time, Geithner appeared unreceptive to the idea, indicating to Fuld that this would not solve Lehman's underlying problem of toxic assets. Not gaining Fed support, Lehman never pursued a formal application. On Sunday, September 21, 2008, Fuld must have been dumbfounded. The idea he had floated to Geithner and that was dismissed just two months ago now got fast-track treatment. From start to finish, it took the Fed only forty-eight hours to evaluate the application and announce that both firms had become bank-holding companies. This decision helped to stabilize Goldman Sachs and Morgan Stanley, marking the legal deaths of the last two bulge-bracket Wall Street investment banks.

Chapter 15

The Enablers and the Deciders

Throughout the history of Lehman Brothers, its success rested squarely on its ability to navigate the capital markets and strike the delicate balance between risk and return. Since inception, Lehman was infused with an entrepreneurial spirit and perceived itself as an underdog. The firm demonstrated through the years its ability to change, find new profit opportunities, and thrive. But by the early 2000s, Lehman had strayed off course, using greater leverage, putting more firm capital at risk, and placing large bets on real estate.

This attraction to uncontrolled risk didn't happen overnight and was not isolated to Lehman. Every bank on Wall Street was drunk on the overinflated real estate market. To survive the financial crisis, many of the major Wall Street risk takers became Troubled Asset Relief Program (TARP) takers. Lehman and these other banks were not blind to the risks of their financial structures, nor were they unaware that risky bets could end up disastrously. But it is safe to assume that the bankers as well as the government agencies responsible for monitoring banks never thought systemic risk was widespread enough to cause the Great Credit Crisis of 2008. Before the House Banking Committee on October 24, 2008, former Federal Reserve (Fed) Chairman Alan Greenspan indicated that the crisis was a "once-in-a-century credit tsunami." If this were true, the storm that hit Lehman was not a natural disaster but man-made.

THE ENABLERS

How could a system as sophisticated as the global financial market, where some of the most educated people on the planet trade and share information at lightning speeds, be brought to its knees? In the wake of this disastrous albeit manmade storm, there has been an ongoing struggle to explain what happened.

A good place to start is the Long-Term Capital Management (LTCM) meltdown, which only a decade earlier demonstrated how leverage combined with excessive risk taking in a single trading firm could affect the global markets. Perhaps because government intervention staved off a worldwide chain reaction then, bankers and policymakers assumed that systemic risk was easily contained. Even more important, there was a general consensus among economists and officials that derivatives—yes, the very financial contracts that led to the LTCM collapse—*protected* the global markets from systemic risk. The theory was that the highly leveraged market provided a cushion by redistributing the risk throughout the global markets. In 1998 Deputy Secretary of the Treasury Lawrence Summers told Congress: ". . . parties to these kinds of contract are largely sophisticated financial institutions that would appear to be eminently capable of protecting themselves from fraud and counterparty insolvencies."[1] And in 2004, referring to derivatives Greenspan said, "Not only have individual financial institutions become less vulnerable to shocks from underlying risk factors, but also the financial system as a whole has become more resilient."[2] Policymakers didn't just understate systemic risk, they also failed to comprehend the extent to which derivative instruments of U.S. banks headquartered in the world's largest economy could magnify risk. Though systemic risk is not strictly an American export, not having a sound U.S. banking regulatory framework impacts the world's entire financial system.

Most observers now also agree that the Fed under Greenspan made an error in judgment by suppressing interest rates too long after the collapse of the dot.com bubble. But this only created the petri dish where the failed experiments took place. Who is to blame for the risky failures themselves? With respect to the role of the federal government, two distinct factions have emerged. One faction insists the government meddled too much with the housing market through the policies of the Federal Housing Administration (FHA). This group also points to the lowered lending standards prescribed by the Department of Housing and Urban Development (HUD) and endorsed by Congress, spurring the derivatives market for subprime lending. On the opposite side is the contingent that argues it was the very lack of government regulation that directly led to the crisis. This camp cites the dismantling of the Glass-Steagall Act, the relaxing of leverage restrictions, and the complete lack of Securities and Exchange Commission (SEC) oversight when it came to banks overdosing on mortgage- and asset-backed securities.

Neither viewpoint is completely off the mark. The U.S. government is so entangled with the capital markets through so many different agencies that it becomes possible for competing interests to emerge from under the same giant umbrella. Having a broader understanding of who should be held accountable is instructive when deciding what reforms are needed to mitigate future systemic risk. Congress, the banking oversight committees, the Fed, and the SEC all played roles—not to mention the media, academics, accountants, independent rating agencies, lobbyists, and consumers. Except for the contrarian who argues that none of the above was to blame—everybody was acting with acceptable (or understandable) levels of self-interest that unfortunately culminated in the crisis—a more assertive analysis might conclude they were all responsible. Collectively, this group might be called the Enablers.

When it comes specifically to Lehman, there has been no shortage of finger pointing at chairman and CEO Dick Fuld and senior management. Perhaps less outrage has been directed at the Lehman board. But any list of enablers must begin at the top with both Fuld and the board of directors.

Dick Fuld

No one has taken more heat for Lehman's downfall than Fuld. Google his name and much of what is written is a social commentary on unbridled greed, anger, and public disgust. Since September 15, 2008, he has been dragged in front of Congress, reportedly punched in the nose by an irate employee, called names, slapped with countless lawsuits, and forced to sell a trophy apartment on Park Avenue. He has also lost a large family fortune. In the process, the prideful Fuld lost something even more valuable—his reputation. The popular view is that Fuld's stewardship was the sole reason for Lehman's demise, suggesting that the more than two hundred partners and twenty-eight thousand employees located in twenty-eight countries were powerless. In this view, Fuld was a master puppeteer, controlling his followers like marionettes. This explanation might make a great movie, but it has one major flaw. It does not account for the many other firms on Wall Street engaged in similar risky and destructive practices.

Many of these firms reported losses exceeding Lehman's. Some even declared bankruptcy before Lehman. From 2008 through 2009, more than

170 banks were shuttered. None of these excessive risk takers were under Fuld's thumb. If Lehman was the only big banking firm engaging in destructive behavior, Treasury Secretary Hank Paulson could have walked away from Lehman without uncorking larger systemic risk, and the Great Credit Crisis might never have occurred. Fuld's leadership during the early 2000s closely resembled that of nearly every Wall Street CEO. Only J.P. Morgan's CEO Jamie Dimon seems to have started, barely, to prepare his institution for the onslaught. This book has suggested that the concentration of risk taking in the hands of one person—in Lehman's case, Fuld—was *partially* responsible for the poor decisions that led to Lehman's demise. Certainly the hyper-growth of Lehman made it a hard firm to manage using Fuld's autocratic approach. Yet Citigroup, where the CEO had little daily oversight over the core risk-taking areas, proves that a bank can go too far in the opposite direction. At Citigroup, risk responsibility appears to have been spread so wide that it was as if nobody could claim it.

As already discussed, there is also the possibility that Fuld simply didn't understand the mechanisms being used to generate such lavish profits. This theme has gained traction among academics and regulators but misses an important point that leads to a broader explanation. If not Fuld, at least somebody—actually numerous people—at Lehman understood the implications of derivatives. Lehman was an originator and purveyor in derivatives. Insider accounts have suggested that Fuld led the firm from such a lofty position that employees who disagreed had no voice. Maybe. Even if we accept the notion that the majority of employees and shareholders were led blindly or forced into submission by Fuld—a dubious claim at best—there is another group that does not deserve a "get out of jail free" card.

Board of Directors

The risk-taking culture of a firm is defined in part by the board of directors. An active board should help determine how much risk to take in the pursuit of profit. It provides a counterbalance to management. Boards, along with CEOs, have a fiduciary duty to represent the best interests of shareholders and protect the long-term interests of the company. This independent voice is essential to good corporate governance. Board participation influences a firm's risk tolerance, especially by looking for danger signs before financial harm is inflicted. Above all, boards are not supposed to be a rubber stamp for management. Boards monitor risk-taking behavior through various subcommittees. Two of the board-level committees at Lehman that were important control points were the Finance and Risk Management Committee (FRMC) and the Compensation and Benefits Committee (Compensation Committee). Lehman also had an Audit Committee and a Nomination and Corporate Governance Committee. Through these four core committees, directors could look into the firm's day-to-day operations.

Lehman's board of directors consisted of ten high-profile individuals, many of whom had served for a decade or more. In 2007, the full board met eight times. For their oversight roles, nine of Lehman's directors each received more than $365,000 in compensation, one-third paid in salary and the rest in stock. Multimillion-dollar error and omission insurance polices were also provided to insulate directors against lawsuits. These directors were busy, serving on an average of three outside boards. Some members continued to operate their own companies. These captains of industry included former CEO John Akers (IBM), John Macomber (Celanese Corp.), Thomas Cruikshank (Halliburton Co.), Sir Christopher Gent (Vodafone PLC), Roland Hernandez (Telemundo), Michael Ainslie (Sotheby's), Roger Berlind (theater producer), and Marsha Johnson Evans (Red Cross). Nine board members were retired, four were more than 75 years old, and only two had financial services experience. Until 2006, actress and socialite Dina Merrill, the eighty-three-year-old daughter of E. F. Hutton, had served eighteen years as a board member. The newest director, Jerry Grundhofer, former chief of US Bancorp, came on board in April 2008 well after the damage was done. At sixty-three, he was the youngest director and had the most current financial industry experience. Rounding out the board was the illustrious eighty-year-old Henry Kaufman.[3]

While skilled in their respective industries, many of Lehman's directors did not have relevant experience or knowledge of securitization, modern financial derivatives instruments (CMBS, RMBS, ABS, CDS), or the type of risk taking Lehman increasingly deployed. Directors were aware that many of these derivative transactions provided double-digit annual returns but did not grasp the potential risk of illiquid derivatives combined with high leverage and inadequate capital. And while it is not realistic to assume that directors would have an intimate knowledge or understanding of complex trading products, directors should understand the broader implication of the type and level of risks being taken. A director might not know how to construct a CMBS, but he or she should know the implications of holding these instruments, and the inherent risk as a percentage of firm capital.

By far Kaufman was (at one time) the most market-savvy and astute board member. He had been on the board since the firm went public in 1994. If there was one board member who should have kept Lehman out of hot soup, it was Kaufman. He was a former Salomon vice chairman and past economist at the Federal Reserve Bank of New York. He had previously served on the Freddie Mac board and had an intimate knowledge of the mortgage markets. He even endowed a chair at Columbia University in the rigorous study of the financial industry. *Business Week* dubbed him one of the greatest financial thinkers of our time. Kaufman's upbringing was also strikingly similar to the firm's three founding brothers, Henry, Emanuel, and Mayer Lehman. Son of a cattle trader, he was born in a small German farming village and immigrated to America in his youth. During his storied Wall Street career, he had developed a reputation as a Cassandra and earned the nickname "Dr. Doom." He had a nose for sniffing out trouble and making profit. In his book *On Money and Markets*, published in 2000, Kaufman identified derivative instruments as fueling a dangerous explosion of credit. He stated that economic conditions have accelerated the growth of such derivatives but cautioned that no one knows how these instruments might perform in an economic downturn—all astute observations prophetically linked to the collapse of Lehman.[4]

Henry Kaufman

Of the ten board members, Kaufman was the most logical choice to head Lehman's FRMC. Part of this committee's role included evaluating the firm's buildup of concentrated bets in commercial and residential real estate. At Lehman, in less than a decade, real estate bets went from being a portion of firm equity to four times greater than firm capital. This concentrated bet on real estate grew under the FRMC's watch. Commercial real estate origination in 2005 was $27 billion, jumping the next year to $34 billion, and in 2007 hitting a record $60 billion. According to a Goldman Sachs' analyst report published in March 2008, Lehman held more commercial real estate on its books than any other Wall Street firm, in excess of $10 billion more than its nearest competitor, Citigroup, and two times more than Bear Stearns, J.P. Morgan, or Morgan Stanley. The board had access to this information long before such a revealing report was published.

An additional risk-management measure that was communicated to the board and highlighted the growing risk trend was daily Value-at-Risk (VaR). From 2004 to 2007, Lehman's VaR jumped fourfold, exceeding $120 million. Simply stated, by 2007 the company increased its wagers. It was now willing to lose up to $120 million in a single trading day. By the first quarter of 2008, the actual losses turned out to be much greater. Even though the FRMC only met twice a year during 2006–2007, the fact that the committee allowed greater concentrated bets to be placed on real estate and had frequent access to VaR reports showing this escalating risk proves the members were willing to accept higher risk taking.

Sitting atop of the FRMC, Kaufman was responsible for providing solid oversight. As the board's chief financial fireman, he had the duty to warn of smoke and to put out the fire. Yet the House of Lehman burned under his watch. In April 2008 Kaufman had the audacity to go on record and comment on the global credit crisis, criticizing the Fed for "providing only tepid oversight of commercial banks."[5] Outside of his Lehman board duties, Kaufman continued to demonstrate trading acumen. In December 2007 and January 2008, he made timely sales of $2 million in Lehman-related stock options. It is surprising that Kaufman did not push for the firm to diversify its trading portfolio. Providing such an independent voice would have been especially valuable in 2006 and 2007.

Not only did Lehman's risk taking increase without greater scrutiny from the Kaufman-run FRMC, but the board also allowed Madelyn Antoncic, Lehman's capable head of risk management, to be demoted and removed from daily assessing the firm's risk taking. Her replacement did not possess nearly the same level of risk management experience, weakening this important control point. The board also permitted Fuld to keep a dual role as chairman and CEO, a role he had since 1994. In many corporations of Lehman's size and complexity, such roles are separated. It is not hard to imagine how beneficial another set of eyes looking at Lehman's mounting risk levels would have been. And by second quarter 2007, as other Wall Street firms reported financial losses and rival boards replaced the CEO in charge, at Lehman no top management change was ever made. Even as Lehman reported historic losses and the stock plummeted, the decisions to replace the firm's president and the CFO were not initiated by the board. The internal fire drill that ensued on September 14, 2008, when Paulson, Treasury Secretary Timothy Geithner, and SEC Chairman Christopher Cox pushed Lehman's board to vote on bankruptcy is further evidence that the board was not proactive.

Lest you think this book is unduly focusing on Lehman's board, take the following into consideration. Since the adoption of the Sarbanes-Oxley Act, there has been increased analysis of corporate governance and Lehman has been no exception. Lehman established a Nomination and Corporate Governance Committee, chaired by Marsha Evans, a retired navy officer. Based on the report card Lehman eventually received, it appears that this committee functioned in name only. The Corporate Library, an independent corporate-governance rating firm located in Portland, Maine, initiated coverage on Lehman in 2002. Using a rating scale of A (strongest) to F (weakest), this firm originally assigned Lehman a D rating. In 2003, the corporate governance rating increased to B but then fell to C. In 2004, the rating dropped to D, and by 2008 it was an F. From a pure corporate governance standpoint, Lehman had been weak for many years. These poor ratings were well known in the industry, yet no material change was made to Lehman's board structure. Increasingly, the level and sophistication of risk taking was greater than the level of board sophistication and oversight. Nell Minow, co-founder of The Corporate Library, reached this same conclusion in prepared testimony to Congress on October 6, 2008. Referring to Lehman, she stated, "A company that had $7 billion in losses after becoming embroiled in the global credit crisis has a risk-management committee that did not understand or manage its risk."[6]

Although the products Lehman was now trading and warehousing on its balance sheet were complex even for the Ph.D. mathematicians who designed them, that was no excuse for board members to avoid understanding the risks involved. Maybe board members were reluctant to learn about the risks because the perceived profits were so significant, or they did not want to rock the boat. This same misguided complacency may have also influenced the incentive system in place at Lehman. The board-appointed Compensation Committee was responsible for ensuring excessive risk taking was not encouraged through excessive compensation. At Lehman, the chair of this four-member committee was John Akers. Since the firm's 1994 initial public offering, Lehman's stock compensation plan was expanded to a larger number of employees. By 2008 approximately 90 percent of employees (twenty-six thousand) participated in some form of compensation in addition to base salary. Lehman was following standard industry practice in setting aside about 50 percent of the firm's gross income for compensation. More than half of Lehman's compensation was paid out in stock, not cash. This made firm stock an important tool to motivate employees.

One of the fastest ways to increase stock price is by increasing revenue. From 1994 to 2007 Lehman's profits had increased from $75 million to $4 billion, more than a fiftyfold increase. This board-approved compensation scheme made Lehman employees the single largest holder of company stock. The second largest single holder was Fuld. The Compensation Committee had an important balance to strike—incentivize employees to make money without blowing up the firm. In 2007, this board also awarded Fuld total estimated compensation in excess of $34 million, making him one of the highest-paid CEOs on Wall Street. Mark Walsh, the firm's risk-taking real estate cowboy, was reportedly paid tens of millions of dollars. It seems uncertain at best that the Compensation Committee struck the balance accordingly. Detailed records of board minutes and activities are not public yet, but it appears that the board just stood idly by or was ill-equipped to fulfill its oversight role.

Congress

Freddie Mac and Fannie Mae were created by Congress. As stated throughout this book, both Democratic and Republican administrations over-promoted home ownership—a policy of good intentions turned bad. Without this initial support and subsequent nurturing, Freddie Mac and Fannie Mae would not have grown into the nation's two largest mortgage-lending factories. By keeping billions of dollars flowing, they were the engines of the housing boom. Their business models were simple: borrow money made cheap by the implied government guarantee and lend it out at higher rates. Greenspan referred to this market advantage as the "big fat gap." At the peak of the housing boom, Freddie Mac and Fannie Mae controlled about half the mortgages in the nation's multitrillion-dollar market. These exchange-traded companies had private and public missions. In the last two decades, the mandate to expand loans to median- and lower-income borrowers increased. Lending standards decreased, setting a lower bar for other mortgage originators. Official oversight of Freddie Mac and Fannie Mae was through the Office of Federal Housing Enterprise Oversight (OFHEOO),[7] an agency that lacked the staff, sophistication, money, and political support needed to be an effective control point. To many in Congress, Freddie Mac and Fannie Mae were the gateway to putting more families in homes. Congressional policy certainly fostered a greater risk-taking environment, which Lehman eagerly participated in.

Congressional Committees

While the daily oversight of financial institutions is left to regulatory agencies such as the Fed and the SEC, Congress has two banking oversight committees specifically designed to ensure that financial institutions were acting according to regulations and laws. The twenty-three-member Senate Banking Committee is chaired by Connecticut Democratic Senator Christopher Dodd. Before 2007, Alabama Republican Senator Richard Shelby was head. This committee is charged with creating broad financial policy and ensuring institutions operate in a healthy, responsible manner. This committee also holds investigative hearings after a financial fire to determine how to minimize future ones.

The second banking committee is the House Financial Services Committee, chaired by Massachusetts Democratic Congressman Barney Frank. He took over this role in 2007 from Mike Oxley Jr., a Republican congressman from Ohio.

These committees are run by elected officials who most often possess no basic working knowledge of complicated capital markets or how regulation, competition, economic growth, and cost of capital combine to influence bank risk-taking behavior. On Capitol Hill possessing an M.B.A. is an oddity. Under the watch of both of these committees, the banking industry experienced its worst financial storm since the Great Depression. While both chairpersons took office well after the seeds of the crisis had been planted, these committees dropped the ball at least a decade ago in not seeing or responding to the growing risk-taking trend of the regulated and shadow banks. In fact, several banking laws were *relaxed* (notably the Glass-Steagall Act), which heightened the crisis. Congressman Frank may be quick to shout back to his detractors that the financial crisis was not his fault, but such comments fail to address why Lehman and many other financial firms failed under his committee's watch. The answer is that there were years of regulatory neglect and weak oversight.

The Fed

As protector of the financial system, the Fed should be independent of the interests of the commercial banks it regulates. While banks have a duty to create shareholder value, which requires taking varying degrees of risk, the Fed's role as central regulator is to ensure that such risk taking does not harm the economy or the financial well-being of citizens. By design, these two parties—regulator and regulated—should not have aligned interests, and the Fed chairman needs to be cognizant of this independent role. It's well documented that many of the largest commercial banks regulated by the Fed increased their risk-taking activities in mortgage securitization. The Fed did not fully embrace the stronger capital requirements outlined in Basel II. Equally well documented is the Fed's inaction as the subprime bubble grew. Since Congress passed the Home Ownership and Equity Protection Act in 1994, the Fed had sweeping powers to regulate predatory lending practices but instead took a hands-off approach. The Fed also supported the repeal of the Glass-Steagall Act in 1999. And while the Fed has no direct oversight responsibility for broker-dealers, the repeal of this act encouraged greater risk taking by commercial banks eager to expand into investment banking. In retaliation,

Lehman and similar firms increased their own risk profiles. The housing bubble had reached its zenith, yet even as late as May 2007 the Fed took the position that the subprime crisis was contained and would not have a spillover effect. In this Wild West atmosphere, the central regulatory body charged with economic forecasting and oversight of banks did not do its job.

When it became obvious in the Lehman crisis that help was needed, the Fed was slow to react. Lehman's financial condition had been deteriorating since 2007, and publicly reported losses surfaced after the first quarter of 2008. Fuld was a sitting member on the Federal Bank of New York's board. Yet the Fed-initiated emergency rescue meeting was not held until three days before Lehman's collapse. If the Fed had set up a meeting even as late as June 2008—immediately after Lehman had announced billions of dollars in losses—it might have given the firm enough time to find a partner.

From a safety and soundness perspective, the Fed has an army of examiners charged with examining banks and assessing risk. Were they not aware of the increase in risky activities? It appears many did not have the training, background, or monitoring systems needed to adequately measure risk before it grew out of control.

The SEC

During the past decade, the SEC allowed risk to accelerate by removing numerous barriers while not rigorously enforcing already existing rules. Most important, the SEC loosened leverage limits on broker-dealers in 2004, and under the guise of modernizing and simplifying, they eliminated the "uptick" rule in 2007. And as the market distorted, the SEC did not enforce laws relating to certain prohibited short-selling activities.

Like the Fed, the SEC seemed woefully unaware of how severe the crisis was until it was too late. By June 2008 the SEC had completed a full written examination report on only 6 of the more than 140 broker-dealers it regulated. The Fed and the SEC need to be held accountable for their contributions to Lehman's failure. These regulatory control points failed to slow down excessive risk taking.

The Media

Timely, accurate, and insightful reporting remains an inherently strong component of a vibrant capital market. Armed with better information, investors make better decisions. Starting in 2003, with rare exceptions, the media—

including TV, print, and the blogosphere—failed to sound a consistent alarm about the growing real estate bubble or the potential consequences.

America has numerous media outlets that race to cover breaking business news and growing trends. Cable television provides three 24/7 stations—CNBC, Bloomberg, and Fox Business—dedicated to business reporting, as well as financial entertainment programs such as Jim Cramer's "Mad Money." All these networks have "experts" with facts, figures, and prognostications who had many opportunities to uncover and report on the looming crisis. It's well documented on YouTube videos how cable TV interviewers routinely laughed and rolled their eyes at stockbroker and pundit Peter Schiff, one of the few investors (and not a committed short-seller) who did consistently sound alarm bells as far back as 2006. Anyone who dares to suggest during a bull market that the economy is fundamentally unstable too frequently receives the moniker "doom and gloomer" or "alarmist."

While it is understandable that soft journalists, those focused on pumping up market confidence, missed the growing danger, it doesn't explain why the more venerable print media such as the *Wall Street Journal*, *New York Times*, or *Financial Times* missed it. Only *The Economist* consistently warned of an American housing bubble. Financial bloggers, who usually take pride in reporting what the "mainstream media" misses, did not fare much better. How to explain this? One school of thought states simply that the warning signs were not picked up by an investment public—including the media—blinded by a bull market. Journalists rely heavily on analysts, executive insiders, investors, and other experts to help shape their view and understanding of financial issues. Yalman Onaran of *Bloomberg News* supports this view, indicating that in such an environment, "if most of the sources provide a similar outlook, it is hard for the contrarian view to shine through." Another reason might be that financial journalists tend to write for Wall Street elites, not for the average consumer, investor, or citizen. Increasingly, media outlets mirror a consumer-driven society, becoming marketing mouthpieces that do more selling than telling. Wall Street was happy to be sold on the idea that all was well. The sophistication gap also has to be considered again. The multitrillion-dollar derivatives market is obscure, and the media did not fully understand the interconnected role that mortgage-backed securities played in the global markets.

Had reporting been more comprehensive and timely, it could have served as a counterbalance to the speculative real estate race to the bottom. The extreme view holds that the media, by building up unrealistic expectations of real estate prices, actually helped fuel the housing bubble. A more nuanced view might suggest that even had there been a louder chorus of warnings, they would have been ignored. Again, few people believed that the failure of one bank would freeze the world's financial markets.

Academics

If journalists get a pass for ignorance or overreliance on unenlightened sources, what about academics? Economists from universities around the world had a unique vantage point to indentify and sound the alarm about risky banking practices and the growing housing bubble. Unlike journalists, they were trained (in theory) on how the financial markets worked. Despite the specialized training, few in academia saw the looming global crisis, or, if they did spot it, they failed to comprehend the widespread damage once the bubble burst. New York University professor Nouriel Roubini was a notable exception. As far back as 2006, Roubini suggested that the country was likely heading toward a catastrophic housing bust that would send shudders through the global markets. Unfortunately for Roubini, naysayers in a bull market tend to get labeled the lunatic. In August 2008 the *New York Times Magazine* ran a profile of Roubini entitled "Dr. Doom."[8]

The Great Credit Crisis of 2008 revealed a blind spot of many economists, in particular the overreliance on models that do not adequately capture the human element of the market. A decade earlier, LTCM demonstrated the weakness in modeling and how seemingly unrelated market events can cause systemic risk. Economists wielding mathematically driven models inappropriately assumed markets were stable and would behave as written on blackboards. But people, not models, move markets. During the Credit Crisis, as the global markets became unhinged, participants behaved in improbable ways. Repo markets, money markets, and commercial paper markets—perceived as lower risk—shut down nearly simultaneously. Many economists understood real estate prices could not increase indefinitely, but they failed to comprehend the impact if this asset class were no longer accepted as collateral. Models failed to measure the profound impact of human panic and liquidity risk.

Faulty models do not fully explain why academics missed the looming crisis, though. In the last thirty years, the economics profession adopted a free-market bias that influenced how risk was measured and policy was shaped. In this environment—which permeated right- and left-leaning professors—financially engineered derivatives that redistributed risk were hailed as proof of market efficiency. Even University of Chicago professor and conservative author Richard Posner admits that academics took a wrong turn. Posner wrote, "Excessive deregulation of the financial industry was a government failure abetted by the political and ideological commitments of mainstream economists, who overlooked the possibility that the financial markets seemed robust because regulation had prevented previous financial crises."[9]

Accountants

Ernst & Young was Lehman's long-standing accounting firm. As a gatekeeper, its primary duty is to evaluate company financials independently and to attest to the accuracy of the balance sheet and income statement. In theory, this independent stamp of approval strengthens the integrity of the financial markets. Financials are evaluated on a quarterly basis. Fees paid by Lehman to Ernst & Young for audit services exceeded $30 million in 2007. To the market, a large portion of Lehman's perceived value and ultimate risk resided in its commercial and residential mortgage holdings. Ernst & Young was charged with applying fair-value accounting principles to ensure that reported financials were accurate. In none of its audits did they issue an ongoing concern letter that would have alerted the investment public to issues of financial stability.

The deterioration of the real estate market began by 2007, but significant balance sheet write-downs by Lehman lagged the industry by more than a year. The ABX index used to price subprime mortgage-backed securities dropped significantly. Competitors with similar portfolios were marking down these positions, realizing billions of dollars in losses by the second quarter of 2007. Lehman was the exception. For the second quarter of 2008, Lehman filed its 10-Q with the SEC. These Ernst & Young–approved financials showed that Lehman's most illiquid assets—those called Level 3 with no direct observable market value—declined only slightly to $41.3 billion from the stated $42 billion at the 2007 fiscal year end. Why didn't the accounting firm push for timelier write-downs? It was the accountant's duty to help investors see through the mist shrouding these crumbling assets. If David Einhorn, a non-CPA, was successful at uncovering trouble, why wasn't Lehman's accounting firm? If Ernst & Young had flagged the toxic assets earlier, market forces would have driven Lehman to address the problem sooner. Conversely, not disclosing these losses sooner should have given Lehman more time to find a buyer.

Credit Rating Agencies

The Fabulous Three credit rating agencies—Moody's, Standard & Poor's, and Fitch—also play an important watchdog role in capital markets. Their ratings, or *opinions*, help investors evaluate the risk of debt instruments.[10] The assigned ratings also help determine an issuer's cost of capital. Credit rating agencies rely on an issuer fee-based revenue model. The more bonds they rate, the more revenue generated. As part of the mortgage securitization process, rating agencies were charged with independently evaluating the strength or weakness of mortgage-linked debt. Once rated, these instruments were then sold to the public.

When accurate, ratings ensure that capital flows to its highest and best use. As the complexity of these mortgage-linked bonds increased, investors relied even more on rating agency guidance. Moody's and Standard & Poor's greatly underestimated the true risk, assigning ratings as high as AAA on billions of dollars in mortgage debt now worth a fraction of original value. Rating agencies using models with flawed assumptions legitimized these otherwise risky investments, sending false pricing signals to the market. Armed with high ratings, investment banks and other financial firms were able to package and sell mortgage-related securities to eager investors. The combination of low perceived risk and higher returns compared to U.S. Treasuries attracted vast inflows of capital, contributing to the housing boom. Pension funds and other institutional investors could buy this debt only if it was highly rated. The rating agencies satisfied this requirement. By second quarter 2007, these same rating agencies, in whipsaw fashion, downgraded thousands of mortgage securities, forcing banks and other investors to take billions of dollars in write-downs. These inevitable ratings actions signaled the end of the U.S. housing bubble, the start of the credit crisis, and Lehman's eventual demise.

Of the Fabulous Three, Moody's has drawn the most investor ire followed by Standard & Poor's as a distant second. In rating mortgage-backed securities, Fitch was basically irrelevant. Credit rating agencies have become more client- and profit-driven. In any other business this is positive. However, for rating agencies this profit-driven strategy reduced the watchdog's bark. Moody's is a prime example of this rating industry shift. In October 2000, Moody's was spun off from Dun & Bradstreet and became a publicly traded company. As expected, it became more profit- and customer-focused. It was now accountable to shareholders. More and more, the firm's focus turned on growing revenue and stock price. To motivate employees, Moody's used stock option–based incentive systems. By the early 2000s, the rapidly emerging mortgage-backed securities (MBS) industry appeared to be the ticket. Moody's serviced this client segment through its structured finance group. Fees associated with MBS were up to three times as profitable as its traditional core business of rating corporate and municipal bonds.[11]

While at Moody's, Scott McCleskey, the senior vice president of compliance, pushed for more frequent monitoring of municipal bonds. In later testimony before a congressional panel on September 30, 2009, he indicated, ". . . while I was there, I found that my guidance was routinely ignored if the guidance meant making less money."[12] By 2007, Moody's structured finance group revenue ballooned to $2 billion. In only a few years, this once smallish group was now contributing half of the company's overall earnings—53 percent in first quarter 2007. Profit margins were topping 50 percent. Moody's stock also responded positively, increasing to more than $73 per share by April 2007, a fivefold increase since going public. Moody's had arrived and was now the most dominant rating agency, even larger than Standard & Poor's.

Dangerously, rating agencies had moved away from a conservative business model where no one customer represented more than 1 percent of revenue. In catering to the mortgage-backed market, investment banks became these agencies' largest customers, representing millions of dollars in fee income. The top five investment banks decided which rating firms got the most lucrative business. Many mortgage originators attempted to shop agencies until they got the "right" rating.

Countless hours of congressional hearings have been held to debate why Moody's and Standard & Poor's failed to perform their gatekeeper role and protect investors. Rating a structured product was complicated, given that there were as many as fifty different tranches with varying qualities of collateral. To decipher this complexity took time. During the market peak, the enormous volume could have put undue pressure on an already stretched rating process. In this environment credit-rating quality slipped. This fact does not excuse the agencies for sloppy ratings. Lastly, model assumptions used by rating agencies were flawed and based on a limited historical data set that quickly fell apart as markets became unhinged.

Regardless of the reasons, some investor trust and confidence have been lost. Instead of capital flowing to its highest and best use, these inaccurate risk ratings allowed billions in capital to be misguided and destroyed. Rating agencies had a dual role: selling needed rating services while maintaining high standards. Part of this included keeping a close eye on the value of collateral used to back the structured products rated. If, starting in early 2004, the credit rating agencies had taken a more conservative posture, the markets might have taken a less risky course.[13] The rating agencies were not the main cause for Lehman's fall, but they left the gate open and allowed the market and its participants to behave in a more destructive manner.

Lobbyists

In the United States, lobbyists and private interest groups influence public policy. Lobbying is a multibillion-dollar business. Annual spending in 2008 and in 2009 exceeded $3 billion in each year. There are approximately 13,400 registered active lobbyists and countless trade organizations. Lobbyists thrive around the Washington Beltway for good reason: it is where deals are cut and bills are passed, watered down, or defeated. Influencing legislation is the name of the game. From a pure economics perspective, the fact that billions of dollars are spent annually is an indication of perceived value.

Since 2000 the financial industry had spent in excess of $5 billion on campaign contributions and lobbying. Academic work has demonstrated this can be a source of systemic risk by defeating legislation aimed at curbing dangerous financial activities.[14] The repeal of the Glass-Steagall Act may have been the ultimate act of lobbyist power.[15] This repeal effort first gained momentum in the 1980s under the deregulation era of Greenspan and the Fed, but it would take $300 million before the banking, insurance, and brokerage industries were able to marshal enough clout to get the job done. Recall that in 1998, Citicorp and Travelers Group merged, placing a bet that Glass-Steagall would be repealed and the universal banking model would take hold. One year later this bet paid off. The Gramm-Leach-Bliley Act was passed and hailed as ushering in a new era for a vibrant financial industry. Sophisticated markets no longer needed to be held back by Depression-era regulation. Lobbyists successfully allowed Citigroup and others to fulfill dreams of becoming financial supermarkets. In the process an important protection against destructive banking behavior was gutted.

The passage of the Commodity Futures Modernization Act in 2000 over the ardent objections of Brooksley Born, then head of the Commodity Futures Trading Commission, was another substantial lobbying victory. Touted as allowing the United States to maintain its competitive position in the OTC derivatives market, it exempted certain OTC derivative contracts, including CDS, from greater regulatory scrutiny. This policy change, aggressively backed by the banking industry lobby, is now seen as a catastrophic mistake.

Lobbying efforts that lead to poor legislative decisions are not limited to Washington, D.C. As with many trends, what happened in California traveled eastward. In the subprime origination business, California was ground zero. Nine of ten of the nation's largest subprime lenders were located in the Golden State. By the peak of the market in 2006, one in every five mortgage loans was subprime. With precision these loans were sold to Wall Street firms such as Lehman, then pooled, repackaged, rated, and resold in the market. Lenders like Countrywide Financial Corporation, Ameriquest Mortgage Company, New Century Financial Corporation, Household International, and Option One Mortgage were California-based but national in scope. They were part of the growing shadow banking system overseen by ill-equipped state regulators. Mortgage lenders understood this relationship, targeting California lawmakers with millions of dollars in an effort to influence legislation. Since 2000, subprime lenders and related participants spent almost $60 million in an attempt to beat back, block, or weaken legislation that sought to restrict risky mortgage lending practices.

From 2000 to 2006, Ameriquest, one of the largest mortgage originators, spent $11.5 million in direct campaign contributions to California politicians. This investment paid off. Between 2001 and 2005, two significant bills that could have curtailed predatory lending practices in California were squashed.

In 2001, Carole Midgen, then an assemblywoman from San Francisco, introduced stronger consumer protection laws through AB 489. Mortgage industry powers mobilized to defeat this early piece of consumer legislation. By 2002, as AB 489 moved closer to a vote, the California Mortgage Association lobbied against the bill. As this bill progressed, Household International spent almost $1 million in lobbying and political donations. (These out-of-pocket expenses pale in comparison to the eventual $484 million settlement Household International reached in 2002 to settle a nationwide predatory lending suit.) By 2002, a watered-down AB 489 was passed. Lobby efforts had been successful.

In 2005, California State Senator Jackie Speier introduced SB 790, establishing additional borrower protection. This time the formidable army of opponents included the California Mortgage Association, California Bankers Association, and California Mortgage Bankers Association. Dead on arrival, SB 790 never got out of committee. Lobbyists had proven their clout and, through efforts in California, had weakened the nation's financial system. By late 2007, many of these risky lending practices came home to roost, and the entire mortgage lending industry began to implode. It is impossible to know for sure what might have happened if AB 489 had not been watered down or if SB 790 had passed, but it seems reasonable that the growth of the risky subprime market would have been slowed.

The banking lobby continues to influence the shape and level of regulatory scrutiny over the financial markets. Post–credit crisis, executives from

TARP-taking banks continue to express public support for re-regulation of the financial markets while their paid lobbyists attempt to defeat or weaken any new regulation. This contradictory message has not gone unnoticed and continues to slow progress toward meaningful regulatory reform.

Consumers

It has been widely demonstrated how banks loosened credit standards, which increased the ease of obtaining loans. Also important to note is that consumers' willingness to plunge deeper into debt contributed to the crisis. Over the last fifty years, the ratio of debt to disposable income has increased in U.S. households. In the 1950s this ratio was about 35 percent, rising to 65 percent by the mid-1960s, where it stayed relatively static until the late 1980s.[16] By 2001 debt to income crossed the dangerous line of 100 percent, hitting an all-time high of 133 percent by 2007. The savings rate that had been as high as 10 percent in the 1980s dropped to negative 1 percent by 2007. In an ominous sign, this was the lowest personal savings rate since the Great Depression. It is true that banks were incentivized to make more loans, but consumers were the ones who agreed to such terms.

THE DECIDERS

So far the focus has been on the Enablers—those entities or individuals that helped sow the seeds of the housing bubble, the tolerance for greater risk taking, and the structure that put the entire financial system in jeopardy if only one major institution were to fail. These seeds were sown through the years. But several major players were involved in the year, months, and weeks immediately before Lehman declared bankruptcy. Collectively, these players were the Deciders. The Financial Accounting Standards Board (FASB), the SEC policy on short-selling, and U.S. Treasury Secretary Paulson all helped seal the deal.

Financial Accounting Standards Board

Since the early 1990s, FASB rules have required financial firms to value assets based on what they could be sold for in a current market transaction. Ideally this would have been done through the use of an independent pricing source. The SEC enforced this mark-to-market requirement. Theoretically, fair value accounting was implemented to give investors a clearer view of firm financial health on a timely basis. In practice, these rules exposed fragile firms to unneeded earnings volatility. During the peak of the real estate boom, banks held large positions in MBS. Many of these highly rated securities were priced to the newly created subprime ABX Index, which uses the price of various credit default swaps as a proxy. To satisfy regulatory capital requirements, many banks opted to hold top-rated MBS. Since ABX's inception through the second quarter of 2007, this index had remained stable at 100. Unfortunately, the ABX Index was only a fair-weather index and proved flawed by the summer of 2007. When the subprime crisis hit that summer, the index exhibited dramatic price swings. Short-sellers piled on and used this index to bet against the entire mortgage market. Increased selling pressure combined with greater market uncertainty pushed the ABX Index down to levels never before seen. Trading in MBS dried up, and no buyers were found at almost any price. Liquidity risk had arrived. By August 2007 the once stable ABX Index dropped to 90; it then dropped to 70 by November. The ABX had morphed into the Wall Street Subprime Fear Index.

In adhering to FASB fair-value accounting rules, banks were forced to deeply discount their assets even if they had no plans of selling them. Many, at least on paper, were becoming balance sheet insolvent. Banks felt that this accounting rule unfairly punished them. In many cases, the cash flow value of the securities was higher than the market value. Fair value accounting also triggered collateral calls. To meet margin calls, some firms had to sell assets in an already down market, forcing MBS prices lower. Banks found that these markdowns reduced regulatory capital and put them in a more vulnerable position. Many banks had to take drastic write-downs, and these accounting losses exacerbated the financial crisis. Such an inflexible accounting rule forced banks' hands. Since the fall of Lehman, fair value rules have been relaxed to better address difficult-to-value and illiquid assets.

SEC Policy on Short-Sellers

The SEC opened the door that allowed short-sellers to help determine Lehman's ultimate fate. In an orderly market, a balance of buyers and sellers provides price discovery. Short-sellers can be an efficient and legitimate means to hedge risk. In the case of Lehman, "naked short-sellers"—a mutation of the legitimate form—were active and made it difficult for the firm's stock to stabilize. Since January 3, 2005, Regulation SHO against naked short-selling had been in place, but the SEC was not diligent about policing or enforcing this rule. What's more, the regulation had no teeth. No monetary penalty is imposed on violators. Lack of SEC enforcement allowed naked short-sellers to become active in Lehman stock and push it down. Had the stock been stabilized, this would have given Lehman more breathing room to find a partner. A stable price would have also produced greater buyer interest. Only after the Lehman bankruptcy, on September 17, 2008, did the SEC approve a more comprehensive order to curb naked short-selling. The SEC was so concerned about the adverse impact of short-sellers that on September 19, 2008, it imposed a temporary ban on legitimate short-selling of nineteen financial stocks.

Hank Paulson

Lehman's risky practices allowed it to dig its own grave, and Hank Paulson was there to shovel on the dirt. He was the ultimate decider. If there is one major criticism that can be waged against Paulson, it is the arbitrary manner in which he picked the winners (Freddie Mac, Fannie Mae, AIG, and to a lesser extent Bear) and decided the loser (Lehman). These actions were a series of missteps that culminated in a full-blown financial crisis. It is nearly impossible to make the case that *not saving* Lehman improved the crisis. One only needs to take a look at the bottom line. To support Lehman would not only have bailed out shareholders. Lehman's investors and employees as well as Fuld would still have taken a significant financial hit even with a bailout. More important, however, is that American taxpayers would have benefited from a bailout. The ensuing panic led to the decision to bail out AIG and ask Congress for enormous sums of money. After Lehman was allowed to die, TARP money was simply transferred to banks so that they could be stabilized, paying out their bonus pools to keep their "talent" from leaving. This is no populist rant. It is exactly what happened.

Though Paulson did attempt to find a partner for Lehman, he did not grasp the severity of the problem soon enough. In April 2008 Paulson had the famous "brand" dinner with Fuld.[17] Some accounts indicate that he expressed more concern about Merrill Lynch than he did about Lehman. Even if Fuld had an overinflated opinion of his firm's value and remained behind the offer curve, Paulson had a duty to make sure that Lehman found a safe home so the economy could be spared. After rescuing Freddie Mac and Fannie Mae on September 7, 2008, Paulson apparently lost his resolve in the face of mounting political opposition. Unwilling to extend financial support to a fragile Lehman, Paulson slit Lehman's main artery.

Some market pundits have claimed that Lehman needed to die in order to defend free market doctrine and reduce moral hazard. This thinking seems dangerously flawed. The global financial system did not *need* to be taken to the brink of collapse with the loss of millions of jobs and trillions of dollars of personal wealth. Furthermore, not finding a way to save Lehman quite possibly had the opposite of its intended effect: it *increased* moral hazard. "Remember Lehman" will be the threat used by big failing interconnected firms that want to be bailed out by the government. Systemic risk existed before Lehman's fall and persists today. The relationship of a single company to the entire financial system should not be ignored.

While it is difficult to determine how much closer to the precipice Lehman's bankruptcy pushed AIG, it is clear Lehman's demise did not help. By one estimate, AIG through its CDS products had Lehman credit exposure for as much as $20 billion. Theoretically, on September 12, an investor could have purchased the entire investment bank for $1.2 billion (based on its market capitalization). The price offered by Barclays proved similar a few days later. In hindsight, such an orchestrated purchase instead of bankruptcy could have created the needed firebreak. If Lehman had been rescued ($1.2 billion spent), would that have reduced or eliminated the $180 billion rescue of AIG? Or the need to pony up $700 billion of taxpayer money for TARP or the more than $9 trillion in government guarantees used to unfreeze the credit markets? Almost assuredly. Saving Lehman would have saved the U.S. government (i.e., taxpayers) money.

As this book has suggested, neither the government nor the CEOs involved in the rescue meeting that fateful weekend in September 2008 had any reliable way of predicting how a Lehman bankruptcy would affect the global economy. Lehman was not an isolated experiment in a safe and controlled environment. Nor should politics have been allowed to cloud decision making. Without any reliable data, given that the decision of the twenty-odd men meeting in Lower Manhattan would affect people all over the planet, it only seems reasonable to err on the side of caution. The fact that the Treasury secretary did not attempt more creative ways to help Lehman reach safe harbor is bewildering. September 15, 2008, should go down in history not only as the day that a once respected firm perished but also as a day when the head of the U.S. Treasury made an egregious error.

UNORDERLY WIND-DOWN

Once the order to let Lehman die was made, everything broke loose. Paulson and Bernanke have argued that Lehman could not be saved because they did not have adequate "resolution authority" to take over Lehman. Even if one accepts that the government's hands were tied, it still had the ability to devise and execute a comprehensive crisis-management action plan to anticipate and respond to the cascade of global financial events that a Lehman bankruptcy might trigger. Once the death sentence was reached, instead of being proactive, the government just walked away, leaving the market in the driver's seat from that point on.

The Treasury secretary and Fed chairman have also claimed they could not have provided needed liquidity to Lehman because its collateral was inadequate. The company was too risky to expose to the American people. In contrast, a few days after the bankruptcy, the same Lehman assets were "miraculously" deemed adequate enough by the Fed to secure a short-term multibillion-dollar funding. On September 15, 2008, this Fed funding was about $63 billion. As soon as Barclays purchased Lehman's North American broker-dealer operations, it repaid the Fed in full. Paulson has also indicated that even if Lehman had adequate collateral, there was no willing buyer. This point is only true if you take into account that a lifeboat was *not* provided to see who else might have emerged. Lehman was a brand-name franchise. Though it was damaged, its core businesses had immense value. Recent strong earnings reported by Barclays and Nomura generated from the former Lehman assets are additional proof. If the government had continued to provide liquidity and given Lehman bank-holding company powers, Lehman would have had more time to find a buyer or be unwound in an orderly manner.

Part of a solid crisis management plan would have included anticipating the impact of pushing Lehman to file for Chapter 11 bankruptcy. Theoretically, companies are given relief from creditors as they attempt to preserve assets and unwind operations. However, the haphazard and last-minute way Lehman was forced to file bankruptcy destroyed franchise value. Once the decision was made to file, no crisis management action plan was created. During that weekend, the government had a working group focus on the option of a Lehman bankruptcy, but neither it nor Lehman developed a crisis management action plan.

Lehman had more than $680 billion in assets, many of which were held at various subsidiaries. When the bankruptcy was announced, it triggered a global termination of 80 percent of trading contracts—a forced sale of more than nine hundred thousand trading contracts in an already down market, with few buyers insuring greater losses.[18] In 2007, the trading and investment area of Lehman had earned $4 billion in annual profits. Post-bankruptcy, these assets were sold for less than $500 million. The bankruptcy filing also put valuable assets in legal limbo. In Europe, Lehman assets were immediately frozen. This meant that clients who had money at Lehman lost access to it. A large number of hedge funds lost legal right to withdrawal billions in cash that otherwise served as liquidity in a turbulent market. They were forced to sell those assets they did control in a falling market. A December 2008 study released by Alvarez and Marsel, Lehman's post-bankruptcy restructuring advisors, estimated that as much as $75 billion in value was destroyed. Like an ice cube in the summer heat, value melted in a matter of minutes.

When Lehman bondholders lost 90 percent of value, shareholders lost everything. It is estimated that the unwinding of Lehman will cost up to $1.4 billion in lawyer and financial advisor costs. Globally, losses to investors were in the trillions of dollars. Taxpayers were eventually exposed to a $700 billion bailout of the economy. The nationalization of Freddie Mac, Fannie Mae, and AIG as well as the significant financial backstop provided to ensure the sale of Bear shifted risk to taxpayers, not to mention the trillions in government guarantees used to stabilize the credit markets. Through all of this, the Fed, who had credit exposure to Lehman in excess of $60 billion, was able to ensure it was paid in full. The Fed did a nice job protecting itself but failed to protect the American people from a Lehman bankruptcy.

It's true that TARP funds have been paid back by many of the largest institutions that received them. But the immediate benefits appear to have been realized more by the risk-taking TARP takers than by the taxpayers forced to bail out these companies. In 2009 five of the largest TARP takers—Bank of America, Citigroup, J.P. Morgan, Morgan Stanley, and Goldman Sachs—set aside approximately $90 billion for compensation. Goldman Sachs received $10 billion, has repaid its debt at lightning speed, and has even had the audacity to suggest that it never really needed the funds. In 2009, Goldman Sachs's accumulated bonus pool was in excess of $16 billion, equating to an average payout of more than $700,000 per employee. With the economy still wobbly and national unemployment at more than 10 percent, this sort of oversized Wall Street payout feels a lot like what got us into financial trouble in the first place. Justifiably, it does not sit well with the average American. In an attempt to quell general outrage, in November 2009, Goldman Sachs CEO Lloyd Blankfein stated, "We participated in things that were clearly wrong and have reason to regret. We apologize."[19] To many, this might have seemed surreal and provided proof that excessive risk taking (and excessive profits) have tainted Wall Street's sense of reality.[20] In spite of Goldman's obvious pandering, the real question remains: Has anything changed?

CONCLUSION

Lehman is no more. Several of the policymakers that set the table for the crisis and then reacted to it have left public office. The demise of Lehman released systemic risk into the global market and demonstrated the importance of taking strong measures to reduce the likelihood of a similar event. Dick Fuld has embarked on a new business venture, working for Matrix Advisors, a New York–based hedge fund. It's safe to say he will never run a large investment bank again. To gain a greater understanding of why so many of the financial system controls and safeguards failed, it is necessary to look beyond Fuld and the personalities that fueled the crisis.

Regulation is at an important crossroad, and significant policy changes need to be made. Tougher federal regulation of commercial, investment, and other shadow banks is in order. Unchecked, Wall Street will always seek the highest profit and ignore many risks. Conversely, excessive government intervention will stifle bank profitability, vital economic growth, and prosperity. Global markets will continue to test the strength of regulation and oversight, and gaps will continue to be exploited, sometimes at a significant cost. Government has a duty to ensure that the next powerful market storm is identified sooner, better contained, or completely averted. At the same time, company executives need to understand that the race is won through measured risk taking and not by uncontrolled gambling.

Epilogue

The Post-Lehman
Financial Landscape

Lessons from the financial collapse are evident, but turning them into action has been slow. Since the Lehman bankruptcy on September 15, 2008, there has been much public discussion and shaming, but little U.S. financial industry reform has occurred.[1] At the time of this writing, proposals on the table include the creation of a systemic risk regulator, a consumer protection agency for financial products, a consolidated bank regulator, stronger capital requirements and caps on leverage for the largest banks, closer oversight of derivatives, resolution authority to aid in the unwinding of mega-insolvent institutions, and curbs on banker pay. Yet with Wall Street banks posting profits again, the stock market up from crisis lows, and bipartisan squabbling, it appears that Capitol Hill has lost any sense of urgency. The financial over-haul bills proposed by the House and Senate are decisively different. The House bill has not received support from a single Republican. The Senate bill shows a willingness to reach across the aisle but still has received considerable pushback from the broader banking community. Until meaningful legislation is passed, the market remains vulnerable to another Lehman-type systemic risk event.

The U.S. government and the Federal Reserve (Fed) made a grave mistake in deciding not to rescue Lehman. In a December 2009 letter, Secretary of the Treasury Timothy Geithner wrote that the administration expects "to recover all but $42 billion of the $364 billion in TARP funds disbursed," which ignores the more than $9 trillion in government-backed guarantees used to shore up the wobbly market.[2] While many of the largest banks have paid back the Troubled Asset Relief Program (TARP), the government still has significant exposure to recipients that remain on financial life support. In May 2009 the Treasury pledged $400 billion to Freddie Mac and Fannie Mae, a doubling since the original bailout. More recently, the financial commitment was increased to unlimited dollar support for these two mortgage giants. AIG and GMAC also show significant weakness as the recession persists. This book has made the case that, in a simple cost-benefit analysis, backstopping a Lehman buyout would have been significantly less expensive than allowing bankruptcy. It is hard to fathom how saving Lehman would have increased the need for creating TARP.

Since Lehman's bankruptcy, much of the public debate has centered on the role of government in the markets precisely because it became so involved *after* refusing to do whatever it took to save Lehman. Such governmental activism in a post-Lehman world has led to a growing sense of schizophrenia, especially among conservative policymakers. Yes, we have to interfere with the market to keep it free. As unsavory as government bailouts may be and in spite of boasts to the contrary from current Goldman Sachs CEO Lloyd Blankfein, Geithner was correct when angrily suggesting that none of the banks "would have survived a situation in which we had let that fire try to burn itself out."[3]

It's impossible to predict when, where, or how the next financial meltdown might begin. But government policymakers and the Fed need to resist the notion that any amount of regulation or deregulation can magically make the system fail-safe. As this book has pointed out, both former Fed Chairman Alan Greenspan and current director of the National Economic Council Lawrence Summers made this mistake. As the *Wall Street Journal* has gleefully reported, Peter Orszag, current director of the Office of Management and Budget, made this same mistake when analyzing Freddie Mac and Fannie Mae. Some hard-nosed American pragmatism is in order—a realistic worldview begets realistic solutions. The best we can hope for are well-placed and nonintrusive regulatory controls that monitor and disallow the outsized risks that firms like Lehman once took. Regulators need to be adequately compensated and trained and must actually enforce the regulations. Government also needs to be well-positioned, when necessary, to step in and wind down failing firms in such a way—these are the key words from Geithner—"that protects taxpayers and the broader economy while ensuring that losses are borne by creditors and other stakeholders."[4]

In the spirit of philosopher George Santayana, who stated, "Those who cannot remember the past are condemned to repeat it," the following ten-point plan will help ensure a better financial future.

1. **We must acknowledge systemic risk exists.** It's official. We can drop the quotation marks around "systemic risk." The stunning collapse of world markets after the Lehman bankruptcy proves that systemic risk exists. Once acknowledged, this risk and its contributing factors can begin to be managed. Outside of the United States, efforts to measure which institutions pose the most systemic risk are already under way. In November 2009 the Financial Stability Board, an international body of regulators and central bankers recently established specifically to address the potential dangers of interconnected firms, compiled a list of thirty cross-border financial firms. This top-thirty list of "too big to fail" institutions includes Goldman Sachs, J.P. Morgan Chase, Morgan Stanley, and Bank of America–Merrill Lynch. Not surprisingly, Barclays and Nomura, the two banks that scooped up Lehman's core operations, are also on this list. In a positive step, those on this watch list are being required to demonstrate they have adequate crisis management plans, including "living wills" outlining how a sudden unwind would be handled.

Regulatory gaps between nations, however, remain sizable. International regulators have not yet found common ground, nor have they sorted out how to work in a fully coordinated fashion. That the international standards set by Basel II have taken so long to gain acceptance and are still not fully embraced by U.S. regulators provides further evidence of the banking community's deep-seated resistance to needed regulatory change. While the U.S. government can help facilitate these cross-border efforts, much work still needs to be completed within our own financial backyard.

2. **The Fed needs to regain credibility at home and abroad.** Similar to the banks it regulates, without credibility, the Fed cannot effectively perform its role. Leading up to the Great Credit Crisis of 2008, the Fed kept interest rates too low for too long. It should have spotted the housing bubble sooner and moved to deflate it. The Fed also failed to identify the escalating risk taking at the major banks it regulated. Once the financial meltdown was in full swing, the Fed delayed its attempt to save Lehman and failed to comprehend the level of collateral damage linked to its bankruptcy. The Fed also failed to fully embrace the higher capital standards imposed by Basel II. In spite of these missteps, there has been a lack of self-criticism and no material changes, including Fed executive firings or reorganizations, have occurred. The Fed

needs to repair its regulatory standing abroad. Many European and Asian countries remain resentful that American banks were permitted to create this contagion and were not stopped from spreading the crisis across the globe. To correct the deficiencies, an independent investigation of why the Fed dropped the ball should be conducted and a full report published.

The Fed also needs to upgrade its examination force, providing the tools and training to keep up with the financial instruments being traded and to ward off excessive risk taking. If the market were a gunfight, the Fed would be carrying pea shooters while Wall Street bankers were carrying AK-47s. Next, the salary gap between regulators and the regulated is staggering. Compared to those who work on Wall Street, and even within the Fed hierarchy, field examiners are viewed as second-class citizens. To attract and retain the best talent requires providing competitive salaries.

Last, the Fed has a responsibility to turn off the fog machine and provide more detailed reporting. One extraordinary reaction to the financial collapse has been the traction Texas Representative Ron Paul has gained with his criticism of the Fed. The Federal Reserve Transparency Act, which would give the Government Accountability Office authority to audit the Fed, had 317 co-sponsors when it passed the House and is heading to a Senate vote as this book goes to press. The Fed does need higher levels of accountability. Since the crisis, it has used significant amounts of taxpayer money, housing billions of toxic mortgage-related assets on its books. But giving Congress a greater say in monetary policy decisions is a dangerous idea—politicians are not trained in market economics. Rather, the Fed should willingly provide reports of how taxpayer money is being spent, how it is reducing the odds of missing the next asset bubble, and how it is helping to manage systemic risk. When all of this happens, the Fed will be back on the road to restored credibility.

3. **An independent systemic risk regulator makes sense.** An idea with widespread support is the creation of an über systemic risk regulator to identify dangerous market trends before they harm the broader economy. Such overseers would perform ongoing financial shock testing and have preemptive authority to help fix system weaknesses. The quantitative skill set needed to oversee this arena would be very specialized, requiring a sophisticated capital markets background and advanced monitoring techniques. Some have proposed that the Fed would fit the bill. In June 2009 I suggested that appointing the Fed as systemic risk regulator was "like a parent giving his son a bigger and faster car right after he crashed the family station wagon," a warning that caught on so rapidly that shortly thereafter Senator Christopher Dodd read this quote into testimony

during a Senate Banking Committee hearing. Since then, I haven't changed my mind. The Fed's lackluster performance in risk detection, monitoring, and management suggests that it needs to fix its existing shortcomings before taking on additional responsibility. Since September 2008 the Fed has also gained oversight responsibilities for Goldman Sachs and Morgan Stanley, two mega-risk takers that further strain existing resources. Instead of anointing the Fed with additional powers, it makes more sense to establish a new agency with no prior baggage to perform this oversight role. Since U.S. banks represent only a small portion of the overall systemic risk watch list, this oversight clearly needs to coordinate with worldwide counterparts.

4. Higher capital levels should be mandated. If anything, Lehman demonstrated that firm capital must be commensurate with the size of risk taking. Capital protects shareholders and provides a degree of insurance to creditors. In times of financial turmoil, there is no substitute for adequate capital. The financial crisis provided a real-life stress test, and many American banks failed. Regulators need to reevaluate existing minimum capital requirements and adjust them to reflect the higher risk-taking trend in banking. The quality of capital is also important. More emphasis should be placed on liquidity and funding through unencumbered common equity. Linking the total amount of bank assets to the amount of capital needed to cushion against unexpected losses is paramount. Banks should be encouraged to maintain capital in excess of the international minimum requirements outlined in Basel II. Requiring higher capital limits will restrict bank profit seeking, spur banker protest, and test the resolve of policymakers. These new limits should be a floor, and well-run firms concerned about sustainability should opt for greater safety. If the risk of a bank's particular strategy is too high, there should be only two viable responses: raise more capital or reduce risk taking. Ongoing monitoring is required. It would be nice to assume that self-preservation alone would inspire senior executives and boards of directors to make these assessments, yet history continues to prove otherwise, making outside regulatory oversight critical. Higher minimum capital requirements will foster a more stable financial system.

5. Leverage constraints must be in place. Leverage is dangerous and can kill. Lehman demonstrated that high leverage is a good predictor of high financial risk. In a strong market, leverage generates magnified profits, but in a down economy it does just the opposite. The more debt a bank piles on, the greater the risk. As a corollary to the capital size requirement, banks need tighter constraints on leverage. Former Morgan Stanley CEO John Mack confirms this view. In testimony before the Financial Crisis Inquiry Commission—a ten-member panel created by Congress—on January 12, 2010, he summed it up well by stating, "In retrospect, many firms were too highly leveraged, took on too much risk, and did not have sufficient resources to manage those risks effectively in a rapidly changing environment."

How leverage is used in pursuing profit is also important to ascertain. Borrowing to buy U.S. Treasury bonds is a lower-risk strategy than using debt to buy subprime securities. Regulators such as the Fed, SEC, and Federal Deposit Insurance Corporation (FDIC)—or if a consolidated bank regulator is created—need to apply conservative leverage limits that take into account economic downturns. The House bill picked an arbitrary leverage cap of 15 to 1. To be meaningful, set limits need to provide banks with enough room to seek profit and remain competitive. In determining the correct limit, more empirical analysis needs to be performed. Once these leverage limits are set and uniformly applied by regulatory agencies, there needs to be clear penalties for noncompliance. Stress testing should be formalized and made part of regulatory oversight practices.

6. **Smarter compensation schemes are critical.** Compensation of Wall Street bankers has come under great scrutiny, and with good reason. Risk-driven compensation schemes contributed to the demise of many brand-name franchises. And though the government has a right to appoint a "pay czar" for the risk takers who became TARP takers, the finger-wagging about executive pay is a passing fad. The debate should not be about those who make a lot and those who make less, nor should it hamper the ability of banks to recruit top talent. Instead, compensation plans should be adjusted for risk and based on profit. Employees who take low risks and make large profits should be rewarded *more* than those who profit from taking oversized bets. Claw-back provisions should account for profits that later turn into losses. In October 2008 the Fed provided banks with compensation guidelines, but these are not mandated and come with no penalty for noncompliance. Last, while many executives walked away from the financial wreck with millions of dollars, shareholders were left with billions of dollars in losses. If anything, this demonstrates that shareholders should more actively participate in influencing executive behavior. Passing shareholder "say on pay" legislation is an important step.

7. **Boards must exercise better oversight.** While a world where shareholders—other than the likes of Carl Ichan—influence company policy may be

science fiction, the board of directors at every financial institution *must* exercise independence and not become an extension of the CEO's friendship network. Boards need to stay current in the risk-taking products and strategies employed by their organizations. And boards need to seek help from outside expert advisors and consultants when they do not possess adequate knowledge concerning risk. Through compensation, audit, nomination, finance, and risk management subcommittees, boards define a firm's risk tolerance. Boards need to ensure that compensation plans are properly aligned with a company's long-term interests and are tracked to risk-adjusted performance measurements. To guarantee robust board oversight, bank regulators should more vigorously examine boardroom activities, including it as part of the overall scoring and reporting process. The services of independent corporate-governance rating agencies should also be used to provide additional oversight in pointing out deficient boards.

8. **Regulations need to remain current.** Congress fails its important banking oversight duties if it just holds blame hearings once the latest financial calamity has already occurred. Congressional banking committees must provide an effective counterbalance to the market's ever-increasing sophistication and risk taking. Keeping regulation current is an iterative process, requiring constant assessment of whether existing laws are meeting goals. Without channeling useful feedback from industry experts and diverse market participants, control mechanisms become quickly outdated—especially in a hyper-competitive market with no protective barrier between commercial banks and investment banks. The banking committees need to strengthen internal staffing by hiring those with market-based expertise who can serve as a counterbalance against the industry lobby. Repealing the protective barrier created by the Glass-Steagall Act was not by itself the mistake. The error in judgment occurred in allowing banks to grow in size and risk-taking activities while not enforcing increased capital requirements, curbing dangerous levels of leverage, or discouraging destructive lending activities. To right this wrong, a modern version of this act setting out permissible activities of all participants—commercial, investment, universal, and shadow banks—needs to be crafted. Such an umbrella law will be challenging to enact, requiring strong bipartisanship support, but it will provide a more comprehensive way to measure and control market-wide risk taking.

Regulators need to better anticipate future risk areas. Greater scrutiny over the global derivatives market needs to be implemented. It appears that CDS will migrate to standardized exchanges, but this does not address products that have not yet been created by a new crop of Wall Street innovators. Lastly, the opportunity for market manipulation must be curbed. The repeal of the SEC uptick rule was a mistake, and the ban on naked short-selling should be aggressively enforced.

9. **A firm policy stance on moral hazard should be taken and articulated.** Economists may be overstating moral hazard as it related to Lehman. Moral hazard obviously played a role in the nearly explicit guarantees offered to quasi-governmental institutions like Fannie Mae and Freddie Mac. But Lehman did not take unprecedented risks based on the assumption that the government would bail it out. Granted, it was shocked, especially after the Bear Stearns rescue, that the government allowed its demise, but the wheels had been put into motion long before September 2008. The inherently competitive and insular nature of investment banks led to all the brand-name firms making similarly outrageous and increasingly leveraged bets concentrated in real estate. If a Lehman bankruptcy was supposed to alleviate moral hazard, it has not radically changed the risk culture of the two remaining bulge-bracket banks. This is evidenced by the size of the bonuses paid out in 2010. But more policy does need to focus on how to approach "too big to fail" institutions. By coming with an implicit government guarantee, TARP has tilted the industry risk-taking equation. As these firms who received government support grow bigger, they continue to become riskier. Yet, simply enacting policy that limits bank size misses the mark. Banks failed not because of their size but because of their excessive risk taking. Simply restricting bank size could have unintended consequences, increasing the cost of services and reducing global competitiveness.

The government needs to take a firm policy stance on moral hazard and clearly articulate it to the market. The Lehman fiasco proved that sending mixed messages can be hazardous to the market's health.

10. **Greater executive accountability.** Better regulatory constraints and oversight can only go so far. There needs to be greater accountability for executives and boards—accountability not necessarily dictated by law. Yes, I am suggesting that institutions and the people we entrust to run them should exhibit a greater standard of financial ethics. In our capital markets, these intermediaries play a vital role and their actions can have far-reaching consequences. Because of this inextricable relationship, it is in the best interest of all

for executives to operate in a responsible, more conservative, and risk-aware manner. It is not sustainable to run a company with a strategy that seeks profit at whatever cost. In December 2009, President Barack Obama laid down an interesting challenge to bankers, saying, "they must ask, not just is it profitable, but is it right."

For proof that these prescriptions maintain healthy markets, one need only look northward. American banks were at the epicenter of the Great Credit Crisis of 2008 while Canadian banks walked away nearly unscathed. Canada was the only G7 country where there was no need for multibillion-dollar taxpayer bailouts or financial regulatory overhaul. This is not a new phenomenon—even during the Great Depression, not one Canadian bank failed—and there is no secret to their success. When it comes to taking risk, Canadian regulators and bankers are more conservative than their southern Wall Street cousins. Since the repeal of the Canadian equivalent of the Glass-Steagall Act in the 1980s, banking oversight has not been loosened. Canada has embraced a universal banking model with its top five banks representing approximately 90 percent of its banking business, and yet these institutions never pose a "too big to fail" threat. Without the ebb and flow of policy change, regulatory oversight has a greater chance to succeed. Canadian regulators avoid systemic risk through *consistently* strict oversight and regulation. Unlike the United States, Canada has only one regulatory body, the Office of the Superintendent of Financial Institutions (OSFI). This prevents agencies from sending mixed signals and banks from the playing the regulatory arbitrage game, seeking the most lenient overseer. The OSFI sets capital constraints more stringent than Basel II guidelines, and banks are required to set internal capital targets to provide cushion against unexpected losses. Capital equity is also emphasized, and minimum common equity of 75 percent is mandated, a much higher standard than those applied by U.S. regulators. Canadian banks tend to maintain leverage ratios of 18 to 1, while at the market peak some American banks were 26 to 1. Investment bank ratios were even higher. In a turbulent market, higher capital cushion and lower leverage is a recipe for success. Compensation schemes also are smaller and not as heavily biased toward stock options. On February 13, 2009, in Toronto, Paul Volcker, the former Fed Chairman who is now a member of President Obama's economic advisory team, argued that the new American system he envisions looks more like the Canadian system.

Our financial markets will continue to evolve and present significant challenges. Financial markets do not heal and repair themselves on their own. How we prepare and respond to the recent crisis will determine the strength and stability of our economy. Good risk management involves preparing for the next flood before it happens. Policymakers on Capitol Hill need to stick to a plan of enacting meaningful financial industry reform. To split this debate along party lines or position it as a Wall Street versus Main Street debate is unnecessarily divisive. One thing the Great Credit Crisis of 2008 taught us is that when the boat began to sink, survival required the resolve of everyone.

Appendix

Lehman Chronology, 1845–2010

Date	Event
1845	Henry Lehman, the oldest of three German brothers, opens a dry goods store—H. Lehman—on Commerce Street in Montgomery, Alabama
1850	The store is renamed Lehman Brothers once the other two brothers arrive from Germany
1858	Lehman remakes itself into a cotton trading firm and establishes a New York City branch at 119 Liberty Street
1861	First major business challenge: Civil War begins, and Lehman's business is disrupted
1865	U.S. Congress creates the House Banking Committee
1868	Lehman moves trading business northward and makes New York City its new headquarters
1899	Lehman's big break: it transacts its first initial public offering (International Steam Pump Company) as it transforms into an investment bank
1906	Lehman teams up with Goldman Sachs and underwrites first initial public offering for Sears, Roebuck & Co.
1912	Lehman sells off all remaining interests in cotton operation to focus entirely on investment banking

Date	Event
1913	Congress creates the Federal Reserve Banking System and the Senate Banking Committee
1925	Robert "Bobbie" Lehman becomes the last family member to run the firm
1929	Stock market crashes due to risky bank lending practices, extreme leverage, and speculation
1933	Congress passes Banking Act of 1933 including Glass-Steagall Act, which separates commercial and investment bank activities
	Commercial banks and investment banks are forced to divest of business interests
	Congress creates the FDIC and gets into the risk management business; depositors are initially insured up to $2,500
1934	SEC is established to regulate broker-dealers such as Lehman; President FDR appoints Joseph P. Kennedy to head SEC
	Congress promotes home ownership as a policy by passing the National Housing Act, creating the Federal Housing Administration
1938	Home ownership policy is expanded further with the creation of government-sponsored entity Fannie Mae
1940s	U.S. home ownership stands at 55 percent
1941	Lehman sends nine of its partners and numerous staff to fight in World War II
1950	Lehman benefits from the post-war economic boom, and investment activities continue to expand
1967	Lehman responsible for $3.5 billion of underwriting
1968	Congress establishes Ginnie Mae to further home ownership policy
1969	Company head Bobbie Lehman dies; there is no successor, and firm is thrown into turmoil
	Dick Fuld is hired; the start of his career as a "Lehman Lifer"
1970s	Rise of trading and growing risk profile as Lehman transforms into a fixed-income trading company; Lewis Glucksman is head of trading
1970	The birth of mortgage-backed securities, with Ginnie Mae issuing $2 million of these instruments
	Congress creates Freddie Mac, further expanding home ownership policy

Date	Event
1971	NYSE allows member broker-dealers to be publically owned, opening up the door for investment banks to go public; Lehman attempts to hold out but succumbs in 1994
1973	Pete Peterson, the first management outsider, is hired to run Lehman
1975	SEC designates Moody's, S&P, and Fitch as official bond raters
1977	Salomon Brothers, working with Bank of America, creates the first nongovernment-issued mortgage-backed securities
1981	Bear Stearns starts its mortgage trading department, a half decade before Lehman
1982	The Garn–St. Germain Act is passed, freeing up S&Ls to engage in risky lending and reducing capital requirements
1983	Salomon Brothers, working with Freddie Mac, issues the first collateralized mortgage obligation
	CEO Pete Peterson is pushed out, and Lewis Glucksman takes over—a loss for investment banking and a win for higher-risk trading activities
1984	Chaos grows under Glucksman and Lehman is quickly sold off to Shearson/ American Express for $360 million; Lehman is no longer a private partnership
	Congress creates a new market for mortgages by passing legislation that lets national banks buy and hold securities on their books
	The "too big to fail" doctrine debuts with the government bailout of Continental Illinois Bank
1986	Congress promotes the growth of CMOs by enacting the Tax Reform Act of 1986, which simplifies tax treatment
	Glass-Steagall Act begins to be dismantled by the Fed as it reinterprets the act, allowing commercial banks to engage in investment banking if less than 5 percent of revenue
1987	First major CMO-related trading loss; Merrill Lynch bond trader loses $377 million—the largest trading loss on Wall Street at that time
	"Black Monday"—stock market drops 22.6 percent in one day
	Alan Greenspan is appointed Federal Reserve Chairman
1988	Mark Walsh, the real estate cowboy, is hired
	Lehman increases trading activities and looks into the rapidly growing securitization business

Date	Event
1989	Fed weakens Glass-Steagall more by allowing commercial banks to increase investment banking activities if they don't exceed 10 percent of revenue
	Dow drops by 6 percent in a single day
	Risky and unconstrained lending practices at S&Ls require a government bailout of $293 billion
	Resolution Trust Company is formed to sell commercial real estate owned by the government; Lehman is quick to buy and profit
	Shearson Lehman can't land the RJR and Nabisco deal; losses from investment banking activities top $1 billion
1990	In the management change, Dick Fuld and Tom Hill are appointed co-CEOs
1992	Lehman moves into mortgage securitization, focusing on the Alt-A mortgage market
1993	Chris Pettit appointed chief operating officer (COO) (joined Lehman in 1977)
	Tom Hill is pushed out and Dick Fuld is appointed sole CEO
	Lehman begins build-out of its risk-management function, and appoints James Vinci as its head
1994	Long-Term Capital Management (LTCM) is started by former Salomon Brothers traders
	Lehman Brothers is spun off from American Express with Dick Fuld as CEO; many feel the ten-year jail term is now over
	Wall Street legend Henry Kaufman joins Lehman's board of directors
	Lehman is weakened by the spin-off and dropped in the investment-banking league tables
	Lehman places large bets on the dollar-denominated Mexican debt *tesobonos* equal to the firm's entire capital; IMF and U.S. government bails out Mexico and Lehman benefits
	Congress passes the Home Ownership and Equity Protection Act, giving the Fed sweeping power to regulate predatory lending; the Fed remains passive
1996	Number-two executive Chris Pettit is fired; position remains vacant for six years, until Joe Gregory is handpicked by Fuld
	Lehman builds out its risk management department, appointing Maureen Miskovic as chief risk officer

Date	Event
1996	Fed weakens Glass-Steagall further, allowing commercial banks to engage in investment banking activities up to 25 percent of revenue
1997	Lehman expands its mortgage securitization business by purchasing Aurora, an Alt-A originator based in Colorado
1998	Fed approves Citicorp-Travelers merger, resulting in the first U.S.–based universal bank
	LTCM fails after using excessive leverage to place derivative bets; Fed convinces Lehman and thirteen other banks to raise $3.65 billion as a rescue plan
	Failure of LTCM causes a run on Lehman; Dick Fuld rises to the challenge and beats back false rumors, elevating his stature on Wall Street
	Brooksley Born, head of the Commodity Futures Trading Commission, warns of the dangers of derivatives and the need for greater regulation
	Lehman greatly expands commercial real estate speculation and securitization through the activities of Mark Walsh
1999	Gramm-Leach-Bliley Act passes, repealing Glass-Steagall Act and the protective barrier between commercial and investment banks
2000	Lehman purchases BNC Mortgage, a West Coast subprime mortgage originator, and increases level of risk taking
	Lehman hires a new CRO, Madelyn Antoncic
	The Commodity Futures Modernization Act is passed over the ardent objections of Brooksley Born, allowing OTC derivatives, including credit default swaps, to remain unregulated
2001	Enron suddenly collapses, exposing weaknesses in credit rating agency ratings processes
	Terrorist attacks of 9/11 force Lehman to find new headquarters
	Post–9/11, the Fed reduces interest rates to lows not seen since President Kennedy's time, fueling the start of the real estate bubble
	Consumer debt-to-income ratio hits 100 percent for the first time in history
2002	Joe Gregory is appointed president, filling a position that was vacant for six years
	Sarbanes-Oxley Act is passed in response to corporate governance failures at Enron, WorldCom, Tyco, and others
	The Corporate Library, an independent corporate-governance rating agency, gives Lehman's board a weak D rating

Date	Event
2002–2005	Aggressive lobbying efforts in California ensure that proconsumer legislation to reduce predatory lending practices is watered down or stopped
2003	Lehman becomes the third largest subprime lender, making more than $18 billion in loans and controlling 9 percent of the market
2004	Basel II tougher banking capital requirements are released; American regulators including FED, FDIC, and OCC resist full adoption
2004	With strong support from Goldman Sachs CEO Henry Paulson, SEC weakens leverage restrictions on investment banks in favor of asset-class-driven capital requirements
	SEC loosens its leverage requirement on broker-dealers such as Lehman Brothers
2005	SEC regulation against naked short-sellers is implemented but not enforced rigorously
	Case-Shiller home price index hits a historical high
	Lehman's average daily Value-at-Risk increases to $38.4 million
	Consumer saving rate drops to negative 1 percentage, the lowest level since the Great Depression; consumers spend more than they make
2006	Lehman bets $2 billion on McAllister Ranch in California in a single deal
	Lehman becomes the largest mortgage originator, churning out more than $4 billion in subprime and Alt-A mortgages per month
	Ben Bernanke replaces Alan Greenspan as chairman of the Federal Reserve
	Lehman CRO Madelyn Antoncic receives "Risk Manager of the Year" award
	Delinquency rate of subprime borrowers increases to 7.5 percent from a low of 2.4 percent
	The Economist and Nouriel Roubini warn of a U.S. housing bubble
	U.S. Senate Banking Committee holds hearings entitled "The Housing Bubble and Its Implications for the Economy"
2007	U.S. home ownership reaches 69 percent
	January: Subprime lending market begins to implode, with originators beginning to declare bankruptcy
	Credit rating agencies see a dramatic increase in mortgage-link bond rating business; such ratings generate 50 percent of Moody's earnings
	Consumer debt-to-income ratio hits 133 percent, a new historical high

Date	Event
2007	Democratic Congressman Barney Frank becomes head of the powerful House Banking Committee
	Democratic Senator Christopher Dodd becomes head of the powerful Senate Banking Committee
	Dow Jones hits all-time high of 14,087.55; Lehman stock is $75 per share
	March 4: HSBC, Europe's largest bank, reports $11 billion write-off to cover losses from subprime and other loans
	July: SEC eliminates "up-tick" rule on short-selling; Bear Stearns shutters both of its subprime hedge funds
	August 1: Countrywide and Ameriquest, two of the largest subprime lenders, fail
	September: Lehman CRO Madelyn Antoncic is replaced by Chris O'Meara
	October: Mark Walsh completes the $22.2 billion Archstone-Smith deal at the very peak of the market
	Lehman participates in the TXU LBO, the largest of the decade
	Credit rating agencies begin downgrading thousands of previously higher-rated mortgage-backed securities
	Lehman generates profit of $4 billion, its highest earnings on record
	Despite escalated risk taking, Lehman's board-level Risk Management Department, headed by Henry Kaufman, meets only once every six months
	Lehman board awards Dick Fuld $34 million, making him one of the highest-paid CEOs on Wall Street
	Lehman's leverage ratio reaches 32 to 1
2008	Lehman's bets on commercial and residential real estate total more than three times more than firm capital; Lehman becomes a real estate hedge fund
	Through its financial products group in London, AIG becomes a CDS bookie, issuing $500 billion in credit default swaps; margin calls increase, and some question whether AIG can honor its bets
	Jim Cramer claims that Bear Stearns is a buy on CNBC's "Mad Money"
	March 16: J.P. Morgan snaps up Bear Stearns, saving it from certain death, and getting a bargain in the process
	March 17: Amidst the collapse of Bear and anxiety about stability, investors push Lehman stock down by 38 percent

Date	Event
2008	March 18: Lehman CFO Erin Callan quells fears during a pushed-up earnings conference call
	May 21: Short-seller David Einhorn publicly questions Lehman's financial health
2008	April 12: Dick Fuld and Hank Paulson have the famous "brand" dinner where Paulson indicates Lehman is important to the economy
	June 9: CFO Callan announces $2.8 billion quarterly loss; first in post-1994 Lehman history
	June 12: President Joe Gregory and CFO Callan are fired
	July: New York Fed president Timothy Geithner is unreceptive to turning Lehman into a bankruptcy holding company
	July 21: SEC institutes emergency order prohibiting short-selling of nineteen financial companies
	August 12: SEC ban on short-selling financial companies is lifted
	September 7: Freddie Mac and Fannie Mae are nationalized; moral hazard is elevated
	September 9: Talks with potential buyer Korea Development Bank break down, and Lehman stock plummets to less than $10 per share
	September 10: Lehman announces $3.9 billion third-quarter losses; stock falls below $5
	September 11: J.P. Morgan clearing bank cuts off credit to Lehman
	September 12: Fed sets up a series of emergency meetings in an attempt to rescue Lehman; Fuld resigns as director of the New York Fed
	September 13: After less than forty-eight hours of due diligence, Bank of America agrees to buy Merrill Lynch, and AIG is on life support
	September 14: Christopher Cox, Timothy Geithner, and Henry Paulson push for a Lehman board vote on bankruptcy
	September 15: After a unanimous board member vote, Lehman files for bankruptcy; Merrill Lynch is rescued by Bank of America
	September 16: Lehman bankruptcy uncorks systemic risk; capital markets become unhinged beginning with money markets, repo markets, and commercial paper markets; AIG is taken over by the government at an eventual cost of $180 billion; Barclays buys Lehman's U.S. operations for $1.7 billion, and Nomura buys the Asian and European operations for $230 million

Date	Event
	September 17–19: After turmoil related to AIG, Lehman, Merrill Lynch, and others, the Dow drops more than 1,000 points
2008	Goldman Sachs and Morgan Stanley receive Fed fast-track approval to become bank-holding companies
	October 2: The $700 billion Toxic Asset Relief Plan (TARP) is approved by Congress; FDIC insurance increases to $250,000 per account
	To stabilize the market, U.S. government extends up to $9 trillion in government-backed guarantees
	October 6: The inquisition of Dick Fuld takes place, as he testifies in front of Congress about Lehman's failure and collapse
	Twenty-four commercial banks fail
2009	Government restricts payment scheme relating to TARP-taking banks; 145 commercial banks fail
	March 3: Dow hits a low of 6,726, a drop of more than 50 percent since the October 1, 2007, high
	Numerous banks rush to repay TARP
	November: Goldman Sachs CEO Lloyd Blankfein apologizes for his firm's role in the crisis, then reveals the firm will pay out more than $16 billion in bonuses
	December 1: $365 billion in TARP funds given out, and moral hazard is fueled
	December: House Banking Committee proposes financial reform legislation, and is unable to garner support from a single Republican; Treasury Secretary Timothy Geithner writes that the administration expects to recover all but $42 billion in dispersed TARP funds; Ben Bernanke is named *Time* "Person of the Year"; the legacy of TARP and its zombie companies remains a taxpayer burden
2010	Canada is the only G7 country that doesn't need a bank bailout
	January 6: Senator Dodd, chairman of the important Senate Banking Committee, announces he will not run for reelection
	February 26: Fannie Mae reports a fourth-quarter loss of $16.3 billion and requests $15.3 billion from the Treasurey to keep a positive net worth
	No meaningful financial industry rebirth occurs in the wake of the 2008 Lehman bankruptcy
	Moral hazard increases and systemic risk of market collapse remains

Notes

Chapter 1

1. U.S. House Committee on Oversight and Government Reform, "Committee Holds Hearings on the Causes and Effects of the Lehman Brothers Bankruptcy," http://oversight.house.gov/index.php?option=com_content&view=article&id=4692:committee-holds-hearing-on-the-causes-and-effects-of-the-lehman-brothers-bankruptcy&catid=42:hearings&Itemid=2 (accessed January 4, 2010).
2. Ibid.
3. Ibid.
4. Ibid.
5. Ibid.
6. Ibid.

Chapter 2

1. Many other investment banks founded by Jewish immigrants can trace their roots back to retail-based businesses. Goldman Sachs was a Pennsylvania clothing store, Lazard Frères began as a dry goods store in New Orleans, and Kuhn Loeb started as a clothier in Cincinnati.
2. Harold D. Woodman, *King Cotton and His Retainers* (University of Kentucky Press, 1968), 81.
3. Brian Trumbore, "Cotton: Eli Whitney Part 2," http://www.buyandhold.com/bh/en/education/history/2001/cotton2.html (accessed January 4, 2010).
4. Woodman, *King Cotton and His Retainers*, 172.
5. Ibid., 10–11.
6. Ibid., 34.
7. Ibid., 169.

8. Lehman Brothers, *A Centennial: Lehman Brothers 1850–1950* (Spiral Press, 1950), 7–8.
9. Ken Auletta, *Greed and Glory on Wall Street: The Fall of the House of Lehman* (Random House, 1986), 27.
10. Lehman Brothers, *A Centennial: Lehman Brothers 1850–1950*, 9.
11. Woodman, *King Cotton and His Retainers*, 203.
12. Lehman Brothers, *A Centennial: Lehman Brothers 1850–1950*, 10.
13. Ibid., 12.
14. Vincent P. Carosso, *Investment Banking in America* (Harvard University Press, 1970), 20.
15. Ibid.
16. Ibid., 8.
17. Ibid., 82.
18. Charles D. Ellis, *The Partnership: The Making of Goldman Sachs* (Penguin Press, 2008), 10.
19. Lehman Brothers, *A Centennial: Lehman Brothers 1850–1950*, 19–20.
20. Herbert H. Lehman would later become a prominent U.S. Senator and then the governor of New York.
21. Lehman Brothers, *A Centennial: Lehman Brothers 1850–1950*, 26.
22. Ibid., 28–29.
23. Ibid., 30.
24. Ellis, *The Partnership: The Making of Goldman Sachs*, 10.
25. Lehman Brothers, *A Centennial: Lehman Brothers 1850–1950*, 32.
26. Ibid., 37.
27. Philip joined Lehman in 1882 at age 21 and became a partner in 1885.
28. Lehman Brothers, *A Centennial: Lehman Brothers 1850–1950*, 39–40.
29. Carosso, *Investment Banking in America*, 322.
30. Contrast FDR's memorable quote with the recent, and perhaps less eloquent, words of President Obama's chief of staff, Rahm Emanuel: "You never want a serious crisis to go to waste."
31. Robert Sobel, *Salomon Brothers 1910–1985* (Salomon Brothers, 1986), 52.
32. "Seligmans to Drop Banking Business," *New York Times*, June 3, 1934, N9.
33. During this period of great American prosperity the heavy regulation from the New Deal era was still in effect. Opponents of stricter market regulation sometimes conveniently overlook this fact.
34. Auletta, *Greed and Glory on Wall Street*, 31.

Chapter 3

1. Ken Auletta, *Greed and Glory on Wall Street: The Fall of the House of Lehman* (Random House, 1986), 31.
2. Ibid., 43.
3. Ibid., 41.
4. Grant Compton, "Back from the Brink Comes Lehman Bros.," *Business Week*, November 10, 1975, 72.

5. Robert Sobel, *Salomon Brothers 1910–1985* (Salomon Brothers, 1986), 78.
6. Rachel S. Epstein, *Investment Banking* (Chelsea House Publishers, 1988), 15.
7. Auletta, *Greed and Glory on Wall Street*, 53.
8. William Street is named after Dutch settler William Beekman, who came to New Amsterdam in the early 1600s. The author of this book is a descendant of William Beekman.
9. Jonathan A. Knee, *The Accidental Investment Banker* (Oxford University Press, 2006), 200.
10. Peterson would leave to found Blackstone Group, a private equity firm. In 2008 he was ranked 149th on the "Forbes 400 Richest Americans" list with a net worth of approximately $2.8 billion.
11. Auletta, *Greed and Glory on Wall Street*, 153.

Chapter 4

1. Vincent P. Carosso, *Investment Banking in America* (Harvard University Press, 1970), 1.
2. Ibid.
3. Alan Greenspan, *The Age of Turbulence* (The Penguin Press, 2007), 424.
4. Carosso, *Investment Banking in America*, 2.
5. Roger T. Johnson, *Historical Beginnings: The Federal Reserve*, rev. (Federal Reserve Bank of Boston, 1999), 20.
6. Edge Act corporations are subsidiaries of bank-holding companies that conduct banking business abroad and are subject to section 25A of the Federal Reserve Act.
7. *Net Encyclopedia*, s.v. "Origins of Commercial Banking in the United States, 1781–1830," http://eh.net/encyclopedia/article/wright.banking.commercial.origins (accessed January 4, 2010).
8. David S. Kidwell and others, *Financial Institutions, Markets and Money* (John Wiley & Sons, Inc., 2006), 586.
9. Ibid.
10. It's worth noting that the crash occurred only sixteen years after the creation of the Fed, which was supposed to stabilize the American markets.
11. Rightfully so. There is substantial evidence that both commercial and investment bankers engaged in risky lending practices, including using depositor monies to speculate in the stock market.
12. In the heat of the Great Credit Crisis of 2008, this government guarantee was temporarily increased to $250,000. The Emergency Economic Stabilization Act of 2008 was signed on October 3, 2008. It increased the FDIC coverage limit to $250,000 per account holder. This limit has been extended through December 31, 2013.
13. Frontline, "The Long Demise of Glass-Steagall," http://www.pbs.org/wgbh/pages/frontline/shows/wallstreet/weill/demise.html (accessed January 4, 2010).

Chapter 5

1. Through its Federal Open Market Committee, the Fed influences short-term interest rates including Fed funds and the discount rate. These rates in turn influence the market cost of borrowing.
2. Central banks might also act as a lender of last resort to the private banking sector during times of financial crisis.
3. Best use is when capital gains the highest risk-adjusted return.
4. Robert G. Eccles and Dwight B. Crane, *Doing Deals* (Harvard Business School Press, 1988), 147.
5. Ibid., 147.
6. Robert Kuhn, *Investment Banking: The Art and Science of High-Stakes Dealmaking* (Longman Higher Education, 1990), 21.
7. A credit default swap is a form of insurance against the likelihood of bond default.
8. Setting VaR dollar limits defines how much a given trading book, portfolio, or division is willing to lose in a day, week, or month before trading is reassessed.
9. The name "bulge-bracket" firm came from the location and size of the firm's name on the public securities offering announcements.
10. Michel Fleuriet, *Investment Banking Explained* (McGraw-Hill Companies, Inc. 2008), 45.
11. These league tables are based on a variety of measurements such as the number of underwriting lead mangers, co-manager, size of deals, type of deals, and number of IPOs in a given year.
12. A bank-holding company is any entity that directly or indirectly owns, controls, or has the power to vote 25 percent or more of a class of securities of a U.S. bank.
13. How rigorous was the Fed when making these spur-of-the-moment approvals? CIT Group, recipient of a similarly rushed approval for a banking charter, received $2.3 billion in TARP funds. It filed for Chapter 11 bankruptcy on November 1, 2009.

Chapter 6

1. To tighten monetary policy, the Fed sells bonds and reduces the amount of money circulating in the economy, which puts upward pressure on interest rates.
2. Edmund L. Andrews, "Greenspan Concedes Error on Regulation," *New York Times*, October 24, 2008, 1.
3. As part of the former CEO's severance agreement, he would receive $55 million from the sale.
4. Edward Robinson, "Last Man Standing," *Bloomberg*, July 2002, 3.
5. W. Braddock Hickman had done previous junk-bond studies dating back to the early 1900s, which Milken studied.
6. Full disclosure: The author's wife worked for Drexel in the late 1980s producing such videos.
7. Today, corporate raiders call themselves "shareholder activists."

8. Brian Burrough and John Helyar, *Barbarians at the Gate* (Harper Perennial, 1990), 187.
9. This term was later reduced, and Milken was released in 1993, having served less than two years in jail.
10. Michael Quint, "Co-President at Shearson Named No.1," *The New York Times*, March 30, 1993.

Chapter 7

1. That same year, Tom Hill joined Blackstone Group, the private equity firm started in 1985 by Pete Peterson, former Lehman CEO. Hill is currently vice chairman of Blackstone Group.
2. In March 1993 Primerica (eventually merged into Travelers) acquired retail brokerage and asset management business of Shearson Lehman Brothers for approximately $2.1 billion and combined the new company to form Smith Barney Shearson, Inc. The name was shortened to Smith Barney in 1994.
3. Jenny Anderson, "The Survivor," *New York Times*, October 28, 2007.
4. Tom Bernard also had worked in fixed-income trading at Salomon Brothers from 1979 to 1990 and received much notoriety as the "human Piranha" in Michael Lewis's book *Liar's Poker*.
5. Joseph Tibman, *The Murder of Lehman Brothers* (Brick Tower Press, 2009), 115.
6. Full disclosure: In 1997, the author became an employee of Citizens Power and eventually became SVP and head of Risk Management.
7. Debbie Galant, "Can Lehman Recapture Its Research Franchise?" *Institutional Investor* 29 (8), 33.
8. It was reported that he would not talk publicly about the matter until many years later.

Chapter 8

1. Bond spreads are expressed in terms of basis points in which 100 basis points are equivalent to 1 percent.
2. Nova Documentary, "Trillion Dollar Bet," produced by Sarah Holt, WGBH, Boston, 1999.
3. Lowenstein, *When Genius Failed*, 134.
4. Ibid., 146.
5. Edward Robinson, "Last Man Standing," *Bloomberg*, July 2002.
6. Lowenstein, *When Genius Failed*, 130.
7. Ibid., 170.
8. Ibid., 194–95.
9. Ibid., 199.
10. Partners at LTCM rejected this offer because they had only hours to review it, and Warren Buffett was vacationing in Alaska, unable to be reached by phone, which complicated negotiations.

Chapter 9

1. Unlike a bank, the government has taxing power and the ability to print money at will, two tools that increase the likelihood of debt repayment.
2. Michael Lewis, *Liar's Poker* (W.W. Norton, 1989), 83.
3. Office of Public Affairs, U.S. Department of Treasury bill signing, November 12, 1999.
4. Lewis, *Liar's Poker*, 88.
5. Ibid., 101.
6. Ibid., 100.
7. Salomon trader Lewis Ranieri has been credited with coining the term "securitization" of mortgage-backed securities.
8. Alyssa Katz, "The Dubious Birth of Mortgage-Backed Securities," www .thebigmoney.com/articles/history-lesson/2009/06/25/dubious-birth-mortgage -backed-securities (accessed January 4, 2010).
9. Some financial historians claim that, in 1987, Drexel Burnham Lambert helped Imperial Savings Association issue the first CDO.
10. U.S. House of Representatives Committee on Banking and Financial Services on October 1, 1998.

Chapter 10

1. GARP was founded as a nonprofit organization in 1996. The author is a past advisory board member of the Boston chapter.
2. Jeff Vanderbeek would eventually rise to EVP and left Lehman in 2004 to become owner of the New Jersey Devils, a professional ice hockey team.
3. Lehman Brothers, *Annual Report* (1999), 19.
4. The 1999 Basel Committee proposal was formally entitled "A Revised Framework on International Convergence of Capital Measurement and Capitals Standards," known informally as Basel II, and was released for industry comment.
5. Miskovic is currently the chief risk officer for State Street Bank in Boston.
6. Lehman Brothers, *Annual Report* (2007), 70.
7. Ibid.
8. David Einhorn and Aaron Brown, "Private Profits and Socialized Risk," *GARP Risk Review*, June/July 2008, 10.
9. Lawrence G. McDonald, *A Colossal Failure of Common Sense* (Crown Business, 2009), 268.
10. Yalman Onaran, "Lehman Fault-Finding Points to Last Man Fuld as Shares Languish," *Bloomberg*, July 22, 2008, http://www.bloomberg.com/apps/news?pid =20601109&refer=home&sid=aKlvv3EUW8lk.

Chapter 11

1. "Danger Time for America," *The Economist*, January 14, 2006, 15.
2. Barbara Kiviat, "A Drag on the Economic Rebound: Consumer Spending," *Time*, June 10, 2009.
3. Professor Stan J. Liebowitz makes the case that adjustable-rate mortgages—not subprime mortgages—might have led to the mortgage crisis of 2008. Stan J. Liebowitz, "ARMs, Not Subprimes, Caused the Mortgage Crisis," *The Economists' Voice* 6 (12), Article 4.
4. Warehouse loans take place when a retail lender borrows funds on a short-term basis using permanent mortgage loans as collateral. This form of interim financing is used to raise funds to make home mortgages and carry them until the mortgages can be packaged and sold "out of the warehouse" to an investor.
5. U.S. Senate Banking Committee, "The Housing Bubble and Its Implications for the Economy," http://banking.senate.gov/public/index.cfm?Fuseaction=Hearings .Hearing&Hearing_ID=bd5181el-1915-4e2d-b721-07e72d883a77 (accessed January 4, 2010).
6. Federal Reserve Bank of Chicago's 43rd Annual Conference on Banking Structure and Competition, Chicago, May 17, 2007.
7. Mark Adelson, *Nomura Securities International Analyst Report*, June 3, 2003, 4.
8. Devin Leonard, "How Lehman Got Its Real Estate Fix," *New York Times*, May 3, 2009.
9. Ibid.
10. Ibid.

Chapter 12

1. William D. Cohan, *House of Cards: A Tale of Hubris and Wretched Excess on Wall Street* (Doubleday, 2009), 168.
2. Ibid, 177.
3. Bryan Burrough, "Bringing Down Bear Stearns," *Vanity Fair*, August 2008.
4. Roddy Boyd, "The Last Days of Bear Stearns," *Fortune* 157 (1), 86.
5. William D. Cohan, "The Rise and Fall of Jimmy Cayne," *Fortune*, August 25, 2008.
6. Landon Thomas Jr., "Quarrel Erupts Between Bear's Elder Statesmen," *The New York Times*, May 7, 2008, http://www.nytimes.com/2008/05/07/business/07bear .html.

Chapter 13

1. David Einhorn claimed that for every stock he was short he was long two.
2. The SEC first adopted the uptick rule (Rule 10a-1) in 1938, when Joseph P. Kennedy Sr. was commissioner.
3. Andrew Ross Sorkin, "Goldman Is Questioned over Wall Street Rumors," *New York Times*, July 16, 2008.

4. Lawrence G. McDonald, *A Colossal Failure of Common Sense* (Crown Business, 2009), 307.

5. Ibid., 306.

6. David Einhorn, "Accounting Ingenuity," Ira W. Sohn Investment Research Conference, May 21, 2008, 7.

7. Ibid., 9.

8. Louise Story, "Lehman Battles an Insurgent Investor," *New York Times*, June 4, 2008.

9. Steve Fishman, "Burning Down His House," *New York Magazine*, November 30, 2008.

10. Yalman Onaran and John Helyar, "Fuld Sought Buffett Offer: He Refused as Lehman Sank," *Bloomberg*, November 10, 2008.

11. As of this writing there are still billions in hedge fund cash that have been frozen as part of the Lehman bankruptcy process. Many of these hedge funds have found themselves in the unsavory position of unsecured creditors.

12. Kenneth Libo, ed., *Lots of Lehmans* (Center for Jewish History, 2007), 8.

Chapter 14

1. Other factors influencing reduced lending standards included excessive profit seeking, lack of lender accountability, historically low interest rates, and passive bank regulatory oversight.

2. Greenspan admitted before a House committee on October 24, 2008, that he saw a flaw in his governing ideology of free markets.

3. In July 2008, Congress had given the U.S. Treasury authority to provide needed loans or equity infusion to Freddie Mac and Fannie Mae.

4. In late December 2009 the government increased its financial support to an unlimited dollar amount.

5. Neuberger Berman was sold but not until a month after the bankruptcy. The planned spin-off would take up to three months to fully meet SEC requirements.

6. James B. Stewart, "Eight Days," *The New Yorker*, September 21, 2009.

7. Ibid.

8. Steve Fishman, "Burning Down His House," *New York Magazine*, November 30, 2008.

9. Ibid.

10. As of the writing of this book, House Democrats and the Obama administration have introduced legislation to give the government "resolution authority" over non-bank financial firms in severe distress that are deemed "too big to fail." If approved this legislation should help plug a clear regulatory gap.

11. U.S. Senate Committee on Banking, Housing and Urban Affairs, "Actions by the Federal Reserve Bank of New York in Response to Liquidity Pressures in Financial Markets," http://banking.senate.gov/public/_files/OpgStmtGeithner4308Testimony.pdf (accessed January 4, 2010).

12. This one-day delay in releasing accurate investor news later generated a formal SEC complaint charging Reserve Fund management with civil fraud for false and misleading statements.

13. Technically, as long as the NAV does not drop below $0.995, the buck is not broken and redemption can remain at $1.

14. Yalman Onaran and John Helyar, "Lehman's Last Days," *Bloomberg*, January 2009.

15. Ibid.

16. In June 2009, Mark Walsh and several of his coworkers were hired by the Lehman bankruptcy trustees to manage the multibillion-dollar private equity real estate portfolio. As the person who created the risk, Walsh was a logical choice to attempt to unwind it.

17. In only one year, Nomura's purchase of Lehman operations allowed it to become a global investment bank. For third-quarter 2009, Nomura reported international revenue exceeded domestic revenue for the first time in firm history.

18. Stewart, "Eight Days."

19. Ibid.

20. The Troubled Asset Relief Program (TARP) was initially rejected by Congress and only approved on October 3, 2008, after last-minute revisions and a plummeting stock market.

Chapter 15

1. U.S. Department of the Treasury, "The CTC Concept Release," July 30, 1988, http://www.ustreas.gov/press/releases/rr2616.htm (accessed January 4, 2010).

2. Alan Greenspan, "Banking," Board of Governors of the Federal Reserve System, October 5, 2004, http://www.federalreserve.gov/BOARDDOCS/ Speeches/2004/20041005/default.htm (accessed January 4, 2010).

3. Henry Kaufman is also a close friend of Alan Greenspan.

4. Henry Kaufman, *On Money and Markets* (McGraw-Hill, 2000).

5. John Parry, "'Dr. Doom' Calls Credit Crisis a 'Global Calamity,'" *Reuters*, April 18, 2008, http://www.reuters.com/article/idUSN1845613820080418.

6. Nell Minow, U.S. Committee on Oversight and Government Reform, "Committee Holds Hearings on the Causes and Effects of the Lehman Brothers Bankruptcy," http://oversight.house.gov/images/stories/Hearings/110th_Congress/Minow _Statement.pdf (accessed January 4, 2010).

7. In July 2008, Congress created the Federal Housing Finance Agency (FHFA), a tough new regulator to oversee Freddie Mac and Fannie Mae.

8. Stephen Mihm, "Dr. Doom," *New York Times Magazine*, August 15, 2008.

9. Richard Posner, *A Failure of Capitalism* (Harvard University Press, 2009), 260.

10. As opinions, credit agency ratings are protected by the First Amendment.

11. Rating-agency fee structure is based on complexity and seasoning of issuance. On a $350 million mortgage pool, Moody's could earn a fee of as much as $250,000 compared to a fee for a similar-size municipal bond of approximately $50,000. Gretchen Morgenson, "Debt Watchdogs: Tamed or Caught Napping," *New York Times*, December 7, 2008.

12. U.S. House Committee on Oversight and Government Reform, "Letter from Scott McCleskey to the Securities and Exchange Commission, Hearing on Credit Rating Agencies and the Next Financial Crisis," http://oversight.house.gov/images/stories /Hearings/Committee_on_Oversight/McCleskey_letter.pdf (accessed January 4, 2010).

13. However, the amount of losses were so large and outside of historical norms, many conservative estimates would have missed the fact that collateral value could fall by 50 percent or more.

14. Deniz Igan, Prachi Mishra, and Tierry Tressel, "A Fistful of Dollars: Lobbying and the Financial Crisis," www.imf.org/external/np/res/seminars/2009/arc/pdf/igan .pdf (accessed January 4, 2010).

15. Similarly, in 1982 in the passage of the Garn–St. Germain Act, lobbyists played a pivotal role in freeing up S&Ls to engage in risky lending and reducing capital requirements. This led to a $293 billion S&L industry bailout by 1989.

16. Barbara Kiviat, "A Drag on the Economic Robound: Consumer Spending," *Time*, June 10, 2009.

17. Fuld indicated that the Treasury secretary valued Lehman's brand, which Fuld perhaps mistook as a confirmation that the government would not let Lehman go into bankruptcy.

18. Jeffrey McCracken, "The Weekend That Wall Street Died," *Wall Street Journal*, December 29, 2008.

19. Christine Harper and Matt Townsend, "Blankfein Apologizes for Goldman Sachs Role in Crisis," Bloomberg.com, November 17, 2009, http://www.bloomberg.com /apps/news?pid=20601103&sid=aeV9jwqKKrEw (accessed January 4, 2010).

20. Another gem demonstrating the disconnect between most Americans and Wall Street CEOs: in the September 19–20 edition of the *Wall Street Journal*, John Thain, the former CEO of Merrill Lynch scorned for the $1.2 million renovation of his executive suite (the one with the infamous $35,000 commode and $6,000 umbrella stand), reportedly joked while speaking at Wharton Business School that he should have furnished his office with Ikea products.

Epilogue

1. The exception was passage of a credit card bill of rights mandating interest rate limits and greater disclosure. Yet, bank credit card lending practices can only be tangentially linked with the credit crisis.

2. U.S. Department of the Treasury, "Treasury Department Releases Text of Letter from Secretary Geithner to Hill Leadership on Administration's Exit Strategy for TARP," http://www.ustreas.gov/press/releases/tg433.htm (accessed January 4, 2010).

3. Robert Schmidt, "Geithner Slams Bonuses, Says Banks Would Have Failed," Bloomberg.com, December 4, 2009.

4. U.S. Department of the Treasury, "Treasury Secretary Timothy F. Geithner Written Testimony, House Financial Services Committee, Financial Regulatory Reform," http://www.ustreas.gov/press/releases/tg296.htm (accessed January 4, 2010).

Index

About the Author

Mark T. Williams has substantial experience in risk management as both a practitioner and as an academic. For more than two decades, he has worked as a trust banker, Federal Reserve Bank examiner, senior trading floor executive for a major energy company, and a business school educator. He has been on the finance and ecomonics faculty at Boston University since 2002, specializing in capital markets. In 2008, he was awarded the Beckwith Prize for excellence in teaching. Williams frequently appears in the national media and has been a guest columnist for Reuters.com, Forbes.com, and the *Boston Globe*. Outside of academics, he conducts risk management seminars, has provided consulting for various Fortune 500 companies, and is a senior advisor at the Brattle Group. He is a graduate of the University of Delaware and Boston University. He resides in Newton, Massachusetts, with his wife and two daughters.